Lecture Notes in Economics and Mathematical Systems

Lecture Notes in Economics and Mathematical Systems

For information about Vols. 1–128, please contact your bookseller or Springer-Verlag

Vol. 129: H.-J. Lüthi, Komplementaritäts- und Fixpunktalgorithmen in der mathematischen Programmierung. Spieltheorie und Ökonomie. VII, 145 Seiten. 1976.

Vol. 130: Multiple Criteria Decision Making, Jouy-en-Josas, France. Proceedings 1975. Edited by H. Thiriez and S. Zionts. VI, 409 pages. 1976.

Vol. 131: Mathematical Systems Theory. Proceedings 1975. Edited by G. Marchesini and S. K. Mitter. X, 408 pages. 1976.

Vol. 132: U. H. Funke, Mathematical Models in Marketing. A Collection of Abstracts. XX, 514 pages. 1976.

Vol. 133: Warsaw Fall Seminars in Mathematical Economics 1975. Edited by M. W. Loś, J. Loś, and A. Wieczorek. V. 159 pages. 1976.

Vol. 134: Computing Methods in Applied Sciences and Engineering. Proceedings 1975. VIII, 390 pages. 1976.

Vol. 135: H. Haga, A Disequilibrium – Equilibrium Model with Money and Bonds. A Keynesian – Walrasian Synthesis. VI, 119 pages. 1976.

Vol. 136: E. Kofler und G. Menges, Entscheidungen bei unvollständiger Information. XII, 357 Seiten. 1976.

Vol. 137: R. Wets, Grundlagen Konvexer Optimierung. VI, 146 Seiten. 1976.

Vol. 138: K. Okuguchi, Expectations and Stability in Oligopoly Models. VI, 103 pages. 1976.

Vol. 139: Production Theory and Its Applications. Proceedings. Edited by H. Albach and G. Bergendahl. VIII, 193 pages. 1977.

Vol. 140: W. Eichhorn and J. Voeller, Theory of the Price Index. Fisher's Test Approach and Generalizations. VII, 95 pages. 1976.

Vol. 141: Mathematical Economics and Game Theory. Essays in Honor of Oskar Morgenstern. Edited by R. Henn and O. Moeschlin. XIV, 703 pages. 1977.

Vol. 142: J. S. Lane, On Optimal Population Paths. V, 123 pages. 1977.

Vol. 143: B. Näslund, An Analysis of Economic Size Distributions. XV, 100 pages. 1977.

Vol. 144: Convex Analysis and Its Applications. Proceedings 1976. Edited by A. Auslender. VI, 219 pages. 1977.

Vol. 145: J. Rosenmüller, Extreme Games and Their Solutions. IV, 126 pages. 1977.

Vol. 146: In Search of Economic Indicators. Edited by W. H. Strigel. XVI, 198 pages. 1977.

Vol. 147: Resource Allocation and Division of Space. Proceedings. Edited by T. Fujii and R. Sato. VIII, 184 pages. 1977.

Vol. 148: C. E. Mandl, Simulationstechnik und Simulationsmodelle in den Sozial- und Wirtschaftswissenschaften. IX, 173 Seiten. 1977.

Vol. 149: Stationäre und schrumpfende Bevölkerungen: Demographisches Null- und Negativwachstum in Österreich. Herausgegeben von G. Feichtinger. VI, 262 Seiten. 1977.

Vol. 150: Bauer et al., Supercritical Wing Sections III. VI, 179 pages. 1977.

Vol. 151: C. A. Schneeweiß, Inventory-Production Theory. VI, 116 pages. 1977.

Vol. 152: Kirsch et al., Notwendige Optimalitätsbedingungen und ihre Anwendung. VI, 157 Seiten. 1978.

Vol. 153: Kombinatorische Entscheidungsprobleme: Methoden und Anwendungen. Herausgegeben von T. M. Liebling und M. Rössler. VIII, 206 Seiten. 1978.

Vol. 154: Problems and Instruments of Business Cycle Analysis. Proceedings 1977. Edited by W. H. Strigel. VI, 442 pages. 1978.

Vol. 155: Multiple Criteria Problem Solving. Proceedings 1977. Edited by S. Zionts. VIII, 567 pages. 1978.

Vol. 156: B. Näslund and B. Sellstedt, Neo-Ricardian Theory. With Applications to Some Current Economic Problems. VI, 165 pages. 1978.

Vol. 157: Optimization and Operations Research. Proceedings 1977. Edited by R. Henn, B. Korte, and W. Oettli. VI, 270 pages. 1978.

Vol. 158: L. J. Cherene, Set Valued Dynamical Systems and Economic Flow. VIII, 83 pages. 1978.

Vol. 159: Some Aspects of the Foundations of General Equilibrium Theory: The Posthumous Papers of Peter J. Kalman. Edited by J. Green. VI, 167 pages. 1978.

Vol. 160: Integer Programming and Related Areas. A Classified Bibliography. Edited by D. Hausmann. XIV, 314 pages. 1978.

Vol. 161: M. J. Beckmann, Rank in Organizations. VIII, 164 pages. 1978.

Vol. 162: Recent Developments in Variable Structure Systems, Economics and Biology. Proceedings 1977. Edited by R. R. Mohler and A. Ruberti. VI, 326 pages. 1978.

Vol. 163: G. Fandel, Optimale Entscheidungen in Organisationen. VI, 143 Seiten. 1979.

Vol. 164: C. L. Hwang and A. S. M. Masud, Multiple Objective Decision Making – Methods and Applications. A State-of-the-Art Survey. XII, 351 pages. 1979.

Vol. 165: A. Maravall, Identification in Dynamic Shock-Error Models. VIII, 158 pages. 1979.

Vol. 166: R. Cuninghame-Green, Minimax Algebra. XI, 258 pages. 1979.

Vol. 167: M. Faber, Introduction to Modern Austrian Capital Theory. X, 196 pages. 1979.

Vol. 168: Convex Analysis and Mathematical Economics. Proceedings 1978. Edited by J. Kriens. V, 136 pages. 1979.

Vol. 169: A. Rapoport et al., Coalition Formation by Sophisticated Players. VII, 170 pages. 1979.

Vol. 170: A. E. Roth, Axiomatic Models of Bargaining. V, 121 pages. 1979.

Vol. 171: G. F. Newell, Approximate Behavior of Tandem Queues. XI, 410 pages. 1979.

Vol. 172: K. Neumann and U. Steinhardt, GERT Networks and the Time-Oriented Evaluation of Projects. 268 pages. 1979.

Vol. 173: S. Erlander, Optimal Spatial Interaction and the Gravity Model. VII, 107 pages. 1980.

Vol. 174: Extremal Methods and Systems Analysis. Edited by A. V. Fiacco and K. O. Kortanek. XI, 545 pages. 1980.

Vol. 175: S. K. Srinivasan and R. Subramanian, Probabilistic Analysis of Redundant Systems. VII, 356 pages. 1980.

Vol. 176: R. Färe, Laws of Diminishing Returns. VIII, 97 pages. 1980.

Vol. 177: Multiple Criteria Decision Making-Theory and Application. Proceedings, 1979. Edited by G. Fandel and T. Gal. XVI, 570 pages. 1980.

Vol. 178: M. N. Bhattacharyya, Comparison of Box-Jenkins and Bonn Monetary Model Prediction Performance. VII, 146 pages. 1980.

Vol. 179: Recent Results in Stochastic Programming. Proceedings, 1979. Edited by P. Kall and A. Prékopa. IX, 237 pages. 1980.

Vol. 180: J. F. Brotchie, J. W. Dickey and R. Sharpe, TOPAZ – General Planning Technique and its Applications at the Regional, Urban, and Facility Planning Levels. VII, 356 pages. 1980.

Vol. 181: H. D. Sherali and C. M. Shetty, Optimization with Disjunctive Constraints. VIII, 156 pages. 1980.

Vol. 182: J. Wolters, Stochastic Dynamic Properties of Linear Econometric Models. VIII, 154 pages. 1980.

Vol. 183: K. Schittkowski, Nonlinear Programming Codes. VIII, 242 pages. 1980.

continuation on page 215

Lecture Notes in Economics and Mathematical Systems

Managing Editors: M. Beckmann and W. Krelle

272

Gerhard Clemenz

Credit Markets with Asymmetric Information

Springer-Verlag

Berlin Heidelberg New York London Paris Tokyo

Author

Dr. Gerhard Clemenz
Institut für Wirtschaftswissenschaften der Universität Wien
Liechtensteinstr. 13/11, A-1090 Wien, Austria

ISBN-13: 978-3-540-16778-5 e-ISBN-13: 978-3-642-45614-5
DOI: 10.1007/978-3-642-45614-5

To my mother

ACKNOWLEDGEMENTS

This research was carried out over the last two years at the University of Vienna, at the Hochschule für Wirtschaft und Politik in Hamburg and at the University of Bonn, and all three provided a favourable environment for my work. My visits in Hamburg and Bonn have been made possible through financial support from the Deutsche Akademische Austauschdienst and the Deutsche Forschungsgemeinschaft, and through the generous granting of leaves from the University of Vienna.
C.Clemenz, R.Flotzinger, F.Haslinger, M.Nermuth, G.Orosel C.Podczeck and G.Winckler have provided most valuable comments on earlier drafts. Furthermore,I received help and encouragement at various stages and in various forms from M.Bray, E.Dierker, M.Hellwig, R.Holzmann, H.Milde, J.Stiglitz, E.Streißler and J.Sutton.

I also benefitted from the response of participants of various meetings and seminars at which I had the opportunity to present some of my work, e.g. at the European Econometric Society Meeting in Madrid, at the Symposium on Money, Banking and Insurance in Karlsruhe, at the 7. Heiligenkreuzer Arbeitskreis der theoretischen Ökonomen Österreichs, at the 2nd International Meeting on Monetary Economics and Banking in Nice and at Research Seminars at the University of Vienna, at the Wirtschaftsuniversität Wien and at the University of Bonn. I wish to thank all my friends and fellow economists as well as all institutions who supported me in undertaking this research and at the same time exempt them from all responsibilities for its shortcomings.

I am indebted to W.Richter for his technical assistance in the production of earlier drafts, and to E.Plakolm for drawing the diagrams. I am particularly grateful to M.Tatzber and H.M.Wurm who struggled with patience and skill not only with my illegible handwriting, but also with the intricacies of a new text processing system.

Finally, I want to thank my wife, whose tireless support in so many ways made it possible to write this book.

CONTENTS

Chapter 0:

INTRODUCTION AND GENERAL OVERVIEW

0.1 Subject and Scope

The main purpose of this study is to apply analytical tools and concepts developed in the "New Information Economics" to credit markets in order to explore the possibility of equilibrium credit rationing and its consequences.
The introduction is divided into two parts: This subsection attempts to motivate the choice of both, subject and approach, while the remainder of the introduction contains a summary of the contents of the book.

Credit markets and, more generally, financial markets, have attracted considerable attention from economists mainly for two reasons:

(i) They perform crucial functions in any advanced, monetary economy, like the sharing of risk between different economic agents, the allocation of loanable funds or the transmission of monetary impulses, to name only the most obvious.

(ii) They have led many observers to conclude that they operate quite differently from most other markets, with non-market clearing, backward-bending supply curves or apparently inefficient equilibria being the rule rather than the exception.

Both points have been recognized by economists of rather different persuasions, though this does not imply agreement on either causes or consequences of the alleged phenomena. So we are told by *Keynes*: "So far ... as bank loans are concerned, lending does not ... take place according to the principles of a perfect market. There is apt to be an unsatisfied fringe of borrowers, the size of which can be expanded or contracted, so that banks can influence the volume of investments by expanding or contracting the volume of their loans, without there being necessarily any change in the level of bank-rate, in the demand schedule of borrowers, or in the volume of lending otherwise than through banks. This phenomenon is capable, when it exists, of having great practical importance." (*Keynes* 1930, p.190).

But also one of the great contemporaries and opponents of *Keynes*, *F.A. von Hayek*, held the view that the banking sector and certain peculiarities of the credit market are crucial for an explanation of business cycles (*Hayek* 1969).

To quite a different camp than *Hayek* belong economists like *Davidson* (1972) or *Minsky* (1975) who also assign great importance to financial markets in their reinterpretation of *Keynes*.

While the authors mentioned so far considered various aspects of credit markets, the proponents of the so-called "availability doctrine" were the first to focus attention on credit-rationing, a phenomenon which is also the central theme of the present book. The contributions of *Roosa* (1951), *Scott* (1957a, b) or *Lindbeck* (1962) were reactions to the then quite commonly held view that monetary policy could exert only little influence on real variables like investment or national income. Availability theorists argued that monetary policy could be used to change aggregate demand even if investment were insensitive to the rate of interest if variations of the money supply were reflected in changes of the availability of loans rather than in changes of the interest rate.

Since then there has been continued interest in credit rationing for at least three reasons:

(i) The first issue under consideration was whether there exist plausible conditions which make rationing compatible with individual rationality without resorting to exogenous factors like interest rate regulations.

(ii) The second problem was to investigate whether rationing implied inefficiency and if so what remedies could be applied.

(iii) The third question was whether credit rationing had any effect on the working of monetary policy.

Despite this interest in credit rationing up to the mid seventies little progress had been achieved in providing a sound and convincing theoretical explanation of this phenomenon. In fact, there was not even full agreement about what the term credit rationing actually meant. As will be argued in some detail later (cf. ch. 1 and 5), a naive application of the concept of excess demand in a conventional goods market to a loan market, can be as misleading as *Keynes'* casual reference to "a fringe of unsatisfied borrowers", which appears too simple for such a complex phenomenon. Of course, one can define any state, in which some or all loan applicants do not get a loan of the size they desire at the ruling rate of interest as credit rationing; and for the purpose of this introduction such a definition will do, but as the analysis proceeds it should become apparent that some care is required when applying this definition to specific credit market equilibria.

In any case, whatever definitions have been used, most of the older models assumed rather than explained credit rationing or introduced ad hoc rigidities which resulted in rationing, as conventional theory would have suggested anyway.

A major breakthrough ocurred in the 1970's, when interest in markets with imperfect information increased and led to many new insights into the functioning of markets and other (economic) organisations. Particularly fruitful proved models of asymmetric quality information as initiated in the seminal paper by *Akerlof* (1970). The basic idea is as simple as it is powerful. For many economic transactions it is true that one party has to pay or to commit itself before knowing with certainty what it will get in exchange. This is the case with "experience" goods where, in contrast to "inspection" goods, the buyer cannot tell the quality on the spot (the terminology is due to *Nelson* (1970)). Usually the seller knows exactly what quality the good has, whereas the buyer knows at best some probability distribution over the quality (assuming it can be defined and measured in an appropriate way). Now, as *Akerlof* (1970) shows for a used cars market, the quality of goods offered may be correlated with the market price, with the possible consequence that buyers will not accept a price below a certain minimum for fear of intolerably low quality, and this can prevent markets from being cleared in equilibrium (*Clemenz* 1983).

Similar problems are likely to arise in all markets, where there is a time lag between payment and delivery, and the "buyer" has no possibility to ensure both punctual delivery and a certain quality standard. This may be the case for many goods markets, but more important and interesting problems of this kind arise in labour markets, insurance markets and credit markets.

The issues involved are most apparent in an insurance market: Suppose a company offers insurance against a particular loss of given size which occurs with probability q. It is plausible that potential buyers of the insurance know their individual probability of loss better than does the company which has only an estimate of the average probability. Now an increase of the insurance premium may in fact reduce the profit of the company for two reasons: Customers with low loss probabilities may drop out of the market, thereby increasing the average probability of loss of the remaining clients: this adverse selection effect may more than offset the increased revenue due to the higher premium. Similarly, clients may become more careless as the premium is increased, and this moral hazard effect will again increase the average probability of loss. *Rothschild and Stiglitz* (1976) were among the first to point out possible implications of these two effects on insurance markets, among which one could mention non-existence of *Nash*-equilibria or separating equilibria where some clients do not get full coverage.

A very similar problem may arise in labour markets: Quite often an employer does not know exactly the productivity of a worker, and situations are conceivable where its level may depend on the wage: A lower wage may induce able workers to drop out (adverse selection) or to reduce the effort (moral hazard) thereby reducing average productivity. Hence, there may be an optimal wage at which the ratio wage/average productivity (often referred to as efficiency wage) reaches a minimum. In that case employers would not reduce the wage even in face of an excess supply of labour (for surveys see *Yellen* 1984, *Schultze* 1985).

Credit markets may also be plagued by adverse selection and moral hazard, and this takes us back to the main topic of this book. The crucial point is that the bank faces the risk of default of borrowers, and this risk may be increased as the loan rate of interest and/or the credit volume are increased, implying that the gross return of a bank need not be a monotonically increasing function of loan rate and loan size. As will be shown in detail below, an increase of the rate of interest may have the following consequences: Relatively safe projects are withdrawn from the market; loan applicants of higher ability drop out of the market; a larger share of borrowers finds it more profitable to declare default rather than to honour their commitments; borrowers reduce their effort and thereby increase the probability of default. All these effects allow for the possible existence of a "bankoptimal" loan rate which would not be changed even if there is an excess demand for loans.

Explanations of credit rationing based on asymmetric information are quite appealing for several reasons:

(i) Unlike most other approaches they do not require any ad hoc assumptions about price or interest rate rigidities: Rationing and interest rate stickiness are the result of rational behaviour of economic agents under plausible informational restrictions.

(ii) Adverse selection and moral hazard explanations appear fairly robust to assumptions concerning the behaviour of economic agents and also to institutional details of the credit market. It is shown at length below that various screening and incentive devices do not rule out the possibility of rationing at least for some approaches. It is interesting to note, however, that the four variants of adverse selection and moral hazard analyzed differ considerably with respect to their power of explaining equilibrium rationing as soon as the models become more general, though they bear some formal resemblance in the simplest case.

(iii) The analysis of credit markets in this book is closely related to some recent work on insurance and labour markets, as mentioned above. This allows, after some adjustments, the application of tools and concepts which are readily available, but at the same time serves to highlight the differences between different markets. A comparison between adverse selection and moral hazard phenomena in different markets, though not explicitly carried out in the present book, is certainly useful in understanding the nature of this type of problems and in distinguishing more clearly between the general structure and specific aspects.

This does not mean that this approach is the only one which can yield useful insights or that it is without its shortcomings. Chapter 1 contains a brief survey of alternative approaches to credit rationing and it should become obvious that most of them are not without merit. It still is my contention, however, that none of these is in any way superior to the adverse selection/moral hazard stories told in this book. Moreover, most of them are compatible with it, and at a later stage one might very well end up with an integrated model that takes account of several aspects now scattered in various models.

As far as shortcomings of the present approach are concerned it is fairly obvious that due to inevitable simplifications some important aspects of credit markets are neglected. A full understanding of the relationship between bank and customer requires a dynamic, i.e. multiperiod perspective, and a fairly detailed description of the organisational structure of both, banks and clients. As far as the first point goes the present approach is basically static, and the dynamic considerations in chapter 3 are no more than a beginning. The bank-client relationship in this book is certainly fairly simple. There are two consolations, however, which make it easier to live with this shortcoming at least for the moment: Alternative approaches as discussed in chapter 1, quite often refer to the importance of such a relationship but, in fact, hardly explain it and satisfy themselves with more or less arbitrary switching costs for customers and screening costs of banks. On the other hand, I am convinced that a plausible modelling and explanation of banking-organisation will contain basically the same elements as the present approach to credit rationing: Rational individuals pursuing their self-interest under informational constraints, and various adverse selection and moral hazard problems. Hence, I am optimistic that the analysis of this book will remain a useful building stone for fuller and richer models in the future.

I do not claim that the shortcomings just mentioned are the only ones, and further critical remarks will be found in each chapter. But it certainly is a bad strategy to dwell at length on the shortcomings of a book before the prospective reader has even started reading it. Hence, I prefer to proceed to a brief summary of the contents.

0.2 Summary of Contents

Chapter 1 introduces the precise definitions of credit rationing employed in subsequent chapters, and provides a brief survey of rationing theories which do not rely on asymmetric information. Basically three such approaches are discussed: The first rests on the role of equity and collateral and shows that with uncertain returns on the project to be financed and the consequent default risk both the loan volume and the loan rate of interest depend on the equity and/or the collateral a borrower is able to provide.

The second approach emphasises that bank services quite often have the character of a joint product. If the demand for banking services of a borrower is positively correlated with the volume of loan he gets then clients with a low propensity to purchase bank services may be rationed.

The third approach uses an implicit contract argument and views a fixed loan rate of interest as part of an agreement to protect borrowers from fluctuations of the deposit rate of interest. In addition, a special bank-customer relationship reflected in administrative and switching costs is invoked in order to generate credit rationing.

Chapter 2 starts the main analysis by formulating a simple credit market model with the following features: The total supply of loans is limited; loan applicants need a loan of fixed size in order to finance a project which yields a random return at the end of one period; banks have to face the risk of default of borrowers. It is shown first that these assumptions do not lead to credit rationing. In addition it has to be assumed that there exists some mechanism such that a change of the interest rate changes the probability of default. Four possible causes for an adverse influence of interest rate increases on the probability of default are identified:

(i) Borrowers differ with repect to their costs of default and a larger portion refuses to repay the loan as the interest rate is increased (model H (for "Honesty")).

(ii) Projects differ with respect to their riskiness and safer projects are withdrawn as the interest rate is increased (model R (for "Riskiness")).

(iii) Borrowers differ with respect to their abilities and the more able borrowers drop out from the market as the interest rate is increased (model A (for "Ability")).

(iv) The probability of default is positively correlated with the unobservable and costly effort of borrowers which is a decreasing function of the interest rate (model E (for "Effort")).

All four models have been criticised because of
a) their static character,
b) the exogeneity of the collateral borrowers have to provide and
c) the fixed loan size.
It has been argued that variations of collateral and loan size serve as signals which can overcome rationing. These points are taken up in the subsequent chapters.

Chapter 3 extends the basic one period model into a multiperiod framework. As far as model H is concerned this allows for the endogenization of the costs of default which are viewed as the loss due to the exclusion of defaulters from the loan market. Differences of default costs can be explained via different abilities.

For model E and model R, if the latter is interpreted as a moral hazard model (borrowers can choose between projects of different riskiness) the introduction of a multiperiod framework yields an additional reason for rationing: the threat of rejection of defaulters in future periods serves as an incentive device, and in order to make it effective some defaulters really have to be denied a credit.

The multiperiod version of model A leads to an interesting dynamic adverse selection problem where banks revise their estimates of individual default probabilities in view of the past performance of borrowers.

Finally it is investigated under what conditions default is declared if it is a joint decision of banks and borrowers. It turns out that an extension of the basic models to many periods strengthens rather than removes the plausibility of equilibrium rationing.

Chapter 4 analyzes the consequences of an endogenously determined collateral for the possibility of credit rationing. The basic idea is that banks could offer different combinations of loan rate of interest and collateral in order to screen loan applicants and overcome adverse selection. It turns out, however, that all models continue to allow for rationing equilibria if borrowers are assumed to be risk neutral. Only if the collateral is raised to a level such that the default risk disappears for the bank will there be no rationing in general.

This result does not hold in general if borrowers are risk averse or if there are costs of default for the bank. Only the credit rationing result of model H is unaffected by such modifications. The adverse selection models R and A, may result in a separating, non-rationing equilibrium but this possibility is sensitive with respect to the precise formulation of the bank's default costs. Moral hazard model E may, but need not, display rationing if borrowers are risk averse.

Chapter 5 relaxes the assumption of a fixed individual loan volume and assumes also an infinitely elastic supply of loanable funds. The return of the project is still random, but its distribution depends now on its size according to a neoclassical production function. It is first shown that some restrictions on the distribution function are required in order to ensure well-behaved iso-profit curves of banks and borrowers. Next, it is demonstrated that with identical borrowers and identical projects there is equilibrium rationing in the sense that borrowers are granted a smaller loan than they desire at the going loan rate of interest. It is shown, however, that such an equilibrium is efficient and it is argued that the term rationing is somewhat misleading in this situation.

Then it is assumed that borrowers differ with respect to their abilities and it is demonstrated that in this case a *Nash*-equilibrium need not exist.

Chapter 6 continues the analysis of the previous chapter, but uses a much simpler stochastic framework: A project either succeeds with probability q or fails with probability 1-q. If it succeeds its return is determined by a production function, if it fails its gross return is zero. Three questions are discussed within this simple framework: First it is shown that alternative equilibrium concepts, known from the literature on insurance markets, imply the existence of equilibria. The *Nash*- and the *Riley*-equilibrium are always separating, the *Wilson*-equilibrium may be a pooling equilibrium, the *Grossman*-equilibrium usually is one. In general, loan applicants need not get the size of loan they demand, but it may be greater or smaller than they desire.

The second question concerns the plausiblity of the (static) equilibria mentioned above if the credit market is modelled as a sequential signaling game. It turns out that the *Wilson*- or *Grossman*-equilibrium constitutes a strategically stable equilibrium under reasonable assumptions.

The third problem analyzed concerns the endogenous determination of the exchange of information about borrowers between banks.

Chapter 7 returns to the assumption of a limited supply of loanable funds in order to investigate whether, even in the case of a variable loan size, some loan applicants may be rejected in equilibrium. It is shown that this possibility depends in general on both the model considered and the equilibrium concept chosen.

In model H rationing by rejection of applicants is ruled out if the loan size is variable.

In models R and A this type of rationing can only occur if there exists a pooling equilibrium. This, in turn, can only be the case if one adheres to the *Wilson*- or the *Grossman*-equilibrium concept.

Finally, model E continues to allow for equilibrium rationing and hence turns out to provide the most robust explanation of this phenomenon.

In a short epilogue there is an outlook on possible future research, in particular, on policy implications of imperfect credit markets as described in this book.

Chapter 1:

APPROACHES TO EQUILIBRIUM CREDIT RATIONING

1.1 A General Description of a Credit Market

The purpose of this chapter is threefold: First, the basic model of a credit market employed throughout this study is introduced. Second, a precise definition of credit rationing is given, and differences between a credit market and a conventional commodity market are discussed. Third, using our basic credit market model, the earlier literature on credit rationing is reviewed. The presentation of various approaches within one model is supposed to facilitate the comparisons between different theories and to highlight the importance of asymmetric information, which is crucial for the analysis in the remaining chapters.

Next, the basic building blocks of a credit market model are introduced.

A bank has to perform at least two tasks: It raises loanable funds and it grants loans. Consequently, a credit market model needs a specification of at least four behavioural functions: A supply function for loanable funds; a bank's demand function for loanable funds; a demand function for loans; and the bank's supply function for loans. Obviously, these functions cannot be mutually independent. In particular, the bank's demand for loanable funds and its supply of loans are closely linked. If non-banks can be either suppliers of loanable funds or loan applicants, the corresponding functions are again interrelated. Since a detailed modelling of the behaviour of all economic agents involved and of their various interactions would become fairly complex it is common usage to introduce several simplifications.

The first concerns the supply of loanable funds. It is assumed that banks can obtain funds by paying a sure rate of interest i. One can imagine that there exists a group of economic subjects who deposit a certain amount of money for one period with the bank and get at the end of the period that amount plus interest payment. Of course it would be possible to derive a supply curve from the utility maximizing behaviour of the savers, but for most of the subsequent analysis it suffices to assume that the supply of loanable funds L^s is a function of the sure (deposit) rate of interest, formally[1)]

$$(1) \quad L^s = L(i), \; L' \geq 0.$$

For $L' = \infty$, i.e. an infinitely elastic supply of loanable funds, a reasonable interpretation is that banks are able to refinance themselves, e.g. through taking loans from the central bank.

In any case, it must be emphasized that the assumption of a supply function like (1) is less innocent than it appears at first sight. In particular, problems that may arise when a bank becomes insolvent or when depositors lose confidence and start a run on the bank are assumed away. Also, it should be noted that rationality is not sufficient to ensure that the supply of loanable funds is nondecreasing in i.

A second set of simplifying assumptions employed in most of the subsequent analysis concerns the banking sector. Banks are assumed to be risk neutral maximizers of their expected profit. Their only cost of raising funds and granting loans is usually assumed to be the payment of i, but in some models other costs are also taken into consideration. In addition, some models exploit the fact that banks offer other services besides the two mentioned above.

A further simplification which will be used in most models to be discussed below is the restriction to only one period. This prevents a full analysis of the ongoing relationship between banks and their clients as well as of the role of different loan maturities, but it facilitates considerably the treatment of those issues which are of central interest for the present analysis.

1) Equations and figures are numbered in each chapter separately. References to equations or figures of other chapters contain first the number of the chapter and then the number of the equation or figure, e.g. (1.1) for the equation below.

Of crucial importance is the specification of the structure of the banking sector. The assumption most frequently encountered is that the banking sector is competitive, implying a zero-profit condition for the equilibrium. Occasionally monopolies or oligopolies are also analyzed.

Last but not least comes the modelling of the bank's decisions concerning its demand for loanable funds and its supply of credits. Both depend crucially on the expected gross return of a loan contract which specifies loan size, loan rate of interest and, in some cases, collateral requirements, maturity and possibly other factors. The expected gross return of a loan contract, on the other hand, cannot be determined in general without some information about the borrower like the distribution of his future income, his willingness to pay, etc. Finally, the bank's actual demand for loanable funds obviously depends also on the demand for loans. Hence, a careful specification of the behaviour of loan applicants is required in order to close the credit market model.

Basically one can distinguish between two types of borrowers and consequently between two types of loans: Loan applicants may be consumers who distribute their income over two (or more) periods via saving or taking loans in order to maximize their total expected utility; or loan applicants may be entrepreneurs who have the knowhow for some investment project but lack the liquid means to implement it without the loan. Formally both types of loan markets look quite often much the same, but we shall concentrate on the second type and cast models which originally were designed for consumption loans within the framework of a market for investment loans.

In order to derive the demand for loans, more precisely, for loan contracts, one has to specify certain characteristics of the loan applicants like size and return of their project and - if the latter is a random variable - its distribution, the costs of default, the attitude towards risk etc. Obviously, information about these factors is also required for an estimation of the expected return of the bank. In particular, one also has to specify the information that is available to the different participants in the credit market under consideration.

In the next section I shall argue that the distinctive feature of a credit market is precisely the fact that the value of a loan contract to the bank depends on - usually incompletely known - characteristics of the borrower.

1.2 Definitions of Credit Rationing

Credit rationing is usually defined as a situation where the demand for loans exceeds their supply at the quoted loan rate of interest. Conventional economic theory has traditionally viewed market clearing and market equilibrium as being one and the same. Consequently, a situation where supply does not equal demand has been thought of as a disequilibrium state which could only persist if forced upon the economy by outside factors like e.g. price regulation.[1] This view is not a consequence of a deficient or misleading equilibrium concept, but arises naturally from the assumptions about the market, in particular about its information structure. According to *Hahn* (1984), "equilibrium is commonly understood as a critical point of an implicit or explicit dynamics ... Consider the supply and demand cross. The resulting price is designated as an equilibrium because we can give no reason why it should change." (*Hahn* 1984, p.22).

Clearly, a point on either the supply or on the demand curve which is not the intersection of both is not an equilibrium at least in a traditional market with perfect information: A Walrasian auctioneer would not stop at this point, and in a non-tâtonnement process agents who are rationed, i.e. cannot sell or buy what they want at the current price would certainly have an incentive to make another price offer. In the traditional theory credit markets are viewed as being perfectly analogous to simple commodity markets. The loan rate of interest is seen as the price per Dollar lent, and it performs exactly

[1] This does not mean that the changes induced by an excess demand (or supply) lead to its reduction or removal, though such a confusion between existence and stability of equilibria has not been (is not?) uncommon. It simply means that something has to change as long as markets are not cleared.

the same market clearing function as the price in any other market. If, at a given loan rate of interest r, the amount of loans demanded exceeds the loanable funds available to the banks it will increase r in order to

a) increase its own gross return per Dollar, which makes it possible to
b) increase the deposit rate of interest i in order to attract additional loanable funds.

In addition, the increase of r will reduce the demand for loans.

This simple picture of a credit market overlooks the fact pointed out in the previous section:

For a bank it is of crucial importance to whom it grants a loan and what actions the borrower takes. For a baker, in contrast, it is immaterial to whom he sells bread and what the buyer does with it (as long as he pays immediately, of course). The aim of a bank is not just to find borrowers, but to find good borrowers. A "good borrower" from the bank's point of view is one who defaults with very small probability (e.g. because his projects are safe or he provides a large collateral), who causes small administrative costs (e.g. because he is an old customer about whom the bank is already well informed), and who uses a lot of services offered by the bank and profitable for her. As will be shown at length below it is exactly this desire to attract "good" borrowers (or to give incentives for a "good" conduct of borrowers) that may prevent banks from changing the loan rate of interest r (or any other component of the loan contract) such that the market is cleared.

To see this point more clearly consider the following example: Suppose a risk-neutral bank grants a loan of size L at interest rate r, and the borrower repays his debt only with probability q, $0 \le q \le 1$. The expected gross return for the bank equals.

(2) $\bar{p}(R,L) = qRL$

where $\bar{p}$ denotes the expected gross return of the loan contract (R,L) and R is the interest rate factor defined as $R := 1+r$. Obviously, $\bar{p}$ is increasing in R and L. Default risk per se does not affect the traditional view that r is adjusted such that supply equals demand.

But suppose that for a particular borrower q depends on R and L with q_R, $q_L < 0$.[1] It is easy to imagine borrowers with $q(R,L) = 0$ for L sufficiently large. Clearly, this would impose an upper limit on L. In any case, if the bank knows the function $q(R,L)$ then the best contract it can get is the solution to the following simple maximization problem

$$(3) \quad \max_{R,L} \bar{p}(R,L) = q(R,L)RL$$

which implies the necessary conditions

$$(4) \quad \frac{\partial \bar{p}}{\partial R} = q_R RL + qL = 0$$

$$(5) \quad \frac{\partial \bar{p}}{\partial L} = q_L RL + qR = 0$$

Denote a solution of (3) as (R^*, L^*). Now it is quite possible, that at R^* the borrower desires a larger loan than L^*. He might even be ready to accept a higher loan rate than R^* in order to obtain a larger loan. The bank, however, would refuse, provided there is no competitive pressure from other banks. We may assume, e.g. that $\bar{p}(R^*,L^*) = (1+i)L$, i.e. the zero-profit condition is satisfied (neglect other costs of raising funds and granting a loan for the moment).

This example illustrates how misleading it can be to treat the loan rate r as the "price" per Dollar lent which is supposed to adjust in order to clear the credit market. A change of r changes in this case the "quality" of the product, i.e. the probability of default. Similarly, an increase of the loan volume may change the risk of the bank and this increase of risk cannot be compensated by increases of

---

[1] Throughout this book we adopt the convention to denote partial derivatives by subscripts, eg. $q_R := \partial q/\partial R$.

r. Loans simply cannot be treated as homogeneous goods measured in monetary units.

This point is reenforced if one considers that the function q(R,L) may be different for different borrowers. Clearly, if the bank knows which customer has which function q it will offer different contracts to different clients. Again, this is impossible in a traditional (perfect information) commodity market, but in a credit market it matters who gets a contract. There is nothing surprising in the observation that not every loan applicant can get the same loan contract if the bank is able to identify relevant characteristics. The really interesting phenomenon which calls for an explanation is different treatment of apparently identical loan applicants, and this problem will be one of the central issues in the remaining chapters.

To sum up the above considerations, the definition of credit rationing at the beginning of this section which refers only to an excess demand for loans at the ruling loan rate is insufficient: It is neither surprising that banks do not grant arbitrarily large loans regardless of R, nor that borrowers with known differences in relevant characteristics get different loan contracts. This point, however, has not always been recognized, and it was only recently that *Keeton* (1979) proposed a sharper distinction between different types of credit rationing:

Type I Rationing: Some or all loan applicants get a smaller loan than they desire at the quoted loan rate of interest.

Type II Rationing: Some loan applicants are denied a loan even though for the bank they are indistinguishable from accepted applicants.

For both types of rationing it is required that applicants strictly prefer a (larger) loan in the sense that they are ready to accept a higher rate of interest in order to obtain one.

Now at first sight Type II Rationing looks like nothing more than a special case of Type I Rationing, because getting no loan is one example for a smaller loan than the desired one. But the requirement of, in the eyes of the bank, homogenous applicants makes Type II

Rationing the really interesting case. Type I Rationing, on the other hand, was used in most of the older literature, and it will also appear in some of the models below.

Having defined credit rationing the question arises whether either type can occur in equilibrium. A satisfactory theoretical explanation requires that all economic agents behave rationally, in particular they do not miss any opportunity of achieving individual advantages, and there are no artificial constraints like interest rate or loan size regulations etc. It will become apparent that it is not always possible to decide whether a particular model is satisfactory, but at least some can be rejected on this criterion.

Virtually all credit market models which attempt to explain the possibility of rationing assume some kind of heterogeneity of loan applicants and loans. The differences between approaches to credit rationing lie firstly, in the choice of the particular characteristic with respect to which applicants and loans are differentiated, and secondly, in the assumptions about the information available to the agents involved. Both aspects are not entirely independent, of course, since it is more likely to be fully informed about some characteristics than about others.

The models reviewed in the remainder of this chapter do not consider informational problems, but concentrate rather on known characteristics of borrowers and their impact on the credit market equilibrium. In the models of section 1.3 borrowers differ with respect to their initial wealth endowment and hence their ability to provide equity and/or collateral. In section 1.4 borrowers differ with respect to their propensity to generate bank business other than granting loans. In section 1.5 rationing may occur because old customers cause lower costs to banks than new ones and therefore get preferential treatment as far as (implicit) insurance contracts against fluctuations of interest rates are concerned.

1.3 Borrowers With Different Wealth Endowments

This section contains a discussion of the main ideas of the traditional approaches to credit rationing including contributions by, among others, *Hodgman* (1960), *Freimer* and *Gordon* (1965), *Jaffee* (1971), *Jaffee* and *Modigliani* (1969, 1976), *Smith* (1972) and *Azzi* and *Cox* (1976).

Most of this literature concentrates on the behaviour of banks and is rather casual in its treatment of other aspects mentioned above. Banks are assumed to have unlimited access to loanable funds at the given sure rate of interest i (e.g. *Jaffee* and *Modigliani* 1969), or they are viewed as acting like any other investor who optimizes the expected utility of his portfolio through diversification of his given wealth endowment, where granting loans is one of several investment opportunities (e.g. *Azzi* and *Cox* 1976). In what follows we shall stick to the former assumption.

The loans are used to finance (part of) some investment project of fixed size which, for convenience, is normalized to equal one. The return of the project is a nonnegative random variable X with commonly known distribution function F(x), density function f(x) and support $[0,m]$, $m < \infty$. It is assumed that the bank can collect costlessly the return x up to an amount RL, where $R = 1 + r$ is the interest factor, and L is the loan size, with $0 \le L \le 1$. Implicitly it is assumed that banks have full control over the amount of credit a borrower can get which implies some exchange of information between banks about loans granted. Borrowers are only liable with their project return and not with their private wealth, hence there is some risk of default, since $x < RL$ with positive probability. Under given assumptions a bank's expected gross return of a loan contract (R,L) equals

$$(6) \quad \bar{p}(R,L) = \int_0^{RL} x dF(x) + RL(1-F(RL))$$

The first term on the right hand side of (6) equals the bank's return if x falls below RL, and the second term is the payment the bank receives if the project is successful, weighted with the success probability. If the banking sector is competitive then one equilibrium condition is

$$(7) \quad \bar{p}(R,L) = IL = (1 + i)L ,$$

i.e. the expected profit per loan equals zero. Combining (6) and (7) we get for dR^p/dL, the slope of the bank's zero-profit curve, which is the locus of all potential equilibrium contracts (R,L):[1]

$$(8) \quad \frac{dR^p}{dL} = -\frac{R(1-F(RL)) - I}{L(1-F(RL))}$$

Now since from (6) and (7)

$$(9) \quad R(1-F(RL)) + \int_0^{RL} (x/L)dF(x) = I$$

the right hand side of (8) is unambigously positive and, not unexpectedly, in equilibrium a borrower cannot get a loan of arbitrary size at a given loan rate r: the larger the loan the higher the interest rate that has to be paid. It would be extremely misleading, however, to call this credit rationing for at least two reasons:

Firstly, considering the discussion in section 1.2, it is obvious that from the bank's point of view, a Dollar lent in contract (R,L) is not homogenous to a Dollar lent in contract (R,L'), L > L'. The probability of default is larger for the first contract, and the bank simply requires compensation for this risk via a higher loan rate. But everybody who can meet the terms of a particular contract will get it, hence there is no rationing in the sense of the definitions in section 1.2. Secondly, and this is a weakness found in most contributions mentioned above, it is impossible to define rationing without knowing the demand for loans. Focusing exclusively on the bank's behaviour is simply not sufficient.

---

[1] Here as elsewhere it is assumed that the conditions required for the admissibility of implicit differentiation are met.

However, *Freimer* and *Gordon* (1965) apparently have an excuse for this omission: They define as rationing the refusal of rational banks to extend individual loans above a certain limit which is smaller than 1 regardless of the loan rate. Now inspection of (9) reveals that under competitive conditions this can only be true if $\bar{x} < I$.[1] In that case banks would at most offer contracts (R,L) such that $RL = m$ and $\bar{x} = IL$, or $L = \bar{x}/I$. That case is perfectly irrelevant, however, since a project with an expected return below the sure rate of interest is not efficient anyway.

Freimer and *Gordon* reach their conclusion through different reasoning. They claim that banks would determine L in such a way that, for given R and I, $\bar{p}(R,L) - IL$ is maximized. Clearly, the first order condition of this is

$$(10) \quad \frac{\partial \bar{p}}{\partial L} = R(1 - F(RL)) = I$$

with the second order condition

$$(11) \quad \frac{\partial^2 \bar{p}}{\partial L^2} = - R^2 f(RL) < 0$$

In order to derive the loan size offered, L*, as a function of R, differentiate (10) with respect to R in order to get

$$(12) \quad \frac{\partial^2 \bar{p}}{\partial L \partial R} = (1-F(RL)) - RLf(RL)$$

which implies together with (11)

[1] Throughout this book expected values of random variables are denoted by putting a bar on the symbol, e.g.

$$\bar{x} := \int_0^m x dF(x).$$

$$(13) \quad \frac{dL}{dR} = + \frac{(1-F(RL)) - RLf(RL)}{R^2 f(RL)}$$

and it is easy to find distribution functions F(x) such that the loan size offered is a concave function of R, and L reaches a maximum at some finite value of R (e.g. take F(x) to be a rectangular distribution). As indicated above *Freimer* and *Gordon* call it rationing if this maximum L is smaller than 1.

The problem is again that rationing cannot be defined in a meaningful way without specification of a demand function. This point has been emphasized by *Jaffee* and *Modigliani* and they tried to overcome this deficiency in their first contribution (1969). They correctly observe that a bank who is a monopolist would not only determine L for a given R, but offer a contract (R,L) which maximizes its expected profit. Differentiating (6) with respect to R yields

$$(14) \quad \frac{\partial \bar{P}}{\partial R} = L(1-F(RL)) > 0 \quad \text{if } F(RL) < 1$$

One implication of (14) is obviously that a bank can always increase its profit by increasing the loan rate, and unless there is some exogenous restriction on R there is no reason why a monopolistic bank should ration a customer rather than raising R. *Jaffee* and *Modigliani* realize this and modify the *Freimer* and *Gordon* model in the following way: They assume that there are two types of projects with different distributions of their return which are known to both, bank and borrower. In addition, they assume that the bank monopolist is forced to charge one and the same interest rate to all borrowers. Finally, they postulate a negatively sloped demand curve for the size of individual loans. Their claim is that the optimal uniform loan rate R* may be such that one of the two types of borrowers is rationed. Their argument can best be explained with the help of Figure 1.

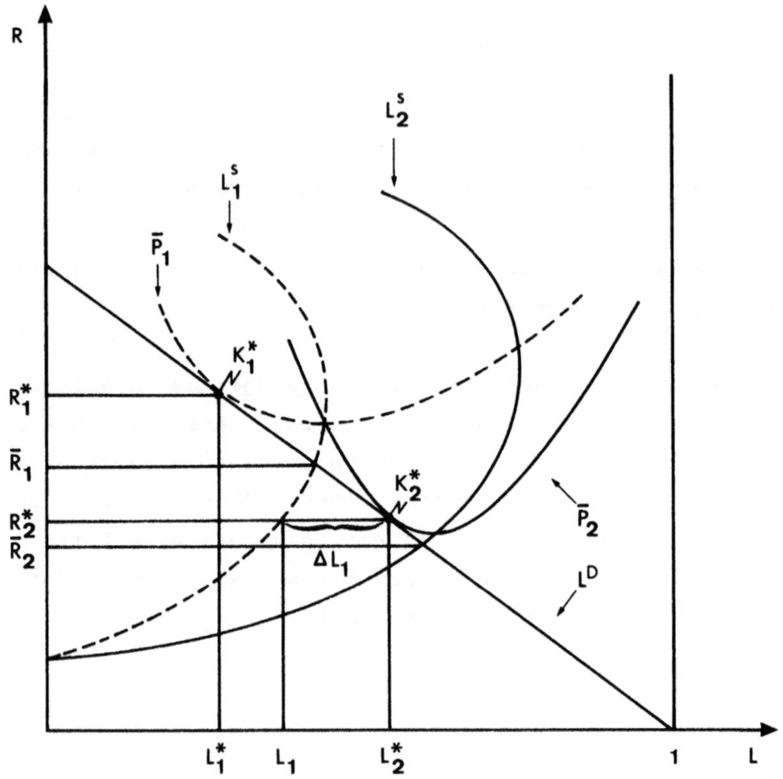

Figure 1

The negatively sloped curve L^D represents the demanded size of a loan as a function of R. Jaffee and Modigliani do not explicitly derive it, and here it is assumed without violation of their argument that it is the same for both types of projects. Dotted lines refer to project 1, solid lines to project 2. The convex curves marked as $\bar{p}_1$ and $\bar{p}_2$ are iso-profit curves of the banks. Their slope equals

$$(8) \quad \frac{dR^p}{dL} = - \frac{R(1-F(RL)) - I}{L(1-F(RL))}$$

which is negative for any $\bar{p} > 0$ and L sufficiently small, with the second derivative

$$(15) \quad \frac{d^2R^p}{dL^2} = \frac{R^2f(RL)+(dR^p/dL)[(dR^p/dL)RLf(RL)+2(1-F(RL)-RLf(RL))]}{L(1-F(RL))}$$

which is unambigously positive for $dR^p/dL = 0$, hence dR^p/dL can change its sign at most once[1]. Higher iso-profit curves indicate higher expected profits. The line connecting all points (R,L), at which $dR^p/dL = 0$ is denoted by L_i^s, i=1,2, and is called by *Jaffee* and *Modigliani* the monopolistic bank's supply curve. Consequently, the intersections of L_i^s and L^D are called the market clearing interest factors $\bar{R}_i$. They are not, however, the bank-optimal interest rates. These are given at the tangency point of L^D and $\bar{p}_i$, denoted as R_i^* where the highest feasible iso-profit curves of the bank are reached, given L^D as the relevant constraint of the optimization problem of the bank. Now suppose R_2^* is the best uniform loan rate of interest a monopolist can charge. Then clearly it is profitable for the bank to grant loans of size L_1 for projects of type 1 which means an excess demand of ΔL_1. Hence, so argue *Jaffee* and *Modigliani*, credit rationing may be rational for a bank which is constrained to charge the same interest rate to all borrowers. This is certainly an improvement as compared to *Freimer* and *Gordon* who would call it credit rationing that L_i^s is backward bending before it reaches L = 1.

The problem with *Jaffee* and *Modigliani* is that they do not explain where L^D comes from. They hint that a loan applicant has some alternative possibility of financing the project, but they do not specify it. They seem to suggest, however, that borrowers have some wealth of their own (see in particular their 1976 reply to *Azzi* and *Cox* (1976)). The opportunity cost of project financing with equity is foregone interest earning on wealth committed to the project, and a natural assumption is that the sure interest rate i could be earned. Given wealth endowment W the expected profit of the borrower equals

$$(16) \quad \bar{g}(R,L) = \int_{RL}^{m} x\,dF(x) - RL(1-F(RL)) + I(W-(1-L))$$

The first term on the right hand side of (16) is the gross return of the project under the condition that it is successful in the sense that x covers the entire loan repayment. The second term equals the

[1] In order to obtain (15) recall that for an implicit function $G(R,L) = 0$ one gets $d^2R/dL^2 = -[G_{RR}(G_L)^2 - 2G_{RL}G_RG_L + G_{LL}(G_R)^2]/(G_R)^3$.

total repayment times the probability of success, and the final term represents the interest earnings of that part of the initial wealth which is not committed to the project. A project will be undertaken if and only if $\bar{g}(R,L)$ is nonnegative. This means that there is a critical zero-profit curve of the borrower with the slope

$$(17) \quad \frac{dR^{g}}{dL} = - \frac{R(1-F(RL)) - I}{L(1-F(RL))}$$

But this is exactly the same as (8), hence iso-profit curves of bank and borrower passing through a point (R,L) coincide. Therefore, the zero-profit curve of the borrower is the highest feasible iso-profit curve of the bank and thus the relevant constraint for a monopolist. Consequently, the diagramatic presentation of the bank's decision problem has to be modified as depicted in Figure 2.

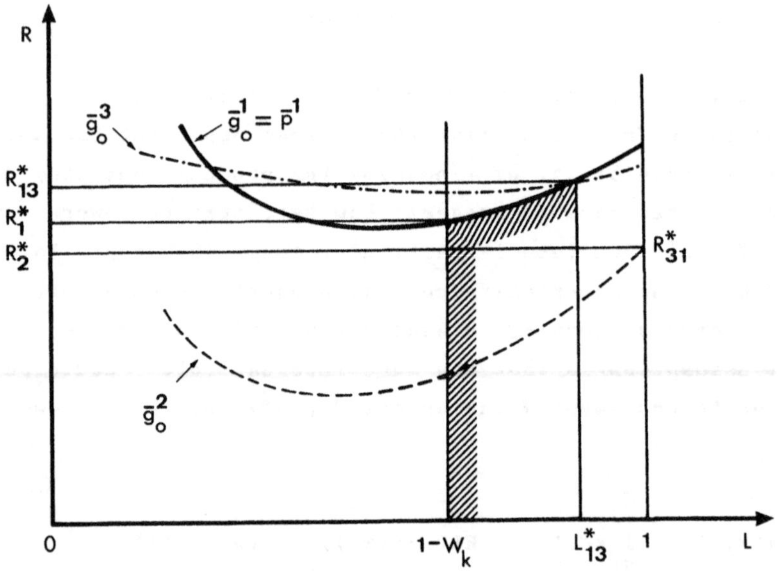

Figure 2

It is reasonable to assume $W < 1$, which ensures the need to apply for a loan in order to finance the project. If the bank wants to grant any loan at all then its minimum size is 1-W because otherwise the project would not be implemented.

Now suppose $\bar{g}_0^i$, i=1,2,3 are borrowers' zero-profit lines for three different types of projects. Basically, there are two possibilities: There may be some contract with R^*_{ij}, $i \neq j$, i,j=1,2,3, which is feasible in the sense that the corresponding L^*_{ij} is larger than $(1-W_k)$, k=1,2,3, and lies on the respective zero-profit curves of the different types of borrowers. This is the case, e.g. for R^*_{13} and R^*_{31} in Figure 2. At R^*_{13} both types of borrowers would get the same loan size L^*_{13}. In a sense they are both rationed since they desire a loan of size 1, but as argued above the term credit rationing is somewhat of a misnomer for this situation.

The second possibility is that there exists no such R^*_{ij}, as is the case with $\bar{g}_0^1$ and $\bar{g}_0^2$. The highest acceptable loan rate for type 2 borrowers is R^*_2, and it may well be that $\bar{p}_1 > \beta\bar{p}_2+(1-\beta)\bar{p}_2(R^*_2,L_2)$, where β denotes the percentage of type 2 borrowers (suppose there are no type 3 borrowers). At R^*_1 type 2 investors would not demand a loan, but this certainly does not constitute credit rationing.

We may conclude, therefore, that differences in the distribution of the project return do not lead to rationing by a fully informed monopolist if the alternative costs of financing the project equals forgone interest earnings of I(1-L).

Jaffee and *Modigliani* suggest that "the negative slope of the demand curve L^D can be derived from the assumption that the firm has only limited access to these alternative means of finance" (1969, p.855). As has been demonstrated, such a limit by itself does not yield the desired result. One possible interpretation of their statement is that the alternative costs of financing the project depend on the size of own wealth committed to the project. Then, instead of (16), we get

$$(18) \quad \bar{g}(R,L) = \int_{RL}^{m} x dF(x) - RL(1-F(RL)) + \sigma(W-(1-L))(W-(1-L))$$

with $\sigma' \geq 0$, meaning that the (sure) interest rate that can be earned on wealth is increasing in wealth.

The slope of an iso-profit curve now becomes

$$(19) \quad \frac{dR^g}{dL} = -\frac{R(1-F(RL)) - \sigma - (W-(1-L))\sigma'(W-(1-L))}{L(1-F(RL))}$$

In general we have $\frac{dR^g}{dL} \neq \frac{dR^p}{dL}$, and there are two possibilities: If $I > \sigma + (W-(1-L))\sigma'(W-(1-L))$ then the bank's iso-profit curve in the increasing branch is steeper at any point (R,L) than the corresponding iso-profit curve of a borrower. Hence, a monopolist will always offer the smallest feasible loan on the zero-profit curve of a borrower. However, the previous arguments concerning the non-optimality of rationing remain true.

Nothing essential is changed if $I < \sigma + (W-(1-L))\sigma'(W-(1-L))$. Since now the bank's iso-profit curve is less steep than that of the borrower, it will always offer the largest possible loan. To see this consider Figure 3

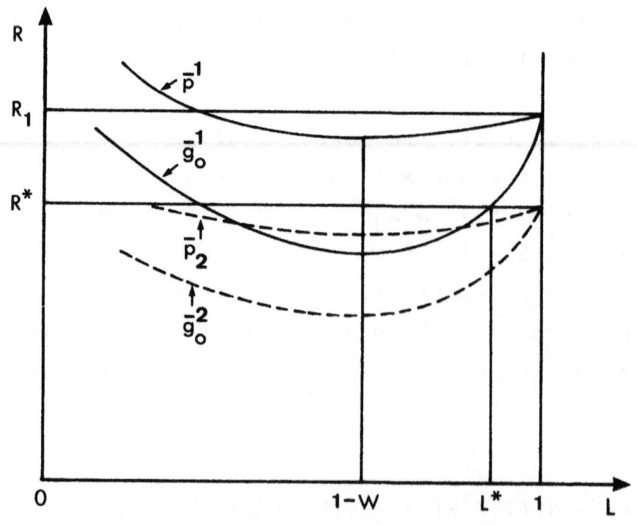

Figure 3

The optimal uniform interest rate factor is either R_1, in which case type 2 borrowers do not demand a loan, or R^*, in which case all borrowers get exactly the loan they desire.

In summing up, the failure of *Jaffee* and *Modigliani* to derive explicitly the demand for loans curve has led them to conclusions which are difficult to substantiate. A credit market with a bank monopolist and borrowers with fixed size projects does not have a nice negatively sloped demand curve as conventional wisdom would have it. Even the restrictive assumption that the monopolist has to charge one and the same loan rate to all borrowers does not lead to equilibrium credit rationing in any meaningful sense.

This basic conclusion is unaffected if some modifications are allowed for. Suppose, e.g. that in a competitive market the supply of loanable funds is an increasing function of I. Now, if there is an excess demand for loans in the sense that the available funds are insufficient to service all loan applicants then it is always possible to raise R in order to increase $\bar{p}$. This, in turn, allows the payment of a larger I and hence the attraction of additional loanable funds. This process will continue until either all loan applicants get a loan or reach their zero-profit curve. In the latter case they are indifferent between getting a loan and being rejected and hence cannot be said to be rationed. (Recall that with a monopolistic bank the loan rate will settle on the borrower's zero-profit curve anyway).

The above analysis remains basically the same if it is assumed that borrowers offer their wealth as collateral and demand always a loan of size 1. Denoting the amount of collateral by C the bank's expected profit becomes

$$(20) \quad \bar{p}(R,C) = \int_0^{\hat{x}} x dF(x) + CF(\hat{x}) + R(1-F(\hat{x}))$$

where $\hat{x}$ is the critical value of the project return which is just sufficient to cover, together with C, the full repayment of the loan, hence $\hat{x} := R - C$. In equilibrium of a competitive market we now have

$\bar{p}(R,C) = I$. The slope of the zero profit curve of a bank in (R,C)-space equals

$$(21)\quad \frac{dR^p}{dC} = -\frac{F(\hat{x})}{1 - F(\hat{x})}$$

which is nothing but the negative of the ratio of probability of default and probability of success.

A borrower's expected profit equals

$$(22)\quad \bar{g}(R,C) = \int_{\hat{x}}^{m} x dF(x) - R(1-F(\hat{x})) - CF(\hat{x})$$

Note, that $\bar{g}(R,C) + \bar{p}(R,C) = \bar{x}$. An iso-profit curve of a borrower has the slope

$$(23)\quad \frac{dR^g}{dC} = -\frac{F(\hat{x})}{1 - F(\hat{x})}$$

which is the same as (21).

As in the case where W is used as equity a monopolistic bank will offer contracts on the zero-profit lines of those borrowers with the most profitable projects. The previous analysis can be easily replicated and the same conclusions are obtained (see *Clemenz* 1984a and Chapter 4).

One final and obvious modification is the admission of variable projects. One consequence is that now it is indeed possible to obtain negatively sloped demand curves for loans. However, some additional problems arise which are analyzed in some detail in chapter 5. There it will become apparent that credit rationing as envisaged by *Jaffee* and *Modigliani* is not a viable equilibrium.

Thus we may conclude this somewhat lengthy section that the older literature on credit rationing, though it offered some valuable insights, did not provide a satisfactory explanation of the phenomenon under consideration.

1.4 The Role of the Horizontal Integration of the Banking Firm

A second approach to credit rationing which has been most clearly formulated by *Cukierman* (1978) rests on the fact that "a banking firm usually handles, besides credit, a number of other activities like demand and time deposits, foreign exchange transactions and in some countries like Israel even brokerage functions" (*Cukierman* 1978, p. 165). The crucial point of this approach is the assumption that the demand for banking services is an increasing function of the loan size, whereby the propensity to buy banking services is different for different loan applicants. Consequently, customers with a lower propensity may be rationed if the monopolistic bank is constrained to charge one loan rate of interest to all clients.

In detail the credit market model analyzed by *Cukierman* is specified as follows:
Banks can get any amount of loanable funds they want at a sure rate of interest i.
Borrowers are assumed to need the loan in order to finance a riskless project. If its return is a concave function of the loan size L, then it is easy to show that their demand for a loan is a decreasing function of R:

(24) $g = x(L) - RL$

(25) $\frac{\partial g}{\partial L} = x'(L) - R = 0$

where $x'(0) = \infty$ and $x'(\infty) = 0$ are assumed to hold.

(26) $$\frac{\partial^2 g}{\partial L^2} = x''(L) < 0$$

(27) $$\frac{\partial^2 g}{\partial L \partial R} = -1 < 0$$

Hence

(28) $$\frac{dL}{dR} = \frac{1}{x''(L)} < 0$$

The projects are assumed to be identical. In addition to the loan, clients also demand some other banking service, the price of which is denoted as b. The demand of the i-th client for the banking service is given by the following function

(29) $D^i = D^i(b, L_i)$, $\partial D^i/\partial L_i > 0$

It is assumed that the n clients of a bank can be indexed in such a way that
$i > j \Rightarrow \partial D^i/\partial L > \partial D^j/\partial L, \ \forall\, L \geq 0, \ i,j = 1,2,\ldots,n.$

Finally, the bank is engaged in monopolistic competition which means according to *Cukierman* that it considers b as given and selects L_i and a uniform R in order to maximize its total profit

(30) $$\max_{(R, L_1, \ldots, L_n)} p = \sum_{i=1}^{n} p_i = \sum_{i=1}^{n} (RL_i + BD^i(L_i)) - I\Sigma L_i$$

$$\text{s.t. } L_i - L^D(R) \leq 0$$

where $B := b-c$ is the net profit per unit of the banking service demanded, c is the constant marginal cost of the banking service. The constraint states that the bank cannot force a larger loan upon a client than he desires.

Supposing the requirements of the Kuhn-Tucker-Theorem are met the necessary conditions implied by (30) are

(31) $R + B(\partial D^j/\partial L_j) - I - \lambda_j = 0$

(32) $\lambda_j(L_j - L^D(R)) = 0$

(33) $\sum_{j=1}^{n} (L_j + \lambda_j(\partial L^D/\partial R)) = 0$

(34) $\lambda_j \geq 0, \quad L_j - L^D(R) \leq 0$

The Lagrangian multiplier λ_j measures the contribution of an increase of L_j to the profit of the bank. Clearly (31) allows for the possibility that $R < I$ and $\lambda_j = 0$ for some clients with $\partial D^j/\partial L$ sufficiently small, which in turn implies the possibility that $L_j < L^D(R)$ for some j. Hence, customers with a low marginal propensity to buy banking services may be rationed in equilibrium.

Note, however, that the rationing result depends crucially on the imposed uniformity of R: If the bank were free to charge different loan rates to different clients rationing would not occur.

Nevertheless, the model of *Cukierman* appears quite interesting: One implication is that R is smaller than I, and therefore loans granted to non rationed customers are larger than they would be without the dependency of the demand for banking services on the loan size. *Cukierman* claims that this is a source of inefficiency in the loan market, and he is quite right: In a more general set up it is possible that a client with a profitable project but a small propensity to buy banking services gets a smaller loan than a client with a bad project and a high propensity to purchase services.

The main conclusions remain unaffected if projects are assumed to be risky: Everything else equal, the possibility of rationing remains intact. The explanation of credit rationing provided by *Cukierman* (1978) appears to be more robust and convincing than those of the previous section, but it suffers from the same weak point: Some unexplained, institutional constraint on the pricing strategies of the bank is required in order to show that equilibrium credit rationing is a theoretical possibility.

1.5 Implicit Contracts and Credit Rationing

For some time implicit contract theory as initiated by *Azariadis* (1975), *Baily* (1974) and *Gordon* (1974) became quite popular as a possible explanation of (relatively) inflexible wages and equilibrium unemployment. The basic idea is that business fluctuations would induce fluctuations of the market clearing wage in the spot market. If workers are more risk averse than employers then a mutually beneficial agreement can be reached which guarantees a wage which fluctuates less than the spot wage or is even fixed, and is smaller than the average spot market wage. The employer insures the worker against wage fluctuations, and the latter may even accept to be unemployed in certain states of the world.

Fried and *Howitt* (1980) have tried to apply this idea to credit markets: They assume that the equilibrium deposit rate of interest is fluctuating. In a spot market this would induce fluctuations of the loan rate. The risk-neutral bank insures its clients against fluctuations of the loan rate by charging a fixed rate which is independent of the actual i and higher than the expected value of r. This arrangement, however, may involve rationing in some states of the world.

The formal structure of this model is the following:
In each period banks can raise funds at the interest rate i, which is, however, a discrete random variable with the probability function q(i). Hence, if i rules it is said that the economy is in state i. There are m identical clients for each bank. Each borrower needs exactly one Dollar in order to finance a project which yields the random return X. He wants to maximize his expected utility for given r, which is defined as

(35) $U(r) := \bar{u}(x-r), \quad u' > 0 > u'', U', U''$

Assuming that the expected utility without the project equals zero there exists a reservation loan rate $\hat{r}$ such that $U(\hat{r}) = 0$. Finally it is assumed that borrowers are always able and willing to fully repay their debt, hence there is no risk of default.

Each bank seeks to maximize its profit which equals in state i

(36) $P(r,n,i) = n(r-i) - c(n), \quad c', c'' > 0$

where n is the number of loans granted and c denotes an administrative cost function which is strictly convex in n.[1] If borrowers can switch costlessly from one bank to another then for a given i the competitive equilibrium loan rate equals

(37) $r = i + c'(m)$

If customers are tied to a particular bank then each bank is a monopolist and charges $\hat{r}$. This case is ruled out by assumption.

Suppose next banks offer an (implicit) contract to borrowers in order to exploit their risk-aversion and to insure them against fluctuations of i and thus r. Borrowers will only accept such a contract specifying r(i) and n(i) for each possible i if its expected utility does not fall below that of the spot market, which is denoted by U*. Hence the bank offers to its m clients (for convenience set m=1) a contract that solves the following optimization problem:

(38) $\max P(r(i),n(i)) = \sum_{i=1}^{k} [n(i)(r(i)-i) - c(n)]q(i)$

s.t.

(39) $\sum_{i=1}^{k} U(r(i))n(i)q(i) - U^* \geq 0$

(40) $1-n(i) \geq 0$

[1] We neglect the problem that n is a natural number and c(n) cannot, strictly speaking, be differentiated with respect to n.

(41) $n(i) \geq 0$

Equation (38) is the bank's expected profit for a given contract $(r(i), n(i), i=1,2,...k)$ which specifies the loan rate and the number of loans for each of the k possible realizations of i. If $n < 1$, i.e. if the number of loans granted is smaller than the number of applicants then rationing is assumed to occur at random. Hence, from a borrower's point of view $n(i)$ is the probability that he gets a loan in state i. (39) is the above mentioned constraint on the utility borrowers derive from the contract, (40) states that the number of loans cannot exceed the number of clients (recall $m=1$) and (41) is the usual nonnegativity constraint on the number of loans.

The Kuhn-Tucker conditions implied by (38) - (40) are

(42) $\{q(i)[r(i)-i-c'(n(i))+\lambda U(r(i))] - \sigma(i)-\mu(i)\} n(i) = 0$

$$n(i) \geq 0, \quad \forall \quad i=1,...,k$$

(43) $\{q(i)[n(i) + \lambda U'(r(i))n(i)]\}r(i) = 0$

(44) $\{\sum_i U(r(i))n(i)q(i) - U^*\} \lambda = 0, \quad \lambda \geq 0$

(45) $[1-n(i)]\sigma(i) = 0$

(46) $n(i)\mu(i) = 0$

where λ, $\sigma(i)$ and $\mu(i)$ are Lagrangian multipliers.

It is easy to see from (43) that $n(i) > 0$ implies that $r(i)$ is independent of i. In order to satisfy condition (43) the term in squared brackets must equal zero, i.e.

(47) $n(i)[1 + \lambda U'(r(i))] = 0$

which implies $r(i) = r^*$, and r^* is implicitly defined through (47). Furthermore, we get

$$(48)\quad \lambda = -1/U'(r^*)$$

This estabilishes the first result, the existence of a rigid loan rate of interest because of an implicit contract.

Next we turn to the possibility that $0 < n(i) < 1$ for some state i. In general, an interior optimum requires that the marginal return of the choice variable equals its marginal cost. We shall now establish that this interpretation applies to credit rationing in the present framework.

Substitute first (48) for λ in (42) in order to obtain

$$(49)\quad \{q(i)[r^*-i-c'(n(i))-U(r^*)/U'(r^*)] - \sigma(i)-\mu(i)\}n(i) = 0$$

From (45) and (46) it can be seen that $0 < n(i) < 1$ implies $\sigma(i) = \mu(i) = 0$. Hence, $0 < n(i) < 1$ requires that the expression in squared brackets of (49) equals zero. Clearly, from a formal point of view this is possible, and credit rationing may exist. But we shall now attempt to provide an economic interpretation of this term. The total expected gross return on loans of a bank equals for a given contract

$$(50)\quad \bar{p} = \sum_{i=1}^{k} q(i)r(i)n(i)$$

Suppose we have $n(j) < 1$, and constraint (39) is satisfied with equality. Consider the effect of a marginal change of n(j) on $\bar{p}$. The first thing to note is that r(j) has to be adjusted in such a way that the expected utility of borrowers remains unchanged. Differentiating (39) totally with respect to n(j) and r(j) yields

$$(51)\quad \frac{dr(j)}{dn(j)} = - \frac{U(r(j))}{U'(r(j))n(j)}$$

Differentiating $\bar{p}$ with respect to n(j) yields therefore

$$(52) \quad \frac{d\bar{p}}{dn(j)} = q(j)[r_j + \frac{dr(j)}{dn(j)}.n(j)] = q(i)[r_j - \frac{U(r(j))}{U'(r(j))}]$$

Hence, the expression in squared brackets is nothing but the marginal return of a loan in state j.

The condition for credit rationing (but $n(i) > 0$) in state i therefore is

$$r^* - U(r^*)/U'(r^*) < i + c'(1)$$

Note, that $c'' = 0$ would imply that this could happen only by chance. $c'' > 0$ on the other hand allows for the possibility that $0 < n(i) < 1$.

Implicit contract theory offers an explanation of credit rationing which does not depend on some arbitrary constraints on the loan rate options of a bank. However, the approach suffers from other weaknesses which are discussed briefly below.

The first point which is left obscure is the determination of i. In particular, it seems generally unreasonable to assume that in state i the interest rate is the same with and without rationing. But how is an equilibrium actually reached? Who can observe what, and at which point of time? The exogeneity of the fluctuations of i is analogous to fluctuations of the wage rate in labour markets, and it appears an unresolved problem to model a general equilibrium with implicit contracts in several markets.

This leads to the next weak point: What prevents banks from offering a fixed deposit rate of interest to the suppliers of loanable funds in order to protect them from fluctuations of i? Admittedly casual empirical observations suggest that the deposit rate i fluctuates far less than the loan rate r, and not the other way round, as the present approach would have it.

Finally, there is the problem of the enforceability of the contract. In the above model it would pay the borrowers to try to renegotiate the terms of the loan or to change the bank whenever $r^* > i+c'(1)$. On the other hand, if $r^* < i+c'(1)$ banks have an incentive to refuse to grant loans at a rate r* and to charge $r = i + c'(1)$. So in general at least one party always has an incentive to break the contract (for a general discussion of this problem see *Bull* 1983).

Fried and *Howitt* are well aware of this point and introduce a distinction between old and new customers of a bank, the former causing lower marginal administrative costs to the bank. This in turn means that they get a lower loan rate than new customers and incur a cost if they switch banks since they would become new customers of the other bank. The cost c' includes screening costs for new clients and costs of opening an account etc. Now first of all it is difficult to see why c(n) should be convex, considering that administrative costs are to a large extent fixed costs. Secondly, it remains unclear how the distinction between old and new customers is maintained in a multiperiod framework. *Fried* and *Howitt* assume that the two types of customers are offered different implicit contracts. But it does not make sense to talk about implicit contracts for "new" customers, since beginning from the second period of their relationship with the bank it is difficult to see what distinguishes them from "old" customers, at least as far as administrative costs are concerned. A more natural assumption seems to be that there exists a spot market for new entrants and a market for implicit contracts for old customers. But if this is so, what is going to prevent an old customer from switching banks if the spot market rate is favourable? He is not risking anything since in the next period he would be an "old" customer anyway, that is a properly screened applicant with an account. Hence it seems doubtful that the implicit contract approach is really going to work. But it points to an aspect which is very important in a credit market, and which has already been emphasized in the joint production model of the previous section: The importance of a special relationship between a bank and its customers. Unfortunately, as yet there is no satisfactory analysis available, and the one period models which are usually employed are obviously inapt for this purpose. On the other hand, it is clearly unsatisfactory to postulate such a relationship more or less ad hoc. As *Baltensperger* and *Devinney* have remarked "while rationing and customer relations can ultimately be viewed as arising from the same source, neither should be viewed as the 'cause' of the other" (*Baltensperger* and *Devinney* 1985, p.493).

1.6 Concluding Remarks

The literature on credit rationing reviewed in this chapter has not come up with a satisfactory explanation of this phenomenon. It is fair to say, however, that it has yielded some valuable insights into the nature and functioning of credit markets. In particular, there are three aspects which are important and differentiate credit markets from most other markets: The risk of default, the joint production of several banking services and the special bank-customer relationship. Though by itself non of these factors can explain credit rationing, they will be part of a full theory of credit markets.

In addition to the articles explicitly referred to there exist several surveys on rationing which discuss some of the approaches presented above. In particular *Baltensperger* (1978) and *Koskela* (1979) cover the older literature. Very akin in spirit to the present description is the survey of *Baltensperger* and *Devinney* (1985) and, not surprisingly, *Clemenz* (1984a), though both also cover more recent approaches which are the subject of the following chapters. A very recent discussion of the basic issues can be found in *Milde, Shim and Yoon* (1985).

Chapter 2:

ADVERSE SELECTION, MORAL HAZARD, AND CREDIT RATIONING

2.1 The Basic Model

It has already been indicated in Chapter 1.2 that credit rationing may occur if $\bar{p}$, the expected gross return per loan of a bank, is not a monotonically increasing function of the loan rate of interest r. This could happen if the probability of default is an increasing function of r, and if this negative effect of raising r outweighs its positive effect on $\bar{p}$. In this section it is shown more precisely how the non-monotonicity of $\bar{p}$ with respect to r creates the possibility of equilibrium credit rationing. The following sections present various mechanisms, based on asymmetric information implying adverse selection and moral hazard, which may induce the existence of a "bank-optimal" loan rate where $\bar{p}$ reaches a maximum.

The credit market analyzed in this and the two following chapters is quite similar to that in section 1.3. The supply of loanable funds in the period considered is a non-decreasing function of the sure deposit rate of interest i, formally

(1) $L^s = L(i), \; \partial L/\partial i \geq 0$

The risk neutral loan applicants are assumed to have no liquid means in order to finance an investment project of fixed size, which is normalized such that it equals 1. The project, if carried through, lasts for one period and yields a random return X with distribution function F(x), density function f(x) and support $[0,m]$, $m < \infty$. The loan applicant desires either a loan of size 1 or no loan at all. He is able, however, to provide some collateral C which can be thought of as some asset which is less liquid than money. A loan contract specifies, apart from the loan volume which always equals 1, the interest factor $R = 1 + r$ and the collateral C, $0 \leq C < R$. The net gain of a borrower at the end of the period for a given contract (R,C) and a project return x equals

(2) $g(R,C,x) = \max\{-C,\ x-R\}$

which means that the maximum loss he can make if the project fails equals C. This follows from the assumption that he is not liable with his private wealth, but the project return accrues to the bank up to a level where it is fully repaid. The critical or default level of X is therefore $\hat{x} := R-C$. The borrower's expected profit of a loan contract (R,C) at the beginning of the period equals

$$(3)\quad \bar{g}(R,C) = \int_{\hat{x}}^{m} x dF(x) - R(1-F(\hat{x})) - CF(\hat{x}) = m - \int_{\hat{x}}^{m} F(x)dx - R$$

The expression in the middle of (3) has the following components: The first term equals the project return under the condition that $x > \hat{x}$, which accrues to the borrower. From this he has to subtract the repayment, which is due with the probability of success $(1-F(\hat{x}))$ and the value of the collateral, which is lost with the probability of default $F(\hat{x})$. The last expression is obtained through integration by parts of the middle one.

Under the assumption that borrowers are risk neutral each demands a loan of size 1 as long as his $\bar{g}(R,C)$ is nonnegative.

Banks, who are also risk neutral, incur a cost of size $I := 1+i$ per loan (other costs as well as other banking activities are neglected) and receive at the end of the period the following gross return, after the project has yielded x

(4) $p(R,C;x) = \min\{C+x,\ R\}$

which implies the expected gross return

$$(5)\quad \bar{p}(R,C) = \int_{0}^{\hat{x}} x dF(x) + R(1-F(\hat{x})) + CF(\hat{x}) = R - \int_{0}^{\hat{x}} F(x)dx$$

The interpretation of (5) is analogous to that of (3) and therefore omitted. Note that $\bar{p} + \bar{g} = \bar{x}$, i.e. a contract (R,C) settles the distribution of the expected project return between bank and borrower. It is easy to see that $\bar{g}$ is decrasing and $\bar{p}$ is increasing in R.

(6) $$\frac{\partial \bar{g}}{\partial R} = -(1-F(\hat{R})) < 0$$

(7) $$\frac{\partial \bar{p}}{\partial R} = 1 - F(\hat{R}) > 0$$

Equation (7) implies that there cannot be equilibrium credit rationing as long as there are no restrictions on R. The only form of rationing which is possible in this model because of the fixed loan size assumption is what we have called Type II Rationing in Chapter 1.2: Some randomly chosen applicants are denied a loan despite their willingness to accept a higher R than the one quoted by the bank. Now if the bank is a monopolist it will always offer a contract such that $\bar{g} = 0$ and $\bar{p} = \bar{x}$. At this contract the risk neutral applicants are indifferent between getting a loan or not, hence there is no rationing. If the banking sector is competitive, as is assumed throughout this chapter, then one equilibrium condition is a zero-profit requirement, formally

(8) $\bar{p}(R,C) = I$

Now if $L^s(i)$ is too small to satisfy the entire demand for loans then this could not be a competitive Nash-equilibrium: Banks could raise R, thereby increasing $\bar{p}$ which enables them to offer a higher I and attract additional loanable funds. In equilibrium either there is no excess demand or $\bar{g}(R,C) = 0$. It is useful to visualize this argument with the help of Figure 1 below.

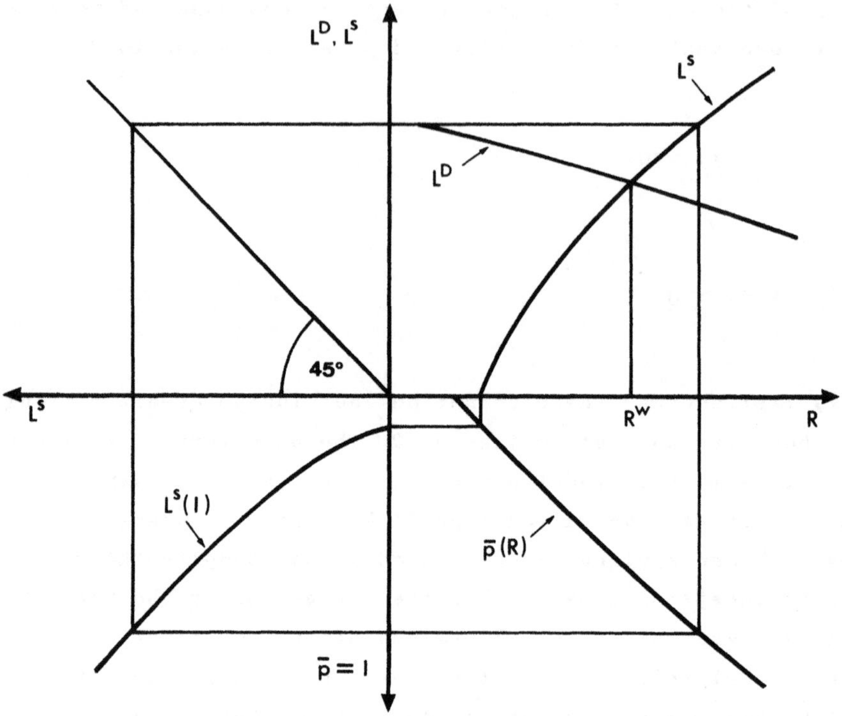

Figure 1

For an interpretation of Figure 1 it is best to start with the lower right-hand side panel. It shows $\bar{p}$ as an increasing function of R. The panel to the left represents the supply of loanable funds as a function of $\bar{p}$ under the condition I = $\bar{p}$. Projecting L and R into the right top panel yields the supply of loanable funds as an increasing function of R. The equilibrium is given at the point where this supply curve crosses the demand curve which is assumed to be decreasing in R. Obviously, in equilibrium the market is cleared.

Consequently, the possibility of equilibrium credit rationing in the present framework requires non-monotonicity of $\bar{p}$ with respect to R. In the following subsections several economically plausible mechanisms are discussed which generate this non-monotonicity, but for the moment assume that $\bar{p}$ is concave in R and decreasing for all $R > R^*$.

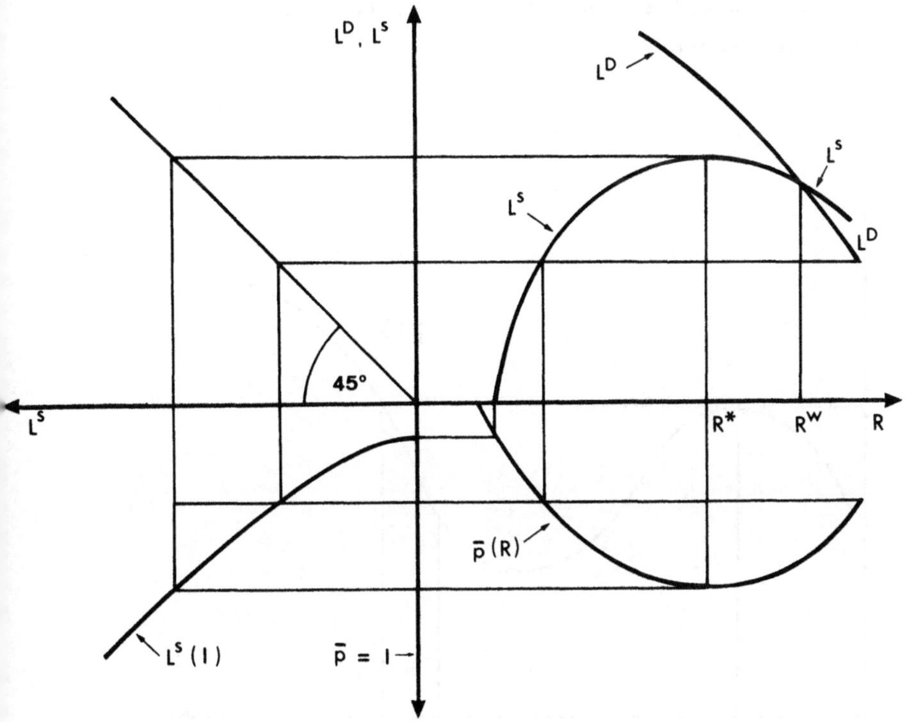

Figure 2

The consequent change of the model can be seen from Figure 2. Now $\bar{p}$ is no longer a monotonically increasing function of R, but reaches its maximum at R*. Consequently, the highest deposit rate banks are ready to pay equals $i^* = \bar{p}(R^*)-1$. Hence, if the demand for loanable funds at R* exceeds the supply at i* an equilibrium with credit rationing will occur. It would not pay a bank to increase R since this would reduce $\bar{p}$ and result in losses for her. Note that at R^w the market would be cleared but it could not be an equilibrium: A bank could attract both borrowers and depositors by reducing R and increasing i and still make a profit.

Stiglitz and *Weiss* (1981) have claimed that for equilibrium rationing to occur it is not necessary that $\bar{p}(R,C)$ has a unique, global maximum with respect to R. If $\bar{p}$ has, say, two local maxima then an equilibrium may exist with two loan rates and rationing at the lower of the two. To see this consider Figure 3.

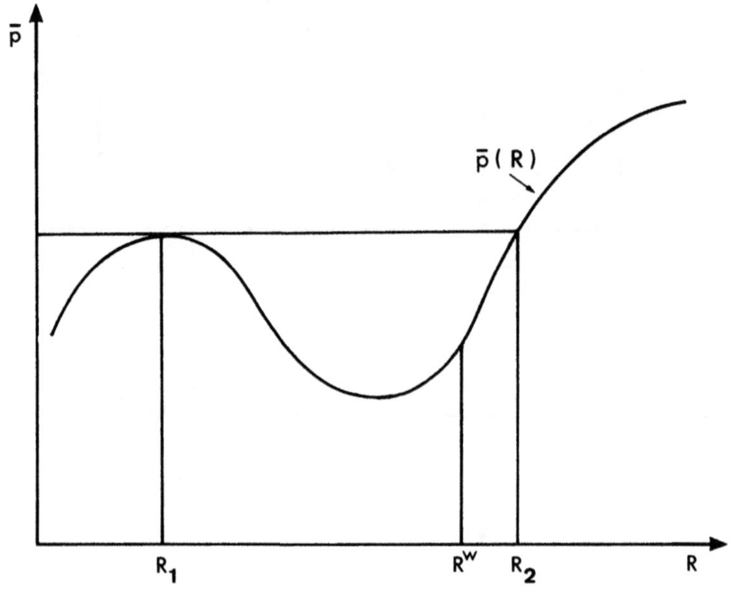

Figure 3

Suppose R^w is a Walrasian, market clearing equilibrium. It is not, according to *Stiglitz* and *Weiss*, the only possible equilibrium. Consider the pair of loan rates R_1, R_2. Both yield the same expected gross return per loan $\bar{p}$. Suppose at R_1 there is excess demand for loans. Clearly, if only R_2 were offered there would be an excess supply of loans. Hence there exists a distribution of loanable funds available to borrowers such that all who are rejected at R_1 get a loan at R_2. Some applicants, however, whose reservation loan rate factor R is between R_1 and R_2 are rationed. We shall discuss this idea in some detail in the next section. In any case, the problem to be solved is to investigate whether there exist economically plausible explanations for the existence of bank-optimal loan rates.

Hence, it seems to be a promising research strategy to consider all factors which may influence $\overline{p}$ and analyze how these in turn can be affected by changes in R. The following list looks rather exhaustive.

Model R:

Projects differ with respect to their riskiness as defined in *Rothschild* and *Stiglitz* (1970) and riskier projects are more profitable for borrowers. This approach has been developed by *Stiglitz* and *Weiss* (1981, 1983; see also *H. Wette* 1983).

Model H:

Borrowers differ with respect to their costs of default, thus an increase of r will increase the share of defaulters. This idea was first presented by *Jaffee* and *Russell* (1976).

Model E:

The return of a project may depend on the effort of the borrower which in turn will be affected by the total cost of the loan.
This moral hazard approach has been analyzed independently by *Clemenz* (1984b), *Watson* (1984) and *Krahnen* (1984).

Model A:

Borrowers differ with respect to their abilities which in turn influence F(x). It has been shown by *Clemenz* (1984b) that this may lead to adverse selection and rationing.

The basic assertion common to all approaches mentioned above is that credit rationing occurs because of asymmetric information about the factors which influence the outcome of the investment projects. It appears that increases of R affect all these factors in the same direction. This, of course, lends more force to each individual approach based on asymmetric information.

The four versions of credit rationing models based on asymmetric information are discussed in more detail in the following sections.

2.2 Projects of Different Riskiness

In this section it is assumed that projects differ with respect to the riskiness of return, where riskiness is defined in the sense of *Rothschild* and *Stiglitz* (1970).[1] Each borrower knows the riskiness of his own project, but banks cannot tell the riskiness of any particular project. One can imagine that the screening of projects by banks has left them with a class of projects with the same expected return, but different risk index k. The risk-index is obtained in the following way: Suppose F(x,k) is a family of distribution functions which differ from each other by mean preserving spreads. A higher value of k corresponds to greater riskiness if and only if the following integral conditions are met:

$$(9) \quad \int_0^m F(x,k_2)dx = \int_0^m F(x,k_1)dx$$

$$(10) \quad \int_0^y F(x,k_2)dx \geq \int_0^y F(x,k_1)dx \qquad \forall y \leq m \text{ and } k_2 > k_1$$

(Recall that [0,m] is the support of f(x)).

Quite often it is convenient to assume that F(x,k) is differentiable with respect to k. Then conditions (9) and (10) become

$$(9') \quad \int_0^m F_k(x,k)dx = 0$$

$$(10') \quad \int_0^y F_k(x,k)dx \geq 0 \qquad \forall y \leq m$$

[1] The intuition behind this concept is that a distribution is riskier than another one if both have the same expected value and the second is preferred by all risk averse individuals. The reader not familiar with this may check that the first point is implied by (9) and the second by (10) below.

Condition (9) (or (9')) implies equal means of all distributions belonging to this family. Condition (10) corresponds to the concept of second degree stochastic dominance (SDSS) and implies, among other things, that distributions with smaller k are preferred by all risk averse agents and have a smaller variance (the latter implication cannot be reversed in general).

One implication of condition (10') can be easily established: Riskier projects yield a higher expected profit for borrowers and a lower one for banks. To see this substitute F(x,k) for F(x) in (3) and (5) and differentiate both with respect to k in order to obtain

$$(11) \quad \frac{\partial \bar{g}}{\partial k} = - \int_{\hat{x}}^{m} F_k(x,k)dx > 0$$

$$(12) \quad \frac{\partial \bar{p}}{\partial k} = - \int_{0}^{\hat{x}} F_k(x,k)dx < 0$$

This result can also be shown by referring to the shape of g(R,C;x) and p(R,C;x): The former is convex in x, the latter is concave, as can also be seen from Figure 4.

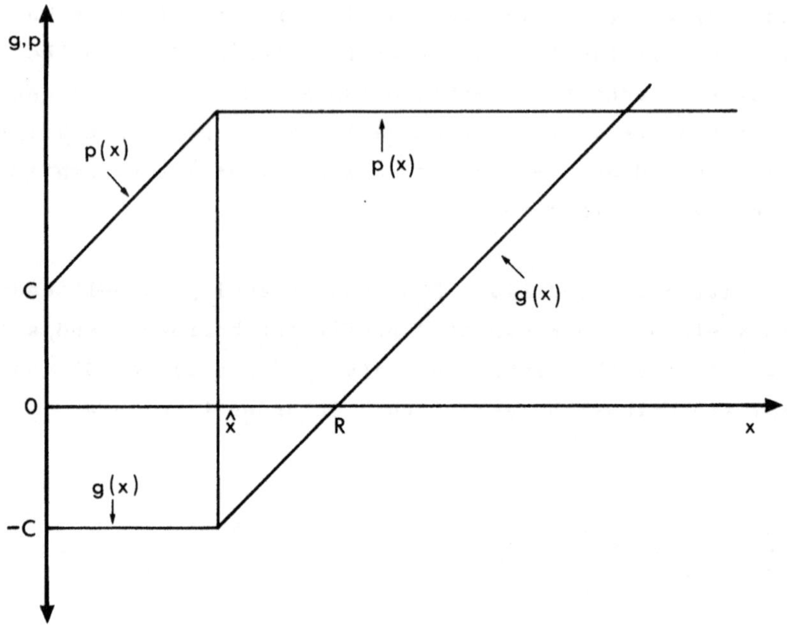

Figure 4

The crucial implication of (11) is that as R is increased the project with the lowest k is the first to become unprofitable and to be withdrawn. If R is further increased the relatively safe projects are withdrawn, and the average riskiness of the remaining projects is increased. Formally this is easy to establish. Denote by $\hat{k}$ the critical level of riskiness, implicitly defined by the condition

$$(13)\quad \tilde{g}(R,C,k) = m - \int_{\hat{x}}^{m} F(x,\hat{k})dx - R = 0$$

Differentiating (13) totally with respect to $\hat{k}$ and R yields

$$(14)\quad \frac{dk}{dR} = \frac{1 - F(\hat{x},\hat{k})}{-\int_{\hat{x}}^{m} F_k(x,\hat{k})dx} > 0$$

Consequently, adverse selection takes place as soon as R is increased above a certain level, and the increase of average riskiness may outweigh the positive effect on $\bar{p}$ of an increase in R. To derive this result formally assume that there is a continuum of projects and that k is distributed over the set of all projects according to a distribution function H(k).

For given C the critical level of riskiness is a function of R, hence $\hat{k} = k(R)$. The bank's expected gross return per loan for a given contract (R,C) equals

$$(15) \quad \bar{\bar{p}}(R,C) = \frac{\int_{k(R)}^{\infty} \bar{p}(k,R,C)dH(k)}{1 - H(k(R))}$$

Differentiating (15) with respect to R yields

$$(16) \quad \frac{\partial \bar{\bar{p}}}{\partial R} = \frac{\int_{\hat{k}}^{\infty} (1-F(R,k))dH(k) - h(\hat{k})(dk/dR)(\bar{p}(\hat{k},C,R)-\bar{\bar{p}}(R,C))}{1 - H(\hat{k})}$$

The first term of the numerator of (16) is clearly positive and represents the expected increase of p due to an increase of R. (Recall that $\partial\bar{p}/\partial R = 1-F(\hat{R}))$. The second term, however, is negative: h(k) is a density function, $\partial\hat{k}/\partial R$ is positive according to (14), and $\bar{p}(k,R,C) > \bar{\bar{p}}(R,C)$, since the former is the return on the least risky, and, because of (12), on the most profitable of all projects undertaken. The second term represents the adverse selection effect, i.e. the deterioration of the riskiness due to an increase of R. With an appropriate choice of H(k) and F(x,k) equation (16) may equal zero for some R = R* with negative second derivative, hence a (local) maximum and a bank optimal loan rate may exist, and the argument of the previous section applies.

It is useful to illustrate the *Stiglitz* and *Weiss* (1981) model by a simple example that has been analyzed in some of the literature criticising and extending their approach and will appear in some of the later chapters.

Example 1: Consider a credit market with only two types of projects. Each project has only two possible outcomes, either x_i with probability q_i or zero with probability $(1-q_i)$, $i = 1,2$. In order to conform with conditions (9) and (10) the expected outcome of both must be equal, say $\bar{x}$, which implies $q_i = \bar{x}/x_i$.

The expected gain of the i-th borrower, given (R,C) equals $\bar{g}_i(R,C) = (\bar{x}/x_i)(x_i-R+C)-C$, implying a maximum acceptable R which is given by $R_i^{\dagger} = x_i - (x_i-\bar{x})C/\bar{x}$, and clearly $R_i^{\dagger}$ is an increasing function of x_i (unless $C = \bar{x}$). Suppose $x_2 > x_1$, and denote the relative share of type 1 projects by β. At $R_1^{\dagger}$ we get

$$\text{(i)} \quad \bar{\bar{p}}(R_1^{\dagger},C) = \beta\bar{x}+(1-\beta)[(R_1^{\dagger}\bar{x}/x_2)+C(x_2-\bar{x})/x_2] < \bar{x}$$

Consequently, at $R_1^{\dagger}$ the bank's gross return reaches a local maximum: If R is decreased then $\bar{\bar{p}}$ falls because $\bar{p}_i$ is smaller for all borrowers. If R is slightly increased then all relatively safe projects are withdrawn, and β can be set equal to zero in (i). On the other hand, there exists an $R_2^{\ddagger}$ such that the bank's profit per loan equals $\bar{x}$ which is larger than $\bar{\bar{p}}(R_1^{\dagger},C)$. But for this example that means that credit rationing in the form described cannot be a Nash-equilibrium. To see this consult Figure 5.

At $R_1^{\dagger}$ the demand for loans falls from the number of total projects, denoted by M, to $(1-\beta)M$. According to a previous argument there are two potential equilibria: The market clearing equilibrium R^w and the pair $(R_1^{\dagger},R_2)$. But even in the latter case there is rationing only in a limited sense: At $R_1^{\dagger}$ type 1 borrowers are indifferent between getting a loan or not, and type 2 borrowers rejected at $R_1^{\dagger}$ get a loan at R_2.

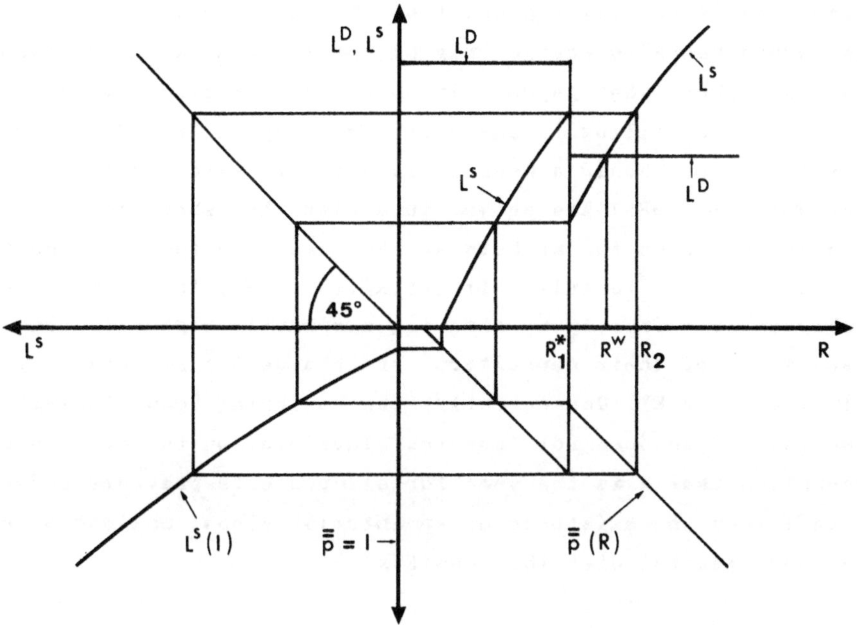

Figure 5

Another problem ist whether (R_1^*, R_2) constitutes a plausible equilibrium. Suppose at $\bar{p}(R_1^*) = \bar{p}(R_2) = I$ the supply of loanable funds equals N, the total number of potential borrowers equals M, and the share of type 1 clients equals β. At R_1^*, the total demand for loans is M > N, at R_2 it is (1-β)M < N. In order to make (R_1^*, R_2) an equilibrium only M applicants are allowed to get a loan, where λ is defined by

(ii) $M + (1-\lambda)(1-\beta)M = N$

or $\lambda = (N-(1-\beta)M/\beta M < 1$

The first question is how banks arrive at an acceptance rate of λ at R_1^*. Which incentive has a single bank to offer R_1^* and R_2 at the same time, and in the right proportion? Would not competition for clients induce banks to charge only R_1^* and to grant as many loans as they can? But then, what happens if there is an excess demand from borrowers who are willing to pay a loan rate up to $R_2^* > R_2$ in order to get a loan? Why should a bank satisfy itself with charging R_2? In fact, as *Yanelle* (1985) has shown, in a situation where an intermediary deals on two markets at the same time the Bertrand-Nash-equilibrium may fail to exist: If (R_2^*, R_2, λ) rules, then a bank can profitably deviate from it by offering a slightly higher I, robbing all competitors of their depositors, and charge $R > R_2$, possibly the monopoly loan rate R_2^*. Consequently, the rationing "equilibrium" with two loan rates does not look too plausible. On the other hand, the assumption that $\bar{x}$ is the same for all projects prevents under given conditions the existence of an interior global maximum of $\bar{p}(R)$ also for more general distributions F(x).

Is there a possibility that R_1^* could be a rationing equilibrium by itself? One way to achieve this is to employ the concept of a local equilibrium: If one assumes that banks consider only very small variations of R, then R_1^* could indeed be such a local equilibrium since a small increase of R above R_1^* leads to a sharp reduction of $\bar{p}$. Such overcautious behaviour of banks does not seem implausible though it is somehow in contrast to their assumed risk neutrality.

A second, economically still more convincing assumption that can make R_1^* the global optimal bank rate is that C is not perfectly liquid. This means that the bank incurs costs if the project fails, which are denoted by Z. The highest gross return a bank can get equals

$$\text{(iii)} \quad \bar{p}_{max}(R,C) = \bar{x} - Z \frac{x-\bar{x}}{x}$$

and $\bar{p}_{max}$ is a decreasing function of x. Hence the highest return a bank can make on the safe project is larger than what it can get on the risky project. The question is whether the difference is big enough to make R_1^*, where both types of borrowers get loans, a global maximum. It is straight forward though tedious, to show that the answer is yes if β, the share of loans used for the safe project, satisfies

$$\text{(iv)} \quad \beta > \bar{x}(1-K)/\bar{x}(1-K)+Z\,\frac{\bar{x}(x_2-x_1)}{x_1 x_2} < 1$$

$$\text{where } K: = x_1/x_2 - C\,\frac{x_1-\bar{x}(1-x_2+\bar{x})}{\bar{x}x_2}$$

Consequently, the introduction of default costs for the bank makes credit rationing more likely to occur in equilibrium, since it allows for the possibility that an interior global maximum of $\bar{p}(R)$ exists.

It follows that the *Stiglitz* and *Weiss* approach is not without its difficulties as it stands. As has been shown the approach seems vulnerable if no additional assumptions are used which allow for the existence of an interior bank optimal loan rate.

Other criticisms have been raised, but since they usually also apply to the other models discussed in the following sections we shall postpone the discussion until the end of this chapter.

One point, however, which is peculiar to the *Stiglitz* and *Weiss* model concerns the magnitude of R at which rationing may occur. For a perfectly safe project with certain return $\bar{x}$ we must have $R > \bar{x}$ in order that it be withdrawn. Consequently, with risky projects R must be well above $\bar{x}$ for credit rationing to occur. We leave it to the reader to judge whether this can be considered a range of R likely to be observed in reality.

Despite these caveats the *Stiglitz* and *Weiss* model is certainly a path breaking and seminal contribution to the rationing literature. Though the basic ideas were present in earlier work by *Jaffee* and *Russell* (1976) and in particular *Keeton* (1979) it was the clearest and most influential statement of the asymmetric information approach to credit markets.

We now turn to other models which are similar to *Stiglitz* and *Weiss* at least in spirit.

2.3 Borrowers of Different Honesty

The following approach to credit rationing proposed by *Jaffee* and *Russell* (1976) differs from all models discussed so far as the default of a borrower is no longer forced upon him because of bad luck with his project, but is at least partly the result of an economic decision: A borrower will default on his loan whenever the costs of default are smaller than full repayment. Costs of default are exogenously given, different for different borrowers and unknown to the bank. An increase of R will induce a larger share of borrowers to opt for default rather than to repay R. Hence a bank optimal loan rate may exist which will not be exceeded even in face of an excess demand for loans.

Formally there are only minor modifications of the models in section 2.1 and 2.2. The supply of loanable funds is given by (1).

The most important change occurs for the loan applicants. In order to make default a choice of borrowers the assumption that banks can get hold of the project return is dropped. If borrowers do not fully repay R then they incur default costs denoted by D. For the sake of simplicity it is assumed in the remainder of this chapter that they have no initial wealth and $C = 0$. Clearly, a borrower will only try to honour his commitment if $R \leq D$ (it is assumed that he prefers to be honest if $R = D$).

The cost of default D requires some interpretation. In the original consumption loan model it can simply be regarded as the disutility of being dishonest, which may differ among consumers. It could also be considered to be some expected penalty, where different agents assign different likelihoods to the possibility of being caught. Probably the most appealing interpretation of D is that it represents the cost of being excluded from the credit market in the future. *Allen* (1983) has given a rigorous formulation of this idea. It seems particularly relevant if credit markets with souvereign borrowers are concerned:

The only possibility for the banking sector to punish defaulters who are national governments is exclusion from the credit market (for a survey of these issues see *Saunders* 1983. Recent contributions in this vein are *Kletzer* 1984, *Eaton and Gersovitz* 1980. See also chapter 3.4 below).

If one accepts that the assumption of substantial exogenous costs of default is reasonable then the profit of a borrower equals

$$(17)\quad g(R,x) = \max\{x-R,\ x-D\}$$

which implies the expected profit

$$(18)\quad \bar{g}(R) = \bar{x} - \min(D,R)(1-F(R)) - DF(R)$$

The right hand side of (18) has the following interpretation: The deduction from the expected return of the project depends on its outcome: If it is successful in the sense that $R \leq x$ then the borrower has a choice between either defaulting and incurring costs D or repaying R. If the project fails and yields only some $x < R$ then he defaults anyway. Such a failure occurs with probability $F(R)$.

If the default costs are sufficiently large (i.e. the borrower is very "honest") $\bar{g}$ will become zero for some $R < \bar{x}$. That critical value $R^*(D)$ is given by

$$(19)\quad D^* = \frac{\bar{x} - R^*(1-F(R^*))}{F(R^*)}$$

with first derivative

$$(20)\quad \frac{dD^*}{dR} = \frac{-F(R^*)(1-F(R^*)) - f(R^*)(x-R^*)}{F(R^*)^2} < 0 \quad \text{for } \bar{x} > R^*$$

Equation (20) says that an increase of R causes borrowers with high costs of default who are good risks for the bank to withdraw their demand. Now suppose there is a continuum of potential loan applicants normalized to be the interval [0,1] and the default costs D are distributed among them according to the distribution function H(D). Total demand for loans as a function of R is given by

$$(21)\quad L^D(R) = H(D^*(R))$$

Only those borrowers are willing to honour their commitment for whom $R \leq D$. Hence, the probability that a particular borrower is honest denoted as q equals

$$(22)\quad q(R) = \frac{H(D^*(R)) - H(R)}{H(D^*(R))}$$

The bank's probability of being repaid, denoted by Q(R), equals the probability of willingness q(R) times the probability of ability (1-F(R)). Hence we have arrived at the formulation of the expected gross return per loan of the bank for given R:

$$(23)\quad \bar{p}(R) = RQ(R)$$

where

$$(24)\quad Q(R) = \frac{(1-F(R))(H(D^*(R)) - H(R))}{H(D^*(R))}$$

The substitution of (23) for (5) is in fact the only change needed for the model of this section as compared to section 2.1 and 2.2 as far as banks go.

The necessary condition for a maximum of $\bar{p}$ implied by (23) equals

$$(25)\quad \frac{d\bar{p}}{dR} = Q(R) + RQ'(R) = 0$$

The term $Q(R)$ is clearly positive, whereas $RQ'(R)$ represents the effect of R on the expected "honesty" and is negative as can be seen below

$$(26) \quad Q'(R) = -\frac{f(R)\ H(D^*) - H(R)}{H(D^*)} - \frac{(1-F(R))[H(D^*)h(R) - H(R)h(D)(\partial D^*/\partial R)]}{H(D^*)^2} < 0$$

In order to show that distribution functions $F(x)$ and $H(D)$ exist such that there is a bank optimal loan rate at which credit rationing may occur consider the following example.

Example 2: Suppose there are only two types of borrowers, the honest and the dishonest ones with corresponding costs of default $D_2 > D_1$. Their projects have two possible outcomes, x with probability $(1-F)$ and a zero return with probability F. If $(1-F)x > D_2$ then there are two potential bank optimal loan rates, either $R = D_1$ or $R = D_2$. Denote the percentage of D_1-borrowers by H. Then we get for the expected gross return of the bank at the two interest rates

(i) $\bar{p}(D_1) = (1-F)D_1$

(ii) $\bar{p}(D_2) = (1-H)(1-F)D_2$

Clearly, $\bar{p}(D_1) > \bar{p}(D_2) \iff H > \dfrac{D_2 - D_1}{D_2}$

and since the last term is strictly between 0 and 1 it is always possible to find a share of "dishonest" borrowers which is large enough to make $R = D_1$ the bank optimal rate and credit rationing in equilibrium a theoretical possibility.

*

It is noteworthy that $\bar{p}(D_1)$ is a global maximum and the problems that arose in the *Stiglitz* and *Weiss* model do not occur.

One obvious objection against the above model concerns the absence of collateral. As I have shown elsewhere (*Clemenz* 1984a) an increase of collateral may also have an adverse selection effect since the very honest applicants drop out from the market for reasons similar to those captured in equation (20). In general, collateral cannot prevent credit rationing to occur, but this point is discussed in more detail in chapter 4 below.

The contribution of *Jaffee* and *Russell* was the first to introduce asymmetric information into the literature on credit rationing. It has gained in importance recently as it became apparent that international credit markets, where no legal authoritiy can enforce repayment, are a good example for the applicability of this approach. The critically minded reader is, however, referred to a recent exchange between *Jaffee* and *Russell* and their critics *Hesse* and *Vandell* (Quarterly Journal of Economics, November 1984). In the opinion of this author the critique is rather besides the point because it misses the crucial information problem present in the *Jaffee* and *Russell* approach.

2.4 Borrowers With Different Abilities

In this section it is assumed that borrowers, who have no wealth of their own, differ with respect to their ability which is denoted by a. Projects appear as identical to the bank, but their return X is stochastically increasing in a, formally,

$$(27) \quad F_a := \frac{\partial F}{\partial a} < 0, \quad \forall a, \ x \geq 0$$

where F(x,a) is the distribution function of the project return for given ability.

It is shown that an increase of the loan rate factor R may cause potential borrowers with relatively high ability to refrain from undertaking their project and to use their ability elsewhere, for example by accepting a job. It is assumed that borrowers can either take the loan and use it for some investment or receive a (wage) income w the amount of which depends on their ability, i.e. w = w(a) with w' > 0. Being risk neutral a potential borrower prefers the loan if and only if the expected net return is greater than w. If high ability clients back out because of an increase of R the average ability of borrowers decreases and the expected return of a loan to the bank may deteriorate despite the higher loan rate of interest.

To see that this may indeed happen consider first the expected net return of a borrower given interest factor R and ability a

$$(28) \quad \bar{g}(R,a) = \int_R^m xf(x,a)dx - R(1-F(R,a))$$

Differentiating (28) with respect to R yields

$$(29) \quad \partial\bar{g}/\partial R = -(1-F(R,a)) < 0$$

Differentiating (29) with respect to a leads to

$$(30) \quad \partial^2\bar{g}/\partial R\partial a = F_a(R,a) < 0$$

Economically (30) implies that borrowers with high ability suffer a bigger reduction of their expected net return if R is increased than less able borrowers. Intuitively, the reason is that able borrowers repay their debts including interest with higher probability than less able ones, hence they suffer more from an increase of the loan rate.

Next we turn to the role of the alternative income w(a). In a full general equilibrium model the source of this income as well as its amount would have to be explained explicitly, but for the present analysis it is assumed to be exogenously given. For the sake of simplicity it is assumed that the difference between the expected gross return of the investment and w(a) is the same for all a, formally

$$(31) \quad \int_0^m xf(x,a)dx - w(a) = \text{constant} > 0$$

We show below that it is the most able potential borrowers who back out first if R is increased above a certain level. Consider the critical interest factor $R^*(a)$, which is obtained from the following equation

$$(32) \quad \int_{R^*(a)}^{m} xf(x,a)dx - R^*(1-F(R^*,a)) = w(a)$$

Differentiating (32) totally with respect to R^* and a yields

$$(33) \quad \frac{dR^*}{da} = - \frac{w'(a) + \int_{R^*}^{m} F_a(x,a)dx}{1-F(R^*)} < 0$$

since (31) implies $w'(a) = -\int_{0}^{m} F_a(x,a)dx > -\int_{R^*}^{m} F_a(x,a)dx > 0$

The backing out of the most able clients leads, of course, to a deterioration of the average ability $\bar{a}$, which is defined as

$$(34) \quad \bar{a} = \frac{\int_{0}^{a^*} ah(a)da}{H(a^*)}$$

where h is the density function of a which is assumed to be distributed in the intervall [0,1], H is the corresponding distribution function, and a^* denotes the ability of the most able client who still applies for a loan at a given r. It is obvious from (34) that $\bar{a}$ is an increasing function of a^* which in turn is decreasing in R because of (33). Formally, $\bar{a}$ is a function of R with $a'(R) < 0$. The magnitude of a' depends on h, i.e. if the share of able borrowers is very high then an increase of R will lead to a large deterioration of $\bar{a}$.

Consider next the expected gross revenue per loan of a bank

$$(35)\quad \bar{\bar{p}}(R) = \frac{\int_0^{a^*(R)} \bar{p}(R,a)\,dH(a)}{H(a^*)}$$

Differentiating (35) with respect to R yields

$$(36)\quad \frac{d\bar{\bar{p}}}{dR} = \frac{(da^*/dR)h(a^*)(\bar{p}(R,a^*)-\bar{\bar{p}}(R))}{H(a^*)} + \frac{\int_0^{a^*(R)} (\partial\bar{p}(R,a)/\partial R)\,dH(a)}{H(a^*)}$$

Since da^*/dR is negative and $\bar{p}(R,a^*)$ is greater than $\bar{\bar{p}}(R)$ the first term is negative and represents the consequences of worse ability of borrowers due to an increase of R. The second term is positive and stands for the increase of the bank return on loans which are repaid. If (36) equals zero then credit may be rationed in equilibrium.

To see that this is a real possibility consider another example, this time numerical.

Example 3: Suppose there are two groups of borrowers, each with a two outcome project: Group one borrowers either make a gross return of $x_1 = 4$ with probability $q_1 = 3/4$ or of zero, and their alternative income w_1 equals 1. Group two borrowers either make a gross return of $x_2 = 3$ with probability $q_2 = 2/3$ or of 0, and their alternative income w_2 equals 1/9.[1] The share of group one borrowers is 3/4. The highest interest factor acceptable for high ability borrowers equals $R^H = 8/3$ which is smaller than the corresponding value for low ability borrowers, namely $R^L = 17/6$ (in order to avoid indeterminate behaviour it is assumed that potential borrowers apply for a loan as long as the

[1] In the numerical example (31) is not satisfied.

expected net return is nonnegative, i.e. as long as $\bar{x} - qR - w \geq 0$). The bank's expected return for $R^H = 8/3$ equals $(8/3)[(3/4)(3/4) + (1/4)(2/3)] = 35/18$. The corresponding figure for $R^L = 17/6$ is (since no high ability investors apply for a loan) $(2/3)(17/6) = 17/9$. Hence it would not pay a bank to increase R above 8/3.

*

2.5 Unobservable Effort of Borrowers

In this section it is assumed that all projects and all borrowers are identical, the latter being risk neutral. Each project requires exactly one unit of money and yields a random return $x \geq 0$. The distribution F(x) depends on the effort e, which is not directly observable by banks, such that an increase of e implies a stochastic increase of x, formally

$$(37)\quad F_e := \frac{\partial F}{\partial e} < 0 \quad \text{or:} \quad F(x,e) < F(x,e'), \quad \forall e > e', \quad x \geq 0$$

Again it is assumed that borrowers have no wealth of their own and service their debt as far as the actual return of the project permits. Hence the expected return of a bank per loan equals

$$(38)\quad \bar{p} = R(1-F(R,e)) + \int_0^R xf(x,e)dx$$

Let c(e) be the cost of effort to the borrower with $c', c'' > 0$. Then his objective function is

$$(39)\quad \max \bar{g} = \int_R^m xf(x,e)dx - R(1-F(R,e)) - c(e)$$

implying the first order condition

$$(40) \quad \partial\bar{g}/\partial e = \int_R^m x f_e(x,e)dx + RF_e(R,e) - c' = 0$$

Differentiating (40) with respect to R yields

$$(41) \quad \partial^2\bar{g}/\partial e\partial R = F_e(R,e^*) < 0$$

The sign of (41) implies, together with the second order condition corresponding to (39)

$$(42) \quad e'(R): = \frac{de}{dR} < 0$$

To see that the set of families of distribution functions for which (42) holds is not empty consider the following example.

Example 4: Suppose the project has two possible outcomes, 0 and 2, effort e can vary between zero and one, the probability of success equals $e^{1/2}$ and the cost of effort is given as $c(e) = e^2$. For any given R the borrower determines his effort e such as to maximize $\bar{g}$, i.e.

$$(i) \quad \max_e \bar{g} = (2-R)e^{1/2} - e^2, \ R \leq 2$$

implying

$$(ii) \quad e = \left(\frac{1-r}{4}\right)^{2/3}$$

with

$$(iii) \ e'(r) = \frac{2}{3}\left(\frac{1-r}{4}\right)^{-1/3}\left(-\frac{1}{4}\right) < 0 \quad \text{for } r < 1$$

By taking (ii) into account a bank maximizes $\bar{p}$ by solving

(iv) $\max \bar{p} = (1+r)(\frac{1-r}{4})^{2/3}$

and from this one gets the optimum loan rate r*.

*

In fact the example has already shown more than the possibility that the effort may be a decreasing function of the rate of interest: it has also shown that this negative incentive effect may become so strong as to outweigh the positive effect on the return per loan to the bank if it raises R. In order to show that this possibility can hold true in more general cases consider again (38). Differentiating $\bar{p}$ with respect to R yields

$$(43) \quad \partial\bar{p}/\partial R = (1-F(R,e(R)) - \int_0^R F_e(x,e)e'(R)dx = 0$$

and equality may hold if -e'(R) is sufficiently large.

The economic interpretation of the above result is straightforward: An increase of the loan rate of interest reduces the expected marginal return to the effort of the borrower. In order to reestablish equality between marginal cost and expected marginal return of effort he decreases his effort. In any case, if (38) has an interior solution a situation as depicted in Figure 2 arises and an equilibrium with credit rationing exists.

2.6 Concluding Remarks

It has been shown that asymmetric information in credit markets allows for the possibility of credit rationing in equilibrium, and to demonstrate this possibility is presumably all that can be hoped for: It seems unlikely that reasonable conditions can be found under which rationing necessarily occurs in equilibrium, and this is also true for other interesting and sensitive markets with imperfect information, like labour markets.

So one could as well stop at this point and proceed immediately to an analysis of macroeconomic implications of credit rationing, as some authors have done. In my view, however, this would be premature for at least two reasons.

Firstly, the models for which equilibrium rationing has been shown to be possible in this chapter share certain grossly simplifying assumptions, and one has to know more about the robustness of the rationing results with respect to a relaxation of these assumptions before drawing further conclusions. In particular, the following assumptions deserve closer attention:

(i) The one-period assumption: Typically, an applicant for a commercial loan maintains his relationship with a bank for several periods in the sense that loans have a maturity of several periods, and borrowers need loans not just in one, but in many periods. It has been argued that rationing may disappear once we enter a mulitperiod framework (*Devinney* 1985a). Unfortunately, a truly dynamic model as would be required for an analysis of these issues is presently beyond the scope of rigorous economic theory, but chapter 3 attempts a few steps in that direction.

(ii) The amount of collateral a borrower has to provide is exogenously given and its use as a screening device is ruled out by assumption. This point is taken up in detail in chapter 4, where also the assumption of risk-neutral borrowers is relaxed.

(iii) Project and loan size are exogenously given. Again this is certainly highly unrealistic, and the abandonement of this assumption leads to a number of new problems which make it necessary to devote chapters 5, 6 and 7 to this case.

Secondly, it is interesting to know whether the four variants of the asymmetric information approach are more or less interchangeable, or whether there are important differences between them in more general settings. It is hoped that the following 5 chapters, which elaborate on the basic models presented above, help to put future investigations of implications for economic policy on a somewhat safer ground than is provided at this stage.

Chapter 3:

CREDIT RATIONING IN MULTI-PERIOD MODELS

3.1 Overview

One of the shortcomings of all models presented so far, particularly in chapter 2, is their static character. In reality it can be observed very often that the relationship between a bank and most of its clients extends over many periods. Many authors have emphasized the importance of this bank-customer relationship, and some have conjectured that credit rationing is a result of the one-period models rather than of asymmetric information and other factors that have been presented as explanations (e.g. *Devinney* 1985a). The aim of this chapter is to make a first step towards an answer of two related questions: a) Why is there a special relationship between banks and its older customers, who are less likely to be rationed and get loans at better terms than newcomers? b) Is there still the possibility of rationing if more than one period is considered?

The analysis below is a fairly straightforward extension of chapter 2. In the next section it is shown how the threat of rationing in future periods can be incorporated in the moral hazard model E of chapter 2.5. Section 3.3 analyzes a simple adverse selection model as presented in section 2.4, where banks observe the performance of borrowers and revise their estimates of the distribution of the project return. Section 3.4 contains a model where default costs of borrowers are endogenized. It is analyzed, whether this version of model H from section 2.3 is compatible with other adverse selection models. In section 3.5 default is considered to be a joint decision of lender and borrower.

3.2 Rationing as an Incentive Device

In this section we return to the assumptions of section 2.5 according to which borrowers can vary their efforts and hence the distribution over the return of their project. The question asked, however, is different, since it is now analyzed whether it is rational for banks to ration new or previously unsuccessful applicants rather than old and successful ones. To answer this question requires a multiperiod model, and for the sake of simplicity it is assumed that each customer lives for two periods. At the beginning of each period he applies for a loan and if he gets one he implements his project for which he receives the return at the end of this period.

To simplify matters further it is assumed that no bank accepts a defaulter of another bank. This assumption can be justified in several ways (see e.g. *Allen* 1983, *Stiglitz* and *Weiss* 1983), for example, banks may sign an agreement that imposes a high penalty on a bank that grants a loan to a defaulter of some other bank, or there may be a law according to which the borrower has to pay first the debt he owes to his previous bank.

3.2.1 Decisions of a Loan Applicant

Given the above assumptions a bank offers to a customer in period 0 a contract specifying five variables: The current loan interest factor R_0, the probability of getting a loan in the next period after having fully repaid the current one, denoted by q_s, the probability of getting a loan next period after defaulting in the current period, q_u, and the corresponding conditional interest factors for the next period, R_s and R_u. In order to create a non-trivial incentive problem it is assumed that there exists an R^* which maximizes the one period return of a loan to a bank, i.e. solves

$$\max \bar{p}(R) = \int_0^R xf(x,e(R))dx + R(1-F(R,e(R))).$$ Denoting the

exogenously given time discount factor common to both, banks and borrowers, by $t > 0$, an applicant has to solve the following maximization problem

(1) $$\max_{e_0, e_s, e_u} \bar{g} = \bar{g}(0) + t(q_s(1-F(R,e))\bar{g}(s) + q_u F(R,e)\bar{g}(u))$$

where $\bar{g}(j) = \int_{R_j}^{\infty} xf(x,e_j)dx - R_j(1-F(R_j,e_j)) - c(e_j), \quad j=0,s,u$

and e_0 and R_0 denote effort and loan rate in the first period, and e_s (e_u) and R_s (R_u) are effort and interest factor of the successful borrower (the defaulter) in the second period.

Differentiating (1) with respect to e_0 yields the following necessary condition

(2) $$\frac{\partial \bar{g}}{\partial e_0} = \int_{R_0}^{\infty} xf_e(x,e_0)dx - c'(e_0) + R_0 F_e(R_0,e_0) +$$
$$+ tF_e(R_0,e_0)(q_u\bar{g}(u) - q_s\bar{g}(s)) = 0$$

Differentiation of (2) with respect to R_0, R_j, q_j ($j=u,s$) yields

(3) $$\frac{\partial^2 \bar{g}}{\partial e_0 \partial R_0} = F_e(R_0,e_0) + tf_e(R_0,e_0)(q_u\bar{g}(u) - q_s\bar{g}(s)) \gtrless 0$$

(4) $$\frac{\partial^2 \bar{g}}{\partial e_0 \partial R_s} = tq_s F_e(R_0,e_0)\{1-F(R_s,e_s)\} < 0$$

(5) $$\frac{\partial^2 \bar{g}}{\partial e_0 \partial R_u} = -tq_u F_e(R_0,e_0)\{1-F(R_u,e_u)\} > 0$$

(6) $$\frac{\partial^2 \bar{g}}{\partial e_0 \partial q_s} = -tF_e(R_0,e_0)\bar{g}(s) > 0$$

(7) $$\frac{\partial^2 \bar{g}}{\partial e_0 \partial q_u} = tF_e(R_0,e_0)\bar{g}(u) < 0$$

It can be seen from (2) that $\partial^2\bar{g}/\partial e_0 \partial e_j = 0$ for $j = s,u$, and it is easy to check that $\partial^2\bar{g}/\partial e_u \partial e_s = 0$. Thus it follows that the second order condition for the solution of (1) implies together with the signs of (4) - (7) without ambiguity that the effort e_0 is an increasing function of R_u and q_s and a decreasing function of R_s and q_u. Ambiguity may arise, however, as far as the effect of R_0 on e_0 is concerned. Even if $f_e(R_0, e_0) > 0$ for the relevant range of R_0, the sign of (3) may still be positive if $q_u\bar{g}(u) - q_s\bar{g}(s)$ is sufficiently large. Fortunately, as will be shown below, it can never be optimal for a bank to fix q_s, q_u, and R_s, R_u such that $q_u\bar{g}(u) > q_s\bar{g}(s)$ which would mean that default is rewarded, hence we may safely assume that e_0 can be written as function of the following form

(8) $e_0 = e(R_0, R_s, R_u, q_s, q_u)$ with $e_{R0}, e_{Rs}, e_{qu} < 0 < e_{Ru}, e_{qs}$

However, it will turn out below that the sign of e_{R0} is immaterial for the results to follow. Obviously, the effort exerted in the second period depends only on the loan rate of interest of this period and, as in the one period model, e_j is a decreasing function of R_j, formally

(9) $e_j = e(R_j)$, $e' < 0$, $j = u,s$

3.2.2 Decision of the Bank

Next we turn to the decision problem of a bank. It is tacitly assumed that borrowers compete for loans, i.e. the demand for loans is high relative to the supply of loanable funds for I and R_0 within the relevant range. The bank offers a contract $K = (R_0, R_s, R_u, q_s, q_u)$ in order to maximize the present value of the expected return of granting a loan in the present period and another loan in the next period conditional on the performance of the borrower. Put formally, the bank solves

(10) $$\max \bar{p}(R_0, R_s, R_u, q_s, q_u) = \bar{p}(0) + (1 - F(R_0, e(R_0, R_s, R_u, q_s, q_u)))tq_s\bar{p}(s) + F(R_0, e(R_0, R_s, R_u, q_s, q_u))tq_u\bar{p}(u)$$

where

$$\bar{p}(0) = \int_0^{R_0} x f(x, e(R_0, R_s, R_u, q_s, q_u))dx + R_0(1-F(R_0, e(R_0, R_s, R_u, q_s, q_u)))$$

$$\bar{p}(s) = \int_0^{R_s} x f(x, e(R_s))dx + R_s(1-F(R_s, e(R_s)))$$

$$\bar{p}(u) = \int_0^{R_u} x f(x, e(R_u))dx + R_u(1-F(R_u, e(R_u)))$$

The following necessary conditions are implied by (10) if a set of bankoptimal interest factors exists

$$(11) \quad \frac{\partial \bar{P}}{\partial R_0} = - \int_0^{R_0} F_e(x, e(R_0, R_s, R_u, q_s, q_u))e_R dx +$$

$$+ (1-F(R_0, e(R_0, R_s, R_u, q_s, q_u))) + t\frac{\partial F}{\partial R_0}[q_u \bar{p}(u) - q_s \bar{p}(s)] = 0$$

where $\frac{\partial F}{\partial R_0} = f(R_0, e(R_0, R_s, R_u, q_s, q_u)) + F_e(R_0, e(R_0, R_s, R_u, q_s, q_u))e_{R0}$

$$(12) \quad \frac{\partial \bar{P}}{\partial R_s} = -\int_0^{R_0} F_e(x, e(R_0, R_s, R_u, q_s, q_u))e_{Rs} dx +$$

$$+ tF_e(R_0, e(R_0, R_s, R_u, q_s, q_u))e_{Rs}[q_u \bar{p}(u) - q_s \bar{p}(s)] +$$

$$+ (1-F(R_0, e(R_0, R_s, R_u, q_s, q_u)))tq_s[-\int_0^{R_s} F_e(x, e(R_s))e_{Rs} dx +$$

$$+ (1-F(R_s, e(R_s)))] = 0$$

$$(13)\quad \frac{\partial \bar{p}}{\partial R_u} = -\int_0^{R_o} F_e(x, e(R_o, R_s, R_u, q_s, q_u))e_{R_u}dx +$$

$$+ (q_u\bar{p}(u) - q_s\bar{p}(s))tF_e(R_o, e(R_o, R_s, R_u, q_s, q_u))e_{R_u} +$$

$$+ F(R_o, e(R_o, R_s, R_u, q_s, q_u))tq_u[(1-F(R_u, e(R_u))) -$$

$$- \int_0^{R_u} F_e(x, e(R_u))e_{R_u}dx] = 0$$

$$(14)\quad \frac{\partial \bar{p}}{\partial q_s} = -\int_0^{R_o} F_e(x, e(R_o, R_s, R_u, q_s, q_u))e_{q_s}dx + t\frac{\partial F}{\partial q_s}[q_u\bar{p}(u) - q_s\bar{p}(s)] +$$

$$+ t(1-F(R_o, e(R_o, R_s, R_u, q_s, q_u)))\bar{p}(s) = 0$$

$$\text{where } \frac{\partial F}{\partial q_s} = F_e(R_o, e(R_o, R_s, R_u, q_s, q_u))e_{q_s} < 0$$

$$(15)\quad \frac{\partial \bar{p}}{\partial q_u} = -\int_0^{R_o} F_e(x, e(R_o, R_s, R_u, q_s, q_u))e_{q_u}dx + t\frac{\partial F}{\partial q_u}[q_u\bar{p}(u) - q_s\bar{p}(s)] +$$

$$+ tF(R_o, e(R_o, R_s, R_u, q_s, q_u))\bar{p}(u) = 0$$

$$\text{where } \frac{\partial F}{\partial q_u} = F_e(R_o, e(R_o, R_s, R_u, q_s, q_u))e_{q_u}$$

3.2.3 Properties of the Optimal Contract

Using equations (1) - (15) we now want to show that there may be an equilibrium with R_o, R_u and R_s such that none of these loan rates of interest will be raised even if there is excess demand for loans, and that $q_s \geq q_u$ always holds, i.e. successful old customers get preferential treatment as compared to defaulters.

The first point, of course, is already contained in the above assumption of an optimal loan rate R^* for the one period model. That this assumption is economically meaningful has been demonstrated in section 2.5. In order to facilitate the following analysis this assumption is slightly strengthened in that the following is supposed to hold

$$(16)\quad \bar{p}'(R) \begin{cases} > 0 & \text{for } R < R^* \\ = 0 & \text{for } R = R^* \\ < 0 & \text{for } R > R^* \end{cases}$$

Next several propositions are stated and proved which contain the main conclusions that can be drawn from the above analysis.

Proposition 1: In a contract that maximizes $\bar{p}(R_0, R_s, R_u, q_s, q_u)$ as defined in (10), the following inequalities can never hold simultanously: $q_u > q_s$ and $R_u < R_s$.

Proof: The proof proceeds by showing that for any contract satisfying the above inequalities $\bar{p}(R_0, R_s, R_u, q_s, q_u)$ can be increased by removing at least one of them.

Suppose $q_u > q_s$ and $R_u < R^* < R_s$. For arbitrary R_0 this contract is dominated by another one specifying $q_u = q_s$ and $R_u = R^* = R_s$. To see this check the following inequality

$$\bar{p}(0|K_1) + t\{(1-F(R_0|K_1))q_s\bar{p}(R_s) + F(R_0|K_1)q_u\bar{p}(R_u)\} <$$
$$< \bar{p}(0|K_2) + t\{(1-F(R|K_2))q_u\bar{p}(R^*) +$$
$$+ F(R|K_2)q_u\bar{p}(R^*) = \bar{p}(R_0, R^*, R^*, q_u, q_u)$$

where K_1 denotes the contract where the inequalities hold and K_2 the contract for which $R_u = R_s = R^*$ and $q_s = q_u$.

Clearly, $\bar{p}(0|K_1) < \bar{p}(0|K_2)$ because (4) - (7) state without ambiguity that a fall in R_s and a rise in R_u and q_s increase the effort and hence the probability of repayment. Since $\bar{p}(R^*) > \max\{\bar{p}(R_u), \bar{p}(R_s)\}$, the expected return per loan granted also increases, and in addition the probability that a loan will be granted is higher for K_2: $F_1 := F(R_0|K_1) > F(R_0|K_2) = F_2$, and the probabilties of granting a loan are:

$$(1-F_1)q_s + F_1 q_u < (1-F_2)q_u + F_2 q_u$$

$$q_s(1-F_1) < q_u(1-F_1)$$

hence the contract with $q_u > q_s$ and $R_u < R^* < R_s$ cannot be optimal.

In similar fashion it can be shown that $q_u > q_s$ and $R_u < R_s < R^*$ or $R^* < R_u < R_s$ cannot be optimal since they are dominated by contracts with $q_s = q_u$ and $R_u = R_s = R^*$.

Q.E.D.

Economically, proposition 1 sounds almost trivial because it simply states that defaulters will never be rewarded by a lower interest rate and a higher probability of getting a loan than borrowers who have honoured their commitments. The following proposition strengthens this statement further.

Proposition 2: For a contract that maximizes $\bar{p}(R_o, R_s, R_u, q_s, q_u)$ the inequality $q_u > q_s$ can never hold.

Proof: For the inequality to hold $q_s < 1$ is required. Because of (14) this implies

$$(14') \quad e_{qs}\{tF_e(R_o, e(R_o, R_s, R_u, q_s, q_u))[q_u\bar{p}(u) - q_s\bar{p}(s)] - \\ - \int_0^{R_o} F_e(x, e(R_o, R_s, R_u, q_s, q_u))dx\} < 0$$

Denoting the term {...} by A and transforming (12) implies that this condition has the form

$$(12') \quad z'(R_o) + (1-F(R_o, e(R_o, R_s, R_u, q_s, q_u)))tq_s[-\int_0^{R_s} F_e(x, e(R_s))e_{Rs}dx + \\ + (1-F(R_s, e(R_s)))] = \\ = z'(R) + (1-F(R_o, e(R_o, R_s, R_u, q_s, q_u)))tq_s p'(R_s) = 0$$

where $z'(R_o) := e_{Rs}A > 0$ since $e_{Rs} < 0$ and $e_{qs} > 0$.

It is easy to see that $z'(R) > 0$ implies $R > R^*$ where the former solves (12') and the latter would be the R that sets the expression in square brackets ($\bar{p}'(R_s)$) equal to zero. Hence $q_s < 1$ implies $R_s > R^*$ and, by using (13) and applying similar reasoning, $R_u < R^*$. But according to proposition 1 a contract with $q_u > q_s$ and $R_s > R^* > R_u$ cannot be optimal and the proposition is proved.

Q.E.D.

Proposition 2 states that defaulters are never more likely to get a loan in the next period than borrowers who have repaid their first period loan. However, a still stronger version of Proposition 2 holds true.

Proposition 3: A contract maximizing $\bar{p}(R_0, R_s, R_u, q_s, q_u)$ satisfies $q_s = 1$.

Proof: Because of Proposition 2, (14) and (12') $q_s < 1$ requires $q_s \geq q_u$, $R_s > R^*$ and $q_u\bar{p}(R_u) > q_s\bar{p}(R_s)$, hence $\bar{p}(R_u) > \bar{p}(R_s)$. However, by an argument similar to that of proposition 1 it can be shown that such a contract cannot be optimal. By changing R_s and R_u such that both equal R^* the $\bar{p}(j)$, $j = 0,s,u$, are all increased, and so is the probability of repayment. Further, it is easy to see that the probability that a loan is granted in the second period is increased as well. Hence a contract with $q_s < 1$ cannot be optimal.

Q.E.D.

Proposition 3 lends strong support to the claim of *Stiglitz* and *Weiss* (1983, p.913) ..."that under a wide range of circumstances, banks lend to borrowers who repaid their previous loans".

It is straightforward to show that propositions 1-3 also rule out $R_u < R_s$ in the optimum. The characterization of an optimal contract is given in the following proposition.

Proposition 4: For a contract maximizing $\bar{p}(R_0, R_s, R_u, q_s, q_u)$ the following hold:

a) $q_s = 1$

b) $q_u \leq q_s$

c) $R_s \leq R^*$, $R_s \leq R_u$

d) $R_0 \geq R^*$

Proof: a) and b) have already been shown. Part c) follows from the fact that $\bar{p}(R_0, R_s > R^*, R_u, q_s, q_u) < \bar{p}(R_0, R^*, R_u, q_s, q_u)$ and $\bar{p}(R_0, R_s, R_u < R_s \leq R^*, q_s, q_u) < \bar{p}(R_0, R_s, R_s \leq R^*, q_s, q_u)$.

Part d) of the proposition follows from (11).

Q.E.D.

Corollary 1: $q_s\bar{g}(s) < q_u\bar{g}(u)$ cannot hold in equilibrium.

This settles the question of the sign of e_{R_0} if $f_e(R_0, e_0) > 0$. Note, however, that this sign has not been needed for any of the above results.

Proposition 4 fully characterizes a contract that maximizes a bank's steady state expected gross return per loan granted to a first period borrower. The most important feature of such a contract for our purpose is the possibility of denying a credit to a defaulter. This result appears to be fairly robust and continues to hold if borrowers are risk-averse.

3.2.4 Equilibrium

As *Stiglitz* and *Weiss* (1983) point out in a similar context the question of the existence of an equilibrium is less straightforward to settle for a multiperiod model than for a one period model. One interesting possibility not further pursued here is that credit rationing may occur even if the supply of funds exceeds the demand (see *Stiglitz* and *Weiss* (1983, pp.920ff.)).

One requirement that ought to be imposed on an equilibrium is "credibility". This term, introduced by Stiglitz and Weiss, means that the commitment of a bank to grant a loan or to accept a deposit can always be honoured. In particular this implies that a fraction of $(1-F(R,e)) + q_u F(R,e)$ [=: $Pr(L_1)$] of the deposits for the first period are committed for the second period as well. This way a bank is prevented from breaking a steady state equilibrium by increasing its proportion of (more profitable) loans to new borrowers and use the higher profits to increase the deposit rate of interest. Hence, in a steady state equilibrium, in each period banks attract loanable funds paying a deposit rate of interest such that $\bar{p}(R_0, R_s, R_u, q_s, q_u) = I + tPr(L_1)I$ and a fraction $Pr(L_1)$ of the current funds is committed for two periods. Under the assumption that, given these interest rates, there is an excess demand for loanable funds not only (some of the) defaulters, but also some new borrowers will be denied a loan in each period.

Before concluding this subsection let us turn to the assumption that banks do not lend to defaulters of other banks. Suppose it is relaxed in such a way that it is possible for a defaulter to declare bankruptcy, thereby eliminating previous debt. In this way a bank knows whether a borrower is new in the market or has defaulted in the previous period. As *Stiglitz* and *Weiss* (1983) have shown in a similar context, it may still be optimal for banks to reject defaulters who apply for loans. The optimal loan rate for a second period borrower who is a new client for a particular bank equals R^*. Now assume that for the optimal contract $q_u = 0$ holds. A bank will pay a deposit rate i^* obtained from the following equation

$$(17) \quad I^*(1+t(1-F(R,e))) = \bar{p}(0) + t(1-F(R,e))\bar{p}(s)$$

But I^* may be greater than $\bar{p}(R^*)$, thus ruling out that banks can lend profitably to defaulters of other banks.

3.2.5 The Stiglitz and Weiss Model

Model E is not the only way to introduce moral hazard in credit markets. *Stiglitz* and *Weiss* (1981) show that model R also works when borrowers are assumed to have a choice between projects of different riskiness. In a multiperiod model this makes sense because the threat of future exclusion from the credit market may induce borrowers to implement safer projects which have a lower one period expected return for them than risky ones. The analysis of this version can be found in *Stiglitz* and *Weiss* (1983) and leads to essentially the same conclusions as the present one.

3.3 Experience Rating of Borrowers

In the preceding section it has been shown that a credit market may display the following features in equilibrium: "New" borrowers are charged a higher loan rate of interest than those old ones who have fully repaid their loan of the previous period. Also, some new clients may be denied a loan. Defaulters are frequently denied a loan and, if not, they have to pay a higher loan rate of interest than old clients, who fully honoured their past obligations. The reason was that borrowers can vary their efforts and banks provide appropriate incentives by offering favourable conditions to well behaved customers.

In this section it is demonstrated that these features may also occur if borrowers differ with respect to their abilities which are evaluated by banks according to their past performance. Hence this section contains an extension of the model of section 2.4 to the two period case.

To keep matters as simple as possible it is assumed that there are only two types of loan applicants, those with the high ability a_2 and opportunity costs w_2 and the others with low ability a_1 and opportunity costs $w_1 < w_2$. Further it is assumed that each project has two possible outcomes, 0 and x_2 or x_1 for the high and low ability group respectively. The shares of the two groups are β and $1-\beta$ respectively, and the probabilities of success are $\pi(s|H)$ and $\pi(s|L)$. Loan applicants live for two periods and appear in overlapping generations, whereas banks live forever. Finally, it is assumed that there exists an R^* that maximizes the expected gross return per loan for the bank in the one period model described in section 2.4 (in particular consider example 2.3).

Banks can only observe whether a borrower defaults or not, and they fully share all their information about borrowers. Borrowers know their own ability with certainty.

Now consider a bank facing first period borrowers. The first period interest factor is denoted by $R \leq R^*$, and R^* will be charged if loanable funds are scarce relative to the demand for loans. The expected gross return of the first period , $\bar{p}_0$, is given by

(18) $\bar{p}_0 = R(\beta\pi(s|H) + (1-\beta)\pi(s|L)) = R\bar{\pi}_s$

where $\bar{\pi}_s = \beta\pi(s|H) + (1-\beta)\pi(s|L)$.

At the end of the period when loans are due for repayment a bank observes who has defaulted and who has not. Then it updates its estimate for each client's probability to belong to the high ability group in a Bayesian fashion, i.e.

(19) $$\pi(H|s) = \frac{\beta\pi(s|H)}{\beta\pi(s|H) + (1-\beta)\pi(s|L)}$$

(20) $$\pi(L|s) = \frac{(1-\beta)\pi(s|L)}{\beta\pi(s|H) + (1-\beta)\pi(s|L)} = 1 - \pi(H|s)$$

It is easy to check that $\pi(H|s) > \beta$. Accordingly the bank will update the estimated probability of success of an old client who has not defaulted

(21) $\pi_s(s) = \pi(H|s)\pi(s|H) + \pi(L|s)\pi(s|L)$

and, with R_s denoting the interest factor for non-defaulters, the expected gross return per loan equals

(22) $\bar{p}_s = R_s\pi_s(s)$

Similarly, one can find the probability of success in the second period of a defaulter

(23) $\pi_s(u) = \pi(H|u)\pi(s|H) + \pi(L|u)\pi(s|L)$

and the corresponding return of a loan

(24) $\bar{p}_u = R_u\pi_s(u)$

Obviously, $\pi_s(s) > \bar{\pi}_s > \pi_s(u)$. Furthermore, in equilibrium with positive credits to each type of applicant $\bar{p}_0 = \bar{p}_s = \bar{p}_u$ must hold since otherwise banks could increase their profits by changing the composition of borrowers. The second equilibrium condition is $I = \bar{p}_0$. The two equilibrium conditions imply together with (21) - (24) $R_s < R < R_u$, where R denotes the interest factor for new borrowers. Now suppose $R = R^*$. Then obviously defaulters are denied a loan because R_u cannot exceed R^* (otherwise the high ability borrowers who were so unlucky as to default would drop out), but $R_u \pi_s(u) < R^* \bar{\pi}_s = I$. Hence there may be an equilibrium where all defaulters are denied a loan in the second period.

However, it may also be the case that only some defaulters are excluded from the credit market. If at $R = R^*$ there is an excess supply of loanable funds, I may be reduced until $I = R^* \pi_s(u)$ with corresponding adjustments of R and R_s. In this situation some defaulters may be granted a loan and some not. Finally, the supply of loanable funds can be so large that there is no credit rationing at all.

The above analysis is only slightly changed if banks are less cooperative and do not exchange all the information they have about their customers. A plausible modification would be that borrowers are always able to prove to any bank the repayment of a previous loan, but that defaulters may be indistinguishable from new market entrants. In that case π_s would change to

(25) $\hat{\pi}_s = (1/(1+\pi(u))[\pi(u)\pi_s(u) + \pi_s]$

where $\pi(u)$: $\beta\pi(u|H) + (1-\beta)\pi(u|L)$

and the analysis can proceed as before.

The analysis of this leads to a similar conclusion as the rather different approach of *Devinney* (1985a,b). He assumes that banks have an imperfect screening mechanism at their disposal which allows them to identify the true ability of a borrower with some probability smaller than one. Since the estimate may be wrong it can happen that a good risk is classified as bad and is offered a contract he does not consider acceptable. As an explanation of rationing this is somewhat unconvincing, however, since it would require that all banks commit the same error. If the classification is based on previous performance, on the other hand, such an error of the entire banking sector is credible, and *Devinney's* rationing example works.

Unfortunately, a more general analysis allowing for arbitrary random returns poses considerable difficulties, so we have to confine the analysis to the simple example of this section though the basic idea appears quite plausible.

3.4 Rationing With Endogenous Costs of Default

3.4.1 Identical Risk Neutral Borrowers

In this section we return to model H presented in chapter 2.3. There the decision to default is left to the borrower and depends on the size of the exogenous cost of default relative to the value of total repayment. Following the first elaboration of this idea by *Jaffee* and *Russell* (1976) there were several attempts, e.g. by *Eaton* and *Gersovitz* (1981, *Allen* (1983) and *Kletzer* (1984), to reformulate the model such that costs of default are endogenous and equal to future earnings foregone because of exclusion from the credit market. The version discussed below is most similar to that of *Kletzer* (1984) except that we stick to the assumption of a fixed project size equal to unity.

It is assumed that borrowers live (or at least expect to live) forever. In each period they can undertake a one-period investment project for which they need a one-period loan of size 1. This implies that there is no possibility for saving and reinvesting the proceeds of one period in the next period.

Let t denote the time preference rate and $T: = \frac{t}{1-t}$. Then the expected value of staying in the credit market forever equals

$$(26)\quad \bar{V}_s = \sum_{j=1}^{\infty} t^j (\bar{x}-R) = T(\bar{x}-R)$$

Here it is tacitly assumed that a borrower is always able to honour his commitments if he wants to.

Now assume that a project has yielded a return x and a borrower has to decide whether to repay R and stay in the market or to keep all of x and default. Assume that the future return of the latter option equals zero. He will default if and only if

$$(27)\quad x > x-R + T(\bar{x}-R)$$

or

$$(28)\quad \frac{R}{\bar{x}} > t$$

i.e. if and only if default is strictly more profitable than repayment. Note, that if borrowers are risk neutral then the decision to default or not to default is independent of the actual project return x: If R is too large with respect to $\bar{x}$ then each borrower will apply only once for a loan and then leave the market.

Things are slightly more complicated if we allow for involuntary default when x < R. Define the expected one period profit of a borrower who does not plan to default as follows:

$$(29)\quad \bar{g}(R) = \int_R^m (x-R)dF + \int_0^R xdF = \bar{x}-R(1-F(R))$$

Then we get for $\bar{V}_s$ instead of (26) (assuming stochastic independence of the project returns of different periods)

$$(30)\quad \bar{V}_s = \sum_{j=1}^{\infty} t^j(1-F(R))^{j-1}(\bar{x}-R(1-F(R)) = \frac{t(\bar{x}-R(1-F(R)))}{1-t(1-F(R))}$$

and it it easy to check that we end up again at condition (28) for default to be preferred by a borrower.

It is noteworthy that with risk-neutral borrowers the bank optimal interest rate $R^* = t\bar{x}$ depends only on the time preference of borrowers and the mean of X, but not on other properties of its distribution. Obviously, with a supply of loanable funds as given by (2.1) the total supply of loans forthcoming at $I = \overline{p}(R^*)$ need not match total demand and some applicants may be denied a loan. It appears somewhat strange, however, to call this credit rationing since rejected applicants are ready to accept a higher loan rate, but they would default with certainty. More interesting cases arise if the endogenous costs of default are different among borrowers. One possibility to model this is to introduce different discount rates t. Obviously this would lead to a simple replication of the analysis in section 2.4.

What seems more interesting is to assume different distributions of the random return since this offers a connection to adverse selection models where projects display different riskiness or borrowers have different abilities.

3.4.2 Endogenous Default Costs and Different Return Distributions

It is obvious from condition (28) that differences in default costs of borrowers may stem either from different time preferences or from different return distributions. As far as the second aspect is concerned it looks particularly interesting since certain types of differences between distributions, more precisely, those which can be expressed in terms of first or second degree stochastic dominance, give rise to the possibility of credit rationing by themselves, as has been shown in chapter 2. The question is whether and how various factors which may account for equilibrium rationing are related. This point is important in view of the difficulty to find screening and signalling mechanisms in markets with asymmetric information about more than one variable (see e.g. *Kohlleppel* (1983a,b), *Wilson* (1983), *Engers* and *Fernandez* (1984)).

The first such factor to be considered is the riskiness of projects as analyzed by *Stiglitz* and *Weiss* (1981). It is obvious from condition (28), however, that the riskiness of projects is irrelevant for the determination of the bank-optimal loan rate in the present multi-period model: All projects under consideration have the same mean return. Adverse selection in the *Stiglitz* and *Weiss* model starts at a level of the loan rate which satisfies $R > \bar{x}$. But according to (28) the critical loan rate equals $R = t\bar{x} < \bar{x}$. Hence the adverse selection effect due to "riskiness" is always dominated by the adverse selection effect due to "honesty".

The second factor of importance is the unobservable ability of borrowers. Under our usual assumption that the project return X is stochastically increasing in ability measured by an index a, there is a distribution of critical interest factors R which corresponds to the distribution of a among loan applicants. The determination of the bank optimal loan rate is basically the same as in chapter 2.3.

But recall that in order to create an adverse selection problem based on different abilities it had to be assumed that loan applicants have an alternative income w(a), w' > 0, which they can only draw upon if their project is not implemented. If the same assumption is entertained in the present model it is clear that the costs of default become smaller. Suppose first that borrowers have some financial backing which allows them to avoid bankruptcy even if their projects fail. Given an actual project return x they prefer to default if and only if

$$(31)\quad x + Tw(a) > x - R + T(\bar{x}(a) - R)$$

or

$$(32)\quad R > t(\bar{x}(a) - w(a))$$

Compared to (28) it is obvious that access to an alternative source of income lowers the value of the critical interest factor R for each risk class. If it is assumed, as in chapter 2.3, that $\bar{x}(a) - w(a)$ is the same for all a then there is the same situation as with identical borrowers, otherwise we get a distribution over the critical R's which is related to the distribution of a and the difference between expected project return and alternative income.

Next the assumption that borrowers never default involuntarily is dropped. If the project return falls short of R they have to declare default and face exclusion from the credit market. If a borrower with a sufficiently large project return stays in the market his expected profit in the next period equals

$$(33)\quad \bar{g}(R) = \bar{x}-R(1-F(R)) + t\bar{g}(R)(1-F(R)) + TwF(R)$$

Equation (33) has the following interpretation: $\bar{x}-R(1-F(R))$ is the expected profit he gets immediately in the period concerned. If he succeeds, which happens with probability $(1-F(R))$ then he is entitled to stay in the market and enjoy $\bar{g}(R)$ in the following period, which is discounted by t. But with probability $F(R)$ the project fails in which case he gets the present value of his alternative future income. After an obvious reformulation of (33) we get

$$(34)\quad \bar{g}(R) = \frac{\bar{x} - R(1-F(R)) + TwF(R)}{1 - t(1-F(R))}$$

A borrower with project return $x \geq R$ will prefer to default if and only if

$$(35)\quad x + Tw > x-R + t\bar{g}(R)$$

which yields, after substituting (34) into (35)

$$(36)\quad (Tw+R)[1-t(1-F(R))] > t[\bar{x}-R(1-F(R))+TwF(R)]$$

or, after some simplifications

$$(37)\quad R > t(\bar{x}(a) - w(a))$$

which is exactly the same as (32). Hence, a previous result has occurred again in a slightly different setting: The critical loan rate of interest is independent of the possibility for the borrower to avoid bankruptcy with certainty. As in the previous case with projects of different riskiness voluntary default because of too high an interest factor relative to default costs dominates adverse selection due to different abilities of borrowers.

The critical interest factor as defined by (37) is smaller than the corresponding R^* of model A in section 2.3, which is defined by

$$(38)\quad m - R^{\#} - \int_{R^{\#}}^{m} F(x)dx \leq w(a)$$

or

$$(39)\quad R^{\#} = m - \int_{R^{\#}}^{m} F(x)dx - w(a)$$

and $R^{\#}$ is simply the interest factor at which a borrower of ability a would switch from the project to his alternative income. Subtracting R of (37) from $R^{\#}$ yields for $R^{\#} > 0$, $t < 1$

$$(40)\quad R^{\#} - R = (1-t)[m - \int_{R^{\#}}^{m} F(x)dx - w(a)] + t \int_{0}^{R^{\#}} F(x)dx > 0$$

and consequently for any a default would occur before according to model A any borrower would drop out from the market. In fact, model A does not work in the present framework since the bank cannot ensure that it gets the proceeds from the project up to an amount R. If it could, on the other hand, then model H would no longer work. Consequently, if costs of default are endogenized in the way just described, combination of adverse selection models based on riskiness and honesty or on ability and honesty are not a relevant possibility: *Depending on the precise specification of the model one of the two mechanisms will always dominate the other*.

3.4.3 Risk Averse Borrowers

Some mild complications arise if borrowers are assumed to be risk averse, but nothing of essence needs to be changed from the conclusions of the preceding analysis.

Given an interest factor R the utility of default after the project has yielded a return of x equals u(x), where $u' > 0 > u''$, which has to be compared with the utility of staying in the market, given by $u(x-R) + tv_s$, where v_s is the present value of optimal behaviour in all future periods. A borrower will default if and only if

$$(41)\quad u(x) - u(x-R) > tv_s$$

Concavity of u implies that if default is optimal for some x it is also optimal for all returns smaller than x since

$$(42)\quad u'(x) - u'(x-R) < 0.$$

This in turn means that if default is optimal for some finite x but not for some larger return then there exists some reservation return x* at which the borrower is indifferent between default and repayment. The value of this critical return can be obtained as follows: Suppose the borrower chooses some x as critical value and repays for larger and defaults for smaller returns. The expected value of this policy is given by

$$(43)\quad v_s(x) = u(x-R) + t\{\int_0^x u(y)dF + Tv_s(x)(1-F(x))\}$$

from which we get after integrating by parts and rearranging

$$(44)\quad v_s(x) = \frac{u(x-R) + t\{u(x)F(x) - \int_0^x u'(y)F(y)dy\}}{1 - tT(1-F(x))}$$

The optimal reservation return x* has to satisfy the following necessary condition

$$(45)\quad \frac{\partial v_s}{\partial x^*} = \frac{u'(x^*-R) + tu(x^*)f(x^*) - v_s(x^*)f(x^*)tT}{1 - tT(1-F(x^*))} = 0$$

Differentiating (45) with respect to R yields

$$(46)\quad \frac{\partial^2 v_s}{\partial x^* \partial R} = - \frac{-u''(x^*-R) + u'(x^*-R)f(x^*)tT}{1 - tT(1-F(x^*))} > 0$$

which implies together with the second order condition corresponding to (45)

$$(47)\quad \frac{dx^*}{dR} > 0$$

The bankoptimal loan rate is therefore obtained from maximizing

$$(48)\quad \bar{p}(R) = R(1-F(x^*(R)))$$

which implies the first order condition

$$(49)\quad \frac{d\bar{p}}{dR} = 1 - F(x^*(R)) - Rf(x^*(R))(dx^*/dR) = 0$$

The main difference to the risk-neutral case is that the borrower's decision to default depends not only on the interest factor, but also on the actual project return. The somewhat counterintuitive looking result that default is preferred for low, but not for very high returns is explained through risk-aversion: the loss x-R weighs heavier than a net gain of equal size.

In any case, risk aversion does not affect the possibility of credit rationing with endogenous costs of default for borrowers.

3.5 Bankruptcy as a Joint Decision of Bank and Borrower

In the preceding section bankruptcy was either the unilateral decision of the borrower or it was forced upon him by the failure of the project to yield a sufficient return. The reason for the passivity of the bank was due to a crucial assumption of model H which reads that the borrower can always keep the entire proceeds of the project if he defaults. As the reader may recall, in other models we employed exactly the opposite assumption, i.e. the bank acquires the return up to an amount sufficient to cover the borrower's debt, and we are now going to investigate the consequences of this assumption for the bankruptcy decision. In particular, it is assumed that bankruptcy can only occur if the actual return of the project falls below the amount required for full debt repayment. This rules out that the bank can declare a borrower to be in default before payments are due on the basis of (contractually specified) evidence that he will be unable to fulfil his obligations.

If the borrower is unable to repay his entire debts, bankruptcy will be declared if at least one of the two parties so wishes. Only if they both agree to continue their relationship can bankruptcy by avoided.

To make things more precise we use a model which bears some resemblance to the analysis of the bankruptcy decision by *Bulow* and *Shoven* (1978). Basically we extend model A of chapter 2.4 to two periods. A borrower wants to implement one project per period and needs a loan of size one. If he has to declare bankruptcy in the first period he is excluded from the credit market in period two. In that case he can recur to an alternative source of income which yields an amount of w with certainty. Suppose that his wealth had to be provided as collateral of value C, and the interest factor R is determined as described in chapter 2.4. The deposit rate is given and equals i. It is assumed that $t = 1$.

Now suppose the return of his project at the end of the first period equals $x_1 < R-C$. If he is declared bankrupt his total income over two periods equals

(50) $g_b = - C + w$

However, he may try to persuade the bank to renounce from declaring bankruptcy and to grant a loan also for the second period with the hope of a return large enough to cover the remaining debt of the first and the entire debt of the second period. If the bank agrees the expected profit of the borrower equals

$$(51)\quad \bar{g}_s = \int_{\hat{x}_2}^{m} x dF - CF(\hat{x}_2) - R(1-F(\hat{x}_2))$$

or, after some manipulations

$$(52)\quad \bar{g}_s = m - R(1+F(\hat{x}_2)) - \int_{\hat{x}_2}^{m} F(x)dx + x_1 F(\hat{x}_2)$$

where $\hat{x}_2 := 2R - x_1 - C$, is the project return required to repay fully the entire debt of both periods.

Clearly, a borrower will prefer bankruptcy if and only if

$$(53)\quad w - C - x_1 F(\hat{x}_2) > m - R(1+F(\hat{x}_2)) - \int_{\hat{x}_2}^{m} F(x)dx$$

Equation (53) shows three things, all of them as expected:

Without alternative income w bankruptcy would never be in the interest of the borrower. Default may become profitable, if the collateral C, or the project return x_1 are very small. This is intuitively plausible since $C+x_1$ is lost if bankruptcy is declared.

Consider next the decision problem of the bank. If the borrower is declared bankrupt the bank retains $C+x_1$, but it may also face some costs, denoted by $Z \geq 0$. This can be thought of as costs the bank has to incur when it liquidates collateral, project proceeds or the plant of the borrower, but it can also be imagined to capture the danger that some depositors lose faith in the bank. In any case, the net return of the bank $_n p_b$ in case of bankruptcy equals

$$(54)\quad {}_n p_b = C + x_1 - Z - I$$

If the bank agrees to wait for some of the payments due at the end of the first period, and to grant a full loan for the second period its expected net profit equals

$$(55)\quad {}_n\bar{p}_s = x_1 + \int_0^{\hat{x}_2} x dF + CF(\hat{x}_2) + R(1-F(\hat{x}_2)) - 2I$$

or, after a few manipulations

$$(56)\quad {}_n\bar{p}_s = x_1(1-F(x_2)) + R(1 + F(x_2)) - \int_0^{\hat{x}_2} F(x)dx - 2I$$

Note, that $\bar{g}_s + {}_n\bar{p}_s = x_1 + \bar{x} - 2I$, i.e. the loan contract distributes the expected total net return of both periods, given x_1 in the first period, between bank and borrower.

A bank prefers bankruptcy of the borrower if and only if

$$(57)\quad C + x_1F(\hat{x}_2) - Z > R(1+F(\hat{x}_2)) - \int_0^{\hat{x}_2} F(x)dx - I$$

It follows that banks are more likely to insist on bankruptcy the larger the collateral, the larger the actual project return, the smaller the bank's bankruptcy cost and the larger I.

According to the assumption stated earlier bankruptcy will be avoided despite an insufficient project return at the end of the first period if both, bank and borrower agree to do so, i.e. if in both equations (53) and (57) the reversed in- equality holds. Adding up these two reveals that the possibility of an agreement to avoid bankruptcy requires the following inequality to hold

$$(58)\quad w - Z < \bar{x} - I$$

Clearly, if the borrower ever enters the credit market then his alternative income w must be smaller then the expected return of his project minus the deposit interest factor, since the latter is the lower bound of R. Therefore, regardless of the bank's bankruptcy costs Z a situation is conceivable where C, x_1 and F(x) are such that both parties agree without much ado to keep the borrower in the market.

Obviously, reversing this argument, it can never be true that both parties prefer bankruptcy at the same time. At least one of them has always an incentive to avoid it, and there is room for bargaining. What could the bargaining be about? The obvious candidate is the interest factor for the second period, denoted by R_2, which has been assumed so far to equal R, the interest factor of the first period.

We shall show now that under the assumptions made so far it is often beneficial for both, bank and borrower, to renegotiate R_2 for the second period rather than to declare bankruptcy. To demonstrate this claim it is sufficient to show that for any first period contract (R,C) and any first period project return x_1 the interest factor R_2 for which $\bar{g}_s(x_1,R,C,R_2) = \bar{g}_b(x_1,R,C,R)$ holds can be larger than the interest factor R_2^* for which $\bar{p}_s(x_1,R,C,R_2^*) = \bar{p}_b(x_1,R,C,R_2^*)$ is satisfied. To see the possibility that $R_2 > R_2^*$, consider the following two equations which show $\bar{g}_s$, $\bar{g}_b$, $\bar{p}_s$ and $\bar{p}_b$ in full detail:

$$(59)\quad w - C - x_1 F(\hat{R}_2) = m - \int_{\hat{R}_2}^{m} F(x)dx - R_2 - RF(\hat{R}_2)$$

where $\hat{R}_2 = R + R_2 - C - x_1$

$$(60)\quad C + x_1 F(\hat{R}_2^*) = R_2^* + RF(\hat{R}_2^*) - \int_{0}^{\hat{R}_2^*} F(x)dx - I$$

where $\hat{R}_2^* = R + R_2^* - C - x_1$

Now, $R_2^* \geq R_2$ may require

$$(61)\quad w \geq x - I$$

since $(R-x_1)([F(\hat{R}_2^*)-F(\hat{R}_2)] - \int_{\hat{R}_2}^{\hat{R}_2^*} F(x)dx > 0$ may hold,

and (61) would contradict the basic assumption of model A. In that case, satisfaction of the reverse of (61) requires $R_2 > R_2^*$.

It is also straightforward to show that the curves $R_2(x_1)$ and $R_2^*(x_1)$, which are implicitly defined by (59) and (60), have positive slope in (R_2,x_1)-space. To see this differentiate (59) and (60) totally with respect to R_2, R_2^* and x_1 respectively. After some simple manipulations one obtains:

$$(62)\quad \frac{dR_2}{dx_1} = \frac{(R-x_1)f(\hat{R}_2)}{(1-F(\hat{R}_2)) + (R-x_1)f(\hat{R}_2)} > 0 \quad \text{since } x_1 < R$$

$$(63)\quad \frac{dR_2^*}{dx_1} = \frac{(R-x_1)f(\hat{R}_2^*)}{1-F(\hat{R}_2^*) + (R-x_1)f(\hat{R}_2^*)} > 0 \quad \text{since } x_1 < R$$

Figure 1 shows what these curves may look like if $R_2(x_1) > R_2^*(x_1)$ for all x_1 satisfying $0 \leq x_1 \leq R$.

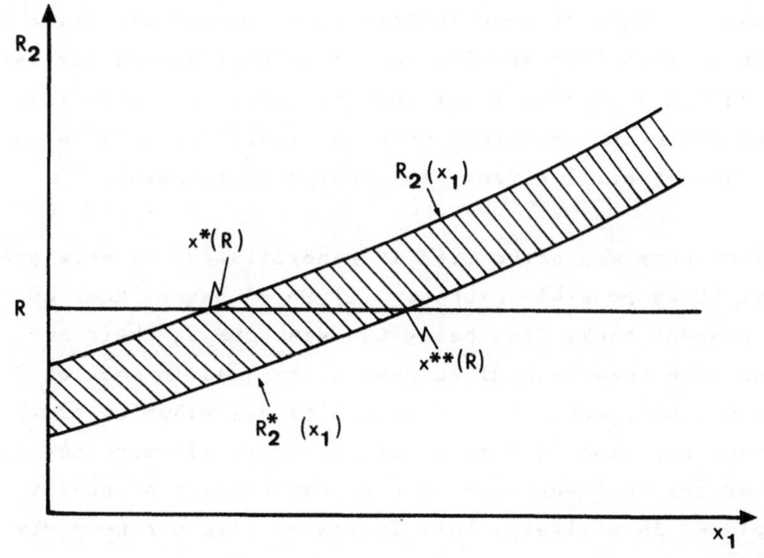

<u>Remark</u>: x^* = switch point of bank
x^{**} = switch point of borrower

<u>Figure 1</u>

The shaded area in Figure 1 shows under the assumption $R_2(x_1) > R_2^*(x_1)$ all combinations of x_1 and R_2 at which both, bank and borrower, agree to avoid bankruptcy. The diagram also shows three ranges of x_1 derived above, at which for $R = R_2$ first only the bank, then bank and borrower, and finally only the borrower would like to avoid bankruptcy.

What are the implications of these simple exercises for credit rationing based on model A?

Firstly, the basic mechanism is not affected, though it has to be modified. The bank considers the expected return for two periods in comparison to the deposit rate, but this does not change the basic fact that its profits are higher with high ability borrowers who, in turn, may drop out of the market if the loan rate is too high.

Secondly, the critique of some authors (e.g. *Howitt* and *Fried* 1980) against adverse selection models, who claim that bankruptcy cases are relatively seldom observed, loses some of its force: Inability of borrowers to honour the contract need not result in a declaration of bankruptcy, but it still affects the profit of the bank.

Thirdly, bankruptcy may occur even if renegotiation is more profitable for at least three possible reasons: (i) Moral hazard and the role of effort may prevent banks from being too generous in their re-negotiations with unsuccessful borrowers. (ii) As in section 3 the revision of a bank's subjective probability distribution of the project return may lead to a shift of its critical curve $R_2^*(x_1)$ above that of the borrower such that no renogiation of credit terms will take place. Intuitively, this indicates also a reason why clients who deal with a particular bank for many periods receive a more generous-treatment in case of failure than relatively new customers: After a while the bank gets a fairly stable opinion about the client's ability which will not be changed much because of a single flop. (iii) As *Bulow* and *Shoven* (1978) show in their treatment of the bankruptcy decision there are other claimants besides the bank who may force bankruptcy upon a borrower, possibly against the will of the bank.

It is hoped that the simple analysis of this section has made clear how crucial the bankruptcy decision is for the working of a credit market and an understanding of the bank-client relationship.

3.6 Concluding Remarks

The analysis of this chapter is the most tentative of the entire study, in spite of (or because of?) the importance of the issues touched upon. There seems to be good reason, however, to conjecture that extensions of the one period to multiperiod models need not imply disappearance of credit rationing. Moral hazard and adverse selection continue to pose a problem, though there are more possibilities for market participants to devise mechanisms to mitigate their negative effects. A more extensive analysis is certainly desirable, but for the time being we have to satisfy ourselves with the present state and concentrate in the following sections again on one period models.

Chapter 4:

SCREENING VS. RATIONING: THE ROLE OF COLLATERAL

4.1 Overview

In this chapter it is investigated how a relaxation of the assumption of an exogenously given amount of collateral may affect the possibility of equilibrium credit rationing as presented in chapter 2. The starting point of the analysis is the stimulating contribution of *Bester* (1984a) who claimed that "rationing is not viable against competition .... banks will compete by choosing contracts with different collateral requirements and interest rates as a self selection mechanism for borrowers ... In equilibrium no borrower ... is rejected." (*Bester* 1984a).

The basic idea of *Bester* is roughly the following: A bank faced with clients whose loans are burdened with different probabilities of default may offer different contracts, i.e. different combinations of interest factor R and collateral C in order to find out the type of each individual borrower. Once this is achieved rationing due to adverse selection disappears since each type would be offered a contract such that either all applicants get a loan or they are indifferent between acceptance and rejection.

It turns out that for none of the four approaches presented in chapter 2 it is generally true that an endogenization of collateral destroys the possibility of equilibrium credit rationing. In particular, if the borrower's initial wealth W, which is assumed to be the upper bound for the amount of collateral C he is able to provide, is smaller than the desired loan (i.e. $W < 1$), then the rationing results are unaffected for risk-neutral borrowers. If risk-aversion is assumed then the *Bester*-critique may, but need not, be valid for some of the four approaches mentioned above.

These results are shown more formally in the following four sections where each of the four basic approaches is taken up in turn. The final section contains some concluding remarks.

4.2 Projects of Different Riskiness

4.2.1 The Stiglitz and Weiss Approach

Since *Bester* (1984a) directed his attack against the model of *Stiglitz* and *Weiss* (1981) it seems appropriate to devote some space to his argument. The analysis of this and the following sections is confined to models with only two types of loan applicants. Recall from chapter 2.2 the *Stiglitz* and *Weiss* model: Given a risk-neutral investor with the distribution function F(x) of his project return, his expected net gain $\bar{g}_F$ of getting a loan contract K:=(R,C) R:=1+r, and undertaking the project equals

$$(1)\quad \bar{g}_F(R,C) = (m-R) - \int_{\hat{R}}^{m} F(x)dx,$$

where m = the maximum value of X, $\hat{R}$:=R-C.

Consider next another borrower whose project return has the distribution H(x), and let F be riskier than H in the sense of *Rothschild* and *Stiglitz* (1970). This implies

$$(2)\quad \bar{g}_F(R,C) - \bar{g}_H(R,C) = \int_{\hat{R}}^{m} [H(x)-F(x)]dx \geq 0$$

i.e. for the borrower the riskier project is at least as profitable as the safer one at any contract (R,C).

The gross return per loan of a bank, denoted by $\bar{p}_j$, j = F,H, is given by

$$(3)\quad \bar{p}_j(R,C) = R - \int_{o}^{\hat{R}} j(x)dx$$

implying

$$(4)\quad \bar{p}_F(R,C) - \bar{p}_H(R,c) = \int_0^{\hat{x}} [H(x)-F(x)]dx \le 0$$

hence for any contract (R,C) the safer project yields the higher gross return for the bank.

Stiglitz and *Weiss* assume that C is exogenously given. Suppose β is the share of projects with the distribution of return H(x). If both groups get loans we have

$$(5)\quad \bar{p}(R,C) := \beta\bar{p}_H(R,C) + (1-\beta)\bar{p}_F(R,C).$$

Suppose at (R^H,C) we have $\bar{g}_H(R^H,C) = 0 < \bar{g}_F(R^H,C)$, hence the safer project would be withdrawn if R is increased any further above R^H, thus for small increases of R, $\bar{p}$ will fall, hence the expected gross return of the bank reaches a local maximum at R^H, given C. Of course, the highest possible gross return per loan for the bank is achieved at a level of R at which $\bar{p}=\bar{x}$, and in that case there would be no credit rationing since $\bar{g}=0$, and loan applicants are indifferent between getting a loan or being rejected. But *Stiglitz* and *Weiss* implicitly assume that a level of R yielding a local maximum of $\bar{p}$ also constitutes an equilibrium, since there is no small variation of R which is profitable. If this weak equilibrium concept is employed, then R^H is indeed an equilibrium, and it would not be changed even if at i, satisfying $1+i=:I=\bar{p}(R^H,C)$ (i.e. the zero-profit condition), the supply of loanable funds is smaller than the total demand. Hence (R^H,C) may be an equilibrium with Type II Rationing.

4.2.2 Bester's Critique and Counterexample

Bester (1984a) objects against the above analysis that "competition will force banks to offer a set of different contracts which act as a self-selection mechanism for borrowers of different risk ... if banks compete by choosing collateral requirements and the rate of interest to screen investors' riskiness, then no borrower will be denied credit in equilibrium." (*Bester* 1984a, p.1).

In order to substantiate this claim Bester offers the following example: There are two groups of two outcome projects with probabilities of success $q_1 > q_2$ and returns $x_2 > x_1$. If a project fails it has return zero (*Rothschild-Stiglitz* increasing riskiness requires $q_1 x_1 = q_2 x_2 = x > 1$).

Loan applicants have initial wealth W, where 0<W<1 (recall that 1 is the loan size). Further, and this will turn out to be crucial, borrowers are risk averse and have identical utility functions u(.). *Stiglitz* and *Weiss* assume risk-neutrality in most of their analysis, but consider risk aversion in their section III which deals with the role of collateral. Given a contract (R,C) an investor will apply for a loan iff

$$(6)\quad \bar{u}(g_j(R,C)) = q_j u(x_j - R + W) + (1-q_j) u(W-C) \geq u_0 := u(W) \qquad j = 1,2$$

The slope of an iso-utility curve in (R,C)-space is given by

$$(7)\quad \frac{dR^*}{dC} = - \frac{(1-q_j) u'(W-C)}{q_j u'(x_j - R + W)} < 0, \qquad j = 1,2$$

and it is easy to check that this curve is concave and steeper at any point (R,C) for the riskier project.

Similar reasoning as in the previous subsection reveals that a rationing equilibrium would have to be on the less risky iso-utility curve satisfying $\bar{u}(g(R,C)) = u_0$. An example is depicted in Figure 1, where dotted lines refer to the riskier project.

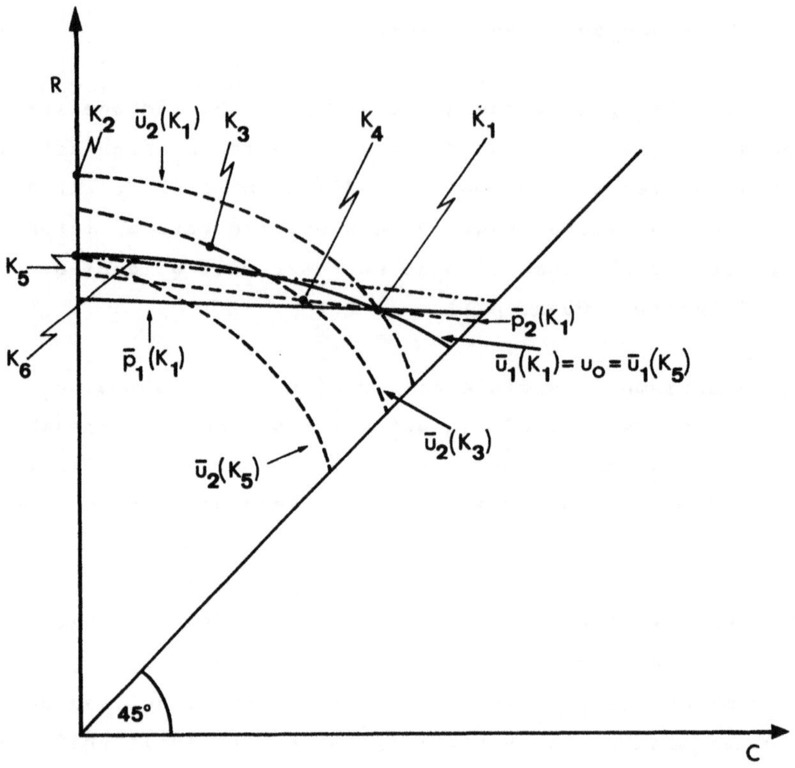

·-·-· bank iso-profit curve for population average through K_5
——— refers to safe projects
- - - refers to risky projects

Figure 1

In addition to the iso-utility curves for the two types of projects Figure 1 also contains iso-gross profit curves of the bank. Their slope dR^P/dC is obtained from the following equation

(8) $\bar{p}(R,C) = q_j R + (1-q_j)C$, hence

(9) $$\frac{dR^P}{dC} = -\frac{1-q_j}{q_j} < 0$$

which implies that borrowers' iso-utility curves are steeper than the bank's iso profit curve at any contract (R,C). Consequently, with perfect information banks would offer contracts without collateral because for each utility level the best contract a bank can get is at the intersection of the iso-utility curve and the ordinate.

From section 2.1 it is clear that a contract with credit rationing would have to lie on the critical iso-utility curve of the safer project. In addition, with imperfect information all contracts offered have to be incentive compatible.

As in all models of this type there are two obvious possibilities to achieve incentive compatibility: Either through a pooling contract or through separating contracts.

The first result shown by *Bester* is that there is no equilibrium pooling contract on the critical iso-utility curve of the safer project: Consider first a contract with strictly positive collateral like K_1 in Figure 1: As has been noted above, to the left of K_1 the iso-utility lines of the borrowers passing through K_1 are strictly above the corresponding iso-profit lines of the bank. Consequently, given K_1 a bank can offer a contract like K_3 which, for the risky project, yields a higher expected profit than K_1 for the bank and at the same time a higher expected utility for the high risk borrowers. A particularly clever bank could even offer a second contract like K_4, which is between the iso-utility and iso-profit curves of low risk borrowers and bank going through K_1 and to the right of the dotted high-risk iso-utility curve passing through K_3, which ensures incentive compatibility. Hence, a contract like K_1 can never be an equilibrium.

A similar argument applies for $C = 0$: Since at $C = 0$ the slopes of the bank's iso-profit line and of a borrower's critical iso-utility line are the same it follows that the iso-profit curve of the bank for the population average is steeper at this point than the iso-utility curve of the safe project. Hence, there is an area to the right of a contract like K_5 in Figure 1 between the safe iso-utility curve and the average iso-profit curve of the bank which contains contracts yielding a higher expected profit than K_5 because they will be bought by borrowers with the safe project only. Moreover, a contract like K_6 would remain profitable even after the withdrawal of K_5. Hence, <u>there does not exist an equilibrium pooling contract with rationing</u>.

The second point to show is that there cannot be equilibrium rationing with separating contracts. Suppose there is a pair of separating contracts like K_1 and K_2 in Figure 1. It would never pay a bank to ration high-risk borrowers at K_2 since they would buy K_1 which is less profitable for the bank. Consequently, a bank would always satisfy the demand for a contract like K_2, which is only demanded by high risk borrowers and deny loans at K_1, if the supply of loanable funds is insufficient. But low risk borrowers are indifferent between acceptance and rejection anyway and cannot be considered as "rationed" in a meaningful way. If the supply of loanable funds is so small that only high-risk borrowers are left then R would be driven up the ordinate until either the entire demand for loans is satisfied or the critical iso-utility curve of high-risk borrowers is reached. Again, the latter case does not constitute rationing even if some borrowers do not get a loan.

Hence it has been shown that in the *Bester*-example, which is some variant of the *Stiglitz* and *Weiss* model, an equilibrium with rationing does not exist, even if the weak concept of a local equilibrium is employed. We shall now take a closer look at the underlying reasons for this result in order to assess its generality.

An obvious way to save the rationing result of *Stiglitz* and *Weiss* from *Bester*'s attack is to assume that borrowers have no wealth of their own and therefore only contracts with $C = 0$ are feasible. In that case a contract like K_5 in figure 1 could be a local equilibrium with rationing. While the assumption $C = W = 0$ quite often simplifies the analysis it is clearly unsatisfactory to make it a necessary condition for equilibrium rationing to exist.

The crucial requirement for *Bester*'s result is the gap between the iso-profit curve of banks and the iso-utility curves of borrowers at any contract (R,C). The fact that in *Bester*'s example the latter is steeper at any contract allows for the possibility that for each contract (R,C) with $C > 0$ there exists a Pareto-dominating contract with larger R and smaller C than the original one. Hence, the first point to discuss concerns the slopes of the iso-utility curves of the different market participants.

Suppose first borrowers are risk-neutral, as in most of *Stiglitz* and *Weiss*, rather than risk-averse. In that case we have

$dR^g/dC = dR^p/dC = -(1-q)/q$, i.e. the requirement of different slopes of the iso-profit curves of banks and borrowers is no longer satisfied.

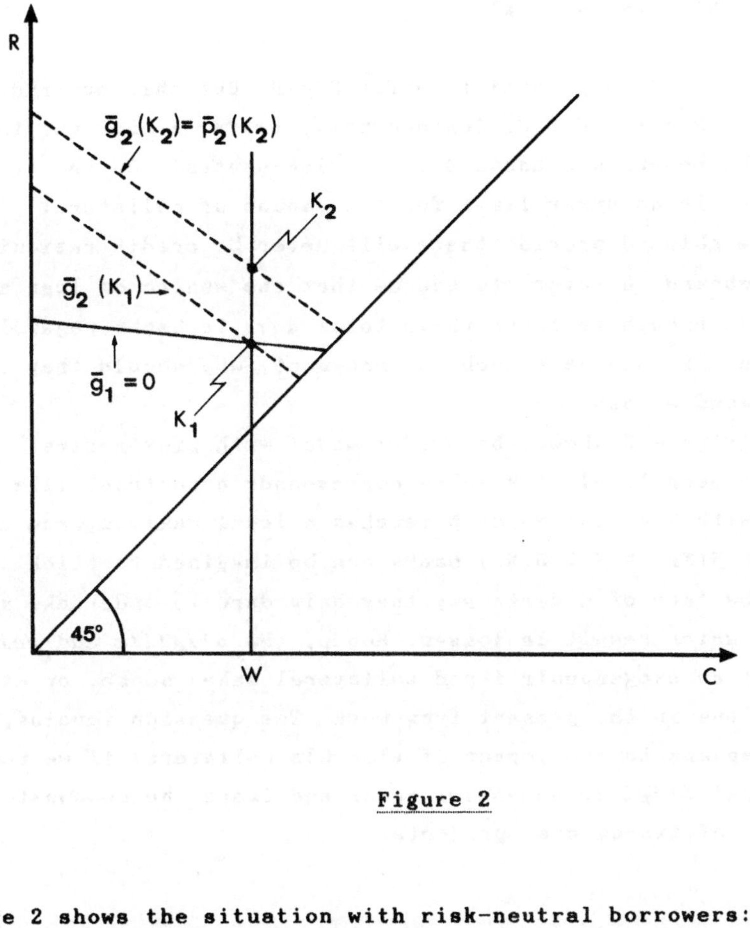

Figure 2

Figure 2 shows the situation with risk-neutral borrowers: The iso-profit curves of banks and borrowers passing through any contract (R,C) coincide. Now consider contract K_1 and suppose there is rationing. Could this be an equilibrium? It depends whether loan applicants have sufficient wealth to provide a larger collateral or not. If they do then it always pays a bank to offer a contract to the right of K_1 on $\bar{g}_1 = 0$: It would attract applicants who have been rejected at K_1, and its profit would be larger than at K_1: It remains the same for low-risk borrowers, but it is higher for the riskier project. Hence, banks have an incentive to go for the contract on $\bar{g}_1$ which is as far right as feasible. The process of pushing the contract to the right if there is excess demand for loans would only end at the intersection of $\bar{g}_1 = (\bar{x}/x_1)(x_1-R)-((x_1-\bar{x})/x_1)C = 0$ and $\bar{g}_2 = (\bar{x}/x_2)(x_2-R)-((x_2-\bar{x})/x_2)C = 0$. Hence, at this intersection the following equality must hold

$$(10)\quad (\bar{x}/x_1)(C-R) = (\bar{x}/x_2)(C-R)$$

and this equality is only satisfied for $C = R$. But this contradicts the assumption $R > 1 > W \geq C$. Consequently, *Bester*'s critique is less forceful if borrowers are assumed to be risk-neutral. On the other hand, if there is no upper limit for the amount of collateral borrowers are able to provide there will never be credit rationing. It is somewhat absurd, however, to assume that the wealth of loan applicants is large enough to cover their total debt to banks regardless of the loan rate. If they have such an endowment, why should they ever bother to demand a loan?

In any case, Figure 2 shows the *Bester* model with risk neutral borrowers. To each level of W there corresponds a contract like $K_1 = (C,R)$, with $C = W$ at which $\bar{p}$ reaches a local maximum, and despite the fact that $\bar{p}(K_2) = \bar{x} > \bar{p}(K_1)$ banks can be imagined to stick to K_1 because in the face of uncertainty they only dare to undertake small changes of R which result in losses. Hence, the *Stiglitz* and *Weiss* assumption of an exogenously fixed collateral makes sense, or at least appears harmless in the present framework. The question remains, however, what happens to the impact of flexible collateral if we return to the original *Stiglitz* and *Weiss* model and leave the somewhat special world of two-outcome projects.

4.2.3 Returns With Arbitrary Distributions and Variable Collateral

Recalling the arguments of the two preceding subsections it is easy to show that the *Bester* critique is not generally valid for the main version of the *Stiglitz* and *Weiss* model, provided their equilibrium concept is accepted: The requirement of diverging iso-profit curves for banks and borrowers is not satisfied.

Consider first the intersection of the two zero-profit lines of the two projects in (R,C)-space. It follows immediately from (2), that $\bar{g}_F(R,C) = \bar{g}_H(R,C)$ can only hold if R = C or, if it holds for some C < R, then the two zero-profit curves coincide to the right of this pair. As in section 2.2 there is no credit rationing if C can be made sufficiently large to make the bank's default risk disappear, a possibility we have already deemed implausible.

But even if the collateral is sufficiently variable such as to prevent credit rationing, there would not be a separating equilibrium, because at any contract (R,C) bank's and a risk-neutral borrower's iso-profit curves passing through have identical slopes. To see this differentiate (1) and (3) in order to obtain

$$(11)\quad dR^g/dC = dR^p/dC = -F(R-C)/(1-F(R-C))$$

Hence there is no profitable opportunity for a bank to break away from a pooling equilibrium. This can be seen from Figure 3: It is assumed that $F(x) = G(x)$ for $x \geq x_1$, hence the iso-profit curves meet at (R,C), $C < W_1$. At K_1 there is no credit- rationing, but it is nevertheless a pooling equilibrium. If W_2 is the relevant wealth constraint then K_2 could be a pooling rationing equilibrium as predicted in the *Stiglitz* and *Weiss* model.

An important assumption in the *Bester* example is the risk aversion of borrowers. It would imply the following objective function of loan applicants.

$$(12)\quad \bar{u}(g(R,C)) = u(m-R+W) - \int_{\ell}^{m} u'(x-R+W)F(x)dx$$

The *Rothschild-Stiglitz*-definition of increasing risk does not rule out

$$(13)\quad \bar{u}_F - \bar{u}_H = \int_{\ell}^{m} u'(x-R+W)[H(x)-F(x)]dx < 0$$

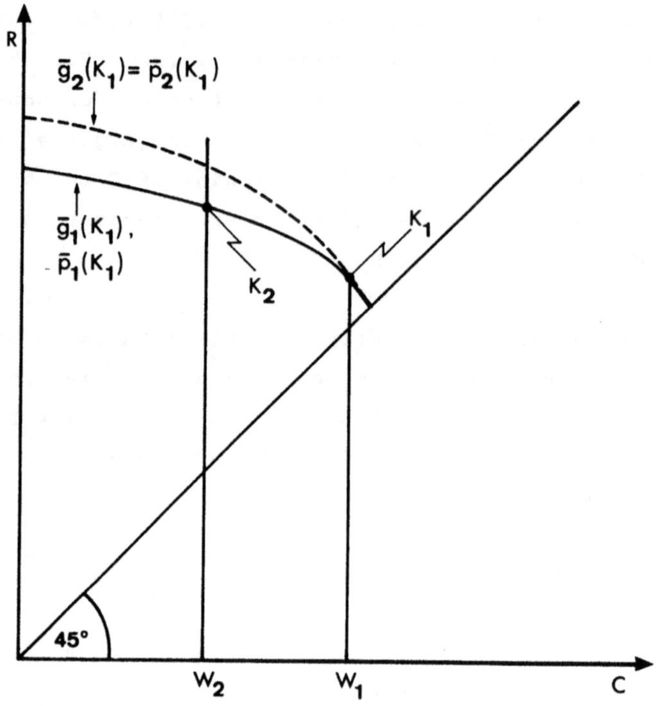

Figure 3

and two iso-utility-curves with the same critical utility u_0 may intersect (inequality (13) would be ruled out if F and H differed with respect to mean utility preserving spreads.) If such an intersection exists then, of course, the riskier project is not the more profitable one for borrowers in general, and the adverse selection mechanism envisaged by *Stiglitz* and *Weiss* would not exist for some range of C. Implicit differentiation of (12) yields

$$(14)\quad dR^{*}/dC = -u'(W-C)F(\hat{x}) \Big/ \int_{\hat{x}}^{m} u'(x-R+W)f(x)dx < 0$$

and the borrowers' iso-utility curve is clearly steeper at any contract (R,C) than the bank's iso-profit curve which has the slope

$-F(\hat{R})/(1-F(\hat{R}))$. Hence, with risk-averse loan applicants and risk-neutral banks we may get exactly the same situation as described by *Bester*: There is only a separating equilibrium without credit rationing rather then the pooling equilibrium with rationing envisaged by *Stiglitz* and *Weiss*.

It would be premature, however, to conclude that the possibility of equilibrium credit rationing in the *Stiglitz* and *Weiss* model depends entirely on the attitude towards risk of loan applicants. As will be shown in the next section things are still more complicated.

4.2.4 The Bank's Costs of Default

One innocent looking assumption of the *Stiglitz* and *Weiss* model is that for the bank the collateral and the acquisition of the project and its return are as good as direct payment from the borrower. In reality, however, it seems unlikely that the bank actually gets the face value of the collateral or the project if the borrower defaults. It is more reasonable to assume that there is a cost the bank incurs which can be thought of as some liquidation cost. For example, it may have to employ a lawyer who takes care of the collateral, there may be transaction costs etc. It is now investigated how such costs affect the conclusions of the two previous subsections.

There are various possibilities to model the bank's costs of default, and we shall confine the analysis to two simple examples: Proportional and fixed costs of default.

4.2.4.1 Proportional Costs of Default

In this subsection it is assumed in accordance with *Stiglitz* and *Weiss* (Section I) that the bank can acquire only a percentage k, $0 < k < 1$ of the collateral it keeps because the project return falls short of R. In other words, it has to bear costs $(1-k)$ times the collateral which has to be used to cover part of the borrower's debt. Consequently, the expected return of a bank is now, instead of (3)

$$(15)\quad \bar{p}(R,C) = R(1-F(\hat{R})) + \int_0^{\hat{R}} x f(x)dx + kCF(\hat{R}) - (1-k)\int_{\hat{R}}^{R} (R-x)f(x)dx$$

which implies the following expression for the slope of an iso-profit curve of the bank at contract (R,C)

$$(16)\quad \frac{dR^p}{dC} = -\frac{kF(\hat{R})}{1-F(\hat{R})-(1-k)[F(R)-F(\hat{R})]} < 0$$

with the second derivative

$$(17)\quad \frac{d^2R^p}{dCdk} = -\frac{1}{DN^2}[F(\hat{R})[1-F(R)]] < 0$$

where $DN := 1-F(\hat{R})-(1-k)[F(R)-F(\hat{R})]$. Equation (17) states that the slope of a bank's iso-profit curve at any (R,C) becomes steeper the larger k, i.e. the smaller the costs of default for the bank are. But this implies that *Bester*'s critique holds even if borrowers are risk-neutral: The iso-profit curve of the bank is flatter than that of a borrower, hence a pooling contract is always dominated by incentive compatible contracts to the left of it.

It is easy to check that this result is also true for Bester's example: The bank's iso-profit curve

$$(18)\quad \bar{p} = q(R) + (1-q)kC$$

implies

$$(19)\quad \frac{dR^p}{dC} = -\frac{(1-q)k}{q} > -\frac{1-q}{q} \qquad \text{for } 0 < k < 1.$$

Consequently, the possibility of credit rationing in the *Stiglitz* and *Weiss* model can disappear even with risk-neutral borrowers.

4.2.4.2 Fixed Costs of Default

The default costs for the bank can also be envisaged to be fixed and independent of the actual size of the borrower's failure: One can imagine that the bank has to employ some agent whenever a borrower fails to fully repay his loan in order to evaluate the proceeds from the project and to handle the liquidation of the assets which accrue to the bank. Denote these costs by Z, which the bank has to incur whenever $x < R$. The expected profit of the bank equals

$$(20) \quad \bar{p} = R(1-F(\hat{R})) + \int_0^{\hat{R}} xf(x)dx + CF(\hat{R}) - ZF(R)$$

which implies for the slope of an iso-profit curve

$$(21) \quad \frac{dR^p}{dC} = - \frac{F(\hat{R})}{1-F(\hat{R})-Zf(R)} < - \frac{F(\hat{R})}{1-F(\hat{R})}$$

as long as the denominator is positive, which is assumed for the relevant range of (C,R). Equation (21) states that now the risk-neutral borrower's iso-profit curve is less steep than that of the bank at any contract (R,C). Moreover, it cannot be ruled out that even risk-averse borrowers have iso-utility curves which are flatter than those of banks at least for some contracts. Consequently, the possibility of credit rationing in the *Stiglitz* and *Weiss* model may continue to hold even with risk-averse borrowers.

This conclusion is not true for the *Bester* example. There the expected utility of a bank is

$$(22) \quad \bar{p} = qR + (1-q)(C-Z)$$

implying

$$(23) \quad \frac{dR^p}{dC} = - \frac{1-q}{q}$$

i.e. the slope of the iso-profit curve is independent of Z. The reason is, of course, that in contrast to the general version the probability of default is not affected by the terms of the credit contract.

4.2.5 Conclusions

The conclusions of this analysis concerning the robustness of the *Stiglitz* and *Weiss*-model are as follows: In their basic version, with no costs of default and risk-neutral borrowers, the mechanism which may lead to credit-rationing is only prevented from functioning if the collateral can be made arbitrary large such as to satisfy R = C. If borrowers are risk-averse, then the model need not work even for fixed collateral since the riskier project need not be more profitable for borrowers in general. The *Stiglitz* and *Weiss* approach to credit rationing is not only sensitive with respect to the risk-attitude of borrowers, but also to the specification of default costs borne by the bank. In any case, the claim of *Bester* "that rationing is not viable against competition" is not generally valid.

4.3. The Jaffee und Russell Model

4.3.1 Identical Borrowers

In the *Jaffee* and *Russell* model of credit rationing an adverse selection problem occurs because loan applicants differ with respect to their costs of default denoted by D. In contrast to other models banks cannot get hold of the project return. The net profit of a borrower at a realized return x equals

(24) $g(R,C,D) = \max \{x-R,\ x-(C+D)\}$

which implies that a borrower defaults whenever R > C + D. It is assumed that D is lost whenever the return x is too small to cover the difference R - C. Hence, the expected net profit of a borrower with default costs D equals

$$
(25)\quad \bar{g} = \begin{cases} \bar{x} - (D+C) & \text{if } R > C + D \\ \int_{\hat{x}}^{m} (x-R)\,dF(x) - (C+D)F(\hat{x}) + \int_{0}^{\hat{x}} x\,dF(x) = & \\ = \bar{x} - R(1-F(\hat{x})) - (C+D)F(\hat{x}) & \text{if } R \le C + D \end{cases}
$$

The slope of an iso-profit curve is

$$
(26)\quad \frac{dR^{g}}{dC} = \begin{cases} -\dfrac{F(R-C) + (R-C-D)\, f(R-C)}{1-F(R-C) - (R-C-D)\, f(R-C)} & \text{for } R \le C+D \\ \infty & \text{for } R > C+D \end{cases}
$$

A bank's gross return equals

$$
(27)\quad \bar{p} = \begin{cases} R(1-F(R-C)) + CF(R-C) & \text{if } R \le D \\ C & \text{if } R > C+D \end{cases}
$$

and consequently

$$
(28)\quad \frac{dR^{p}}{dC} = \begin{cases} -\dfrac{F(R-C) + (R-C)\, f(R-C)}{1 - F(R-C) - (R-C)\, f(R-C)} < 0 & \text{if } R \le C+D \\ \infty & \text{if } R > C+D \end{cases}
$$

where I restrict attention to distribution functions which satisfy $1-F(x) > xf(x)$ in the relevant range of R, C and D. Clearly, for any pair (R,C) the bank's iso-profit curve is steeper than that of the borrower. To see this note that (26) equals (28) if D = 0. Differentiating (26) with respect to D yields

$$
(29)\quad \frac{d^{2}R^{g}}{dCdD} = \frac{f(R-C)(1-dR^{g}/dC)}{1-F(R-C)-(R-C-D)f(R-C)} > 0
$$

and consequently $0 > \dfrac{dR^{g}}{dC} > \dfrac{dR^{p}}{dC}$

Assume again $W < 1$. Figure 4 shows the equilibrium if all borrowers are equally dishonest.

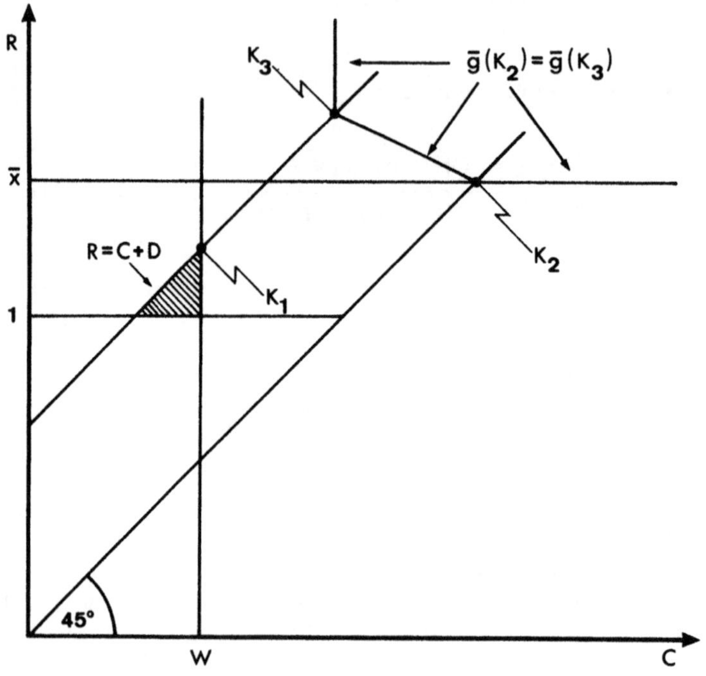

Figure 4

In Figure 4 only contracts in the shaded area are both acceptable for borrowers and profitable for the bank: Contracts above the line $R = C+D$ result in default and banks are left only with collateral $C < 1$. Contracts with $C > 1$ are not feasible for the borrowers and contracts with $R < 1$ result in a loss for the bank even if all borrowers are willing to fulfill their obligations. Obviously, of all feasible contracts K_1 is the most profitable for the bank. If some borrowers have to be denied a loan at K_1 there is no possibility for the bank to offer an alternative contract which would allow to raise additional funds, hence there is "credit rationing" in equilibrium. The use of this term is somewhat strange, however, because it seems odd to speak of credit rationing if applicants are only ready to accept a higher loan rate because they are planning to default.

As in the previous model there is no credit rationing if collateral has no upper bound. If there is an excess demand for loans, competition between borrowers would drive the contract to the zero-profit line of loan applicants, which passes through K_2 and K_3. At K_3 we have $C = R = \bar{x}$, hence $\bar{g} = 0$, and the default costs become irrelevant: $C = R$ implies that there never is any default. Clearly, $\bar{p}$ reaches its maximum at K_3, namely $\bar{x}$.

An economically meaningfull definition of credit rationing in this framework requires that applicants are rejected who are not only willing to accept a contract with larger collateral and/or higher loan rate than the going one, but also to fulfill it. This in turn means that we need again at least two groups of borrowers with default costs $D_2 > D_1$ and β as the relative share of "honest" borrowers.

4.3.2 Two Types of Borrowers

Inspection of (25) and (26) reveals, that $\bar{g}(R,C,D)$ is decreasing in D, and that the iso-profit curve of the less honest borrower is steeper. The situation of a credit market with applicants of different honesty is depicted in Figure 5.

Consider first the case with $W < 1$ as the upper limit of the collateral. Similar reasoning as in the previous subsection shows that there are two possible equilibria (provided the demand for loans is large relative to the supply of loanable funds): either K_1, the intersection of $R = C + D_1$ and $C = W$, or K_2, the intersection of $R = C + D_2$ and $C = W$. At the former contract $K_1 = (C+D_1, W)$ there is credit rationing in the sense that honest applicants are rejected despite their willingness to accept and honour a contract with larger R. Banks refuse to grant such a loan because they cannot tell the honest borrowers from the dishonest ones. At K_2, on the other hand, borrowers are rejected, but they would be unwilling to honour a contract with a higher loan rate. Formally, the condition that K_1 rather than K_2 is the equilibrium, can be written as

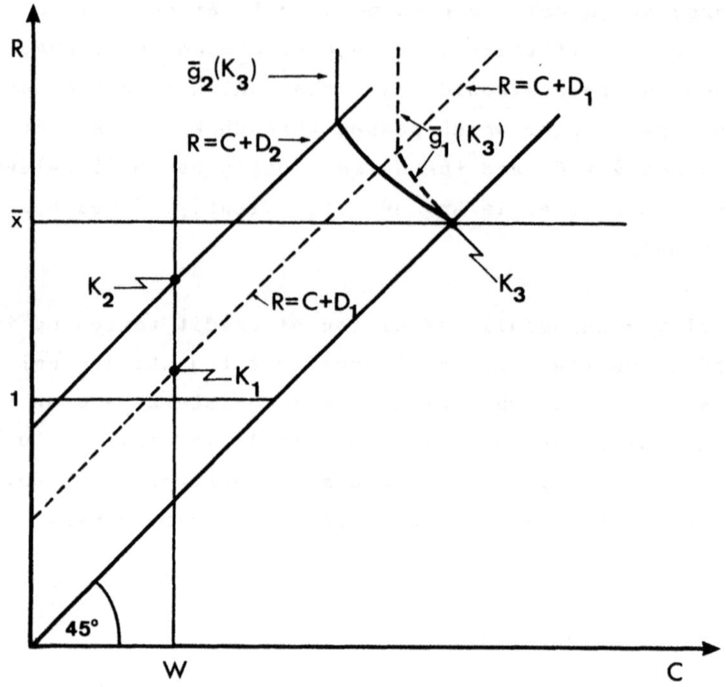

Figure 5

$$(30) \quad \frac{D_1(1-F(D_1))}{D_2(1-F(D_2))} > \beta$$

which is obtained from calculating $\bar{p}$ for R = D_1 and for R = D_2 respectively, and since the left hand side of this inequality is strictly positive it is always possible to find some β sufficiently small to make K_1 the rationing equilibrium.

Of course a contract like K_1 could not be an equilibrium for $W \geq \bar{x}$. If there is an excess demand for loans at K_1 there exist contracts with larger collateral which increase the bank's expected gross profit and make it possible to attract additional loanable funds through granting a higher deposit rate. This process comes to an end either if all applicants get a loan or if the contract K_3 is offered, with $K_3 = (\bar{x},\bar{x})$, $\bar{g}(K_3) = 0$. At this point all zero-profit curves of the different types of borrowers intersect. In fact, we obtain the same result as in section 2: If the collateral can be raised to the level $C = R = \bar{x}$, then all adverse selection and rationing problems disappear. If wealth, and thus the maximum collateral, is limited and smaller than the required loan, then a credit rationing equilibrium may exist.

4.3.3 Risk Aversion

In the ***Stiglitz*** and ***Weiss*** model it turned out that the assumption of risk neutrality is rather helpful, though by no means necessary, for the credit rationing result. It is interesting, therefore, to check how risk aversion affects the ***Jaffee*** and ***Russell*** approach. The expected utility of a contract with $R \le C + D$ equals

$$(31)\quad \bar{u}(g(R,C)) = \int_0^{\hat{x}} u(x-C-D+W)dF(x) + \int_{\hat{x}}^{m} u(x-R+W)dF$$

and it is obvious that $\bar{u}$ is decreasing in D, and that iso-utility curves of different types of borrowers with the same utility level intersect at $R = C$ because then $\hat{x} = 0$. Default is profitable whenever $R > C+D$. Hence the analysis of the case with risk aversion parallels that of the two preceding subsections dealing with risk-neutrality.

It is also obvious that default costs of banks have no substantial effect on the above analyis. The conclusion of this section is therefore that variability of the collateral does not affect the possibility of equilibrium credit rationing in the ***Jaffee*** and ***Russell*** model unless we admit the economically implausible possibility that collateral can be raised up to a level of $\bar{x}$.

4.4 Borrowers With Different Abilities

In chapter 2.4 it has been shown that credit rationing may occur if the abilities of borrowers are different and cannot be observed directly by banks. The question addressed in this section is whether variations of the collateral can serve as a remedy for adverse selection and remove credit rationing. Let 'a' measure ability, then we assume

$$(32) \quad \partial F(x,a)/\partial a = F_a(x,a) \leq 0$$

Suppose again there are two types of applicants with abilities $a_2 > a_1$ and β as the relative size of able a_2-borrowers. From chapter 2.4 we know that for each contract (R,C) the expected net profit of an investment project is increasing in a, formally

$$(33) \quad \partial \bar{g}(R,C,a)/\partial a = - \int_{\hat{R}}^{m} F_a(x,a)dx > 0$$

The slope of an iso-profit curve equals

$$(12) \quad dR^g/dC = - F(\hat{R},a)/(1-F(\hat{R},a)) \qquad \text{implying}$$

$$(25) \quad d(dR^g/dC)/da = - F_a(\hat{R},a)/(1-F(\hat{R},a))^2 \geq 0$$

i.e. the iso-profit curve of the less able borrower is steeper. Graphically the above described situation can be depicted as in Figure 6.

In the original model it is assumed that C = W = 0. Credit rationing may occur if $\beta\bar{p}_2(K_2^0) + (1-\beta)\bar{p}_1(K_2^0) > \bar{p}_1(K_1)$ where K_2^0 is the intersection of the "critical" iso-profit line g_2^* and the ordinate. High ability applicants will turn to their alternative income source at any contract above g_2^*.

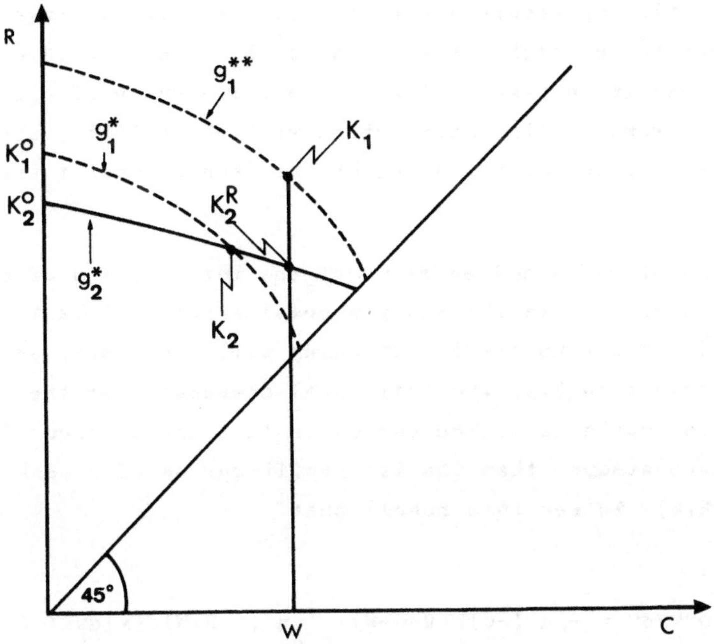

If g_1^{**} and W are the critical iso-profit-line and wealth, then $K^R{}_2$ may be a rationing equilibrium if $\beta p_2(K^R{}_2) + (1-\beta)p_1(K^R{}_2) > p_1(K_1)$

Figure 6

Whether equilibrium credit rationing continues to exist after C has been allowed to take on arbitrary values between 0 and $W > 0$ depends on the location of the intersection of the two critical profit lines g_1^* and g_2^*. If it is strictly to the left of W then no credit rationing will occur. The equilibrium will be separating but it need not be unique. Since the bank's and the borrowers' iso-profit curves have the same slope at any contract, any set of pairs of contracts consisting of a contract (C_2, R_2) to the right of K_2 on g_2^* and a contract (C_1, R_1) to the left of K_2 on g_1^* form an equilibrium. Clearly, banks will only reject high ability borrowers after all low ability applicants have already been denied a loan.

Credit rationing requires that the two critical iso-profit curves intersect to the right of W. This is the case in Figure 6 if g_1^{**} rather than g_1^* represents the relevant minimum profit curve of unable borrowers. Its intersection with g_2^* is to the right of the 45°-line, a case not ruled out by the assumptions of the present model.

As in the *Stiglitz* and *Weiss* model the introduction of risk aversion of borrowers affects the analyis considerably: If banks do not face costs of default no credit rationing will occur and, as in the *Bester*-model of section 2.2, the collateral demanded from the less able borrowers equals zero. The reason is that the borrowers' iso-utility-curves are steeper than the iso-profit-curves of a bank at each contract (R,C). To see this recall that

$$(34) \qquad dR^{g}/dC = -\ u'(-C)F(R-C+W)/\int_{R-C}^{m} u'(x-R+W)f(x)dx < 0$$

$$(12') \qquad dR^{p}/dC = -\ F(R-C)/(1-F(R-C))$$

It follows that the analysis of the present model parallels that of the *Stiglitz* and *Weiss* model in section 2. The same is true if default costs of banks are taken into account.

Thus we can conclude that in the model of *Clemenz* (1984b) with different abilities admission of variable collateral need not destroy the possibility of credit rationing.

4.5 Borrowers With Unobservable Effort

In chapter 2.5 it has been shown that credit rationing may occur if the return of a project depends on the costly effort of borrowers which cannot be observed by banks. At a given level of collateral borrowers will reduce their effort if R is increased because now their expected marginal return of effort is decreased. This in turn may imply that a bank's expected profit is nonmonotonic in R.

As *Watson* (1984) has shown $\bar{p}(R,C)$ becomes monotonic in R again if C is kept equal to R. To see this consider the determination of effort e by a borrower. He maximizes

$$(35)\quad \bar{g}(R,C,e) = (m-R) - \int_{\hat{R}}^{m} F(x,e)dx - c(e)$$

where c(e) is the positive, convex cost of effort function. The first order condition is

$$(36)\quad c'(e) = - \int_{\hat{R}}^{m} F_e(x,e)dx$$

Clearly, if $\hat{R} = R - C = 0$, then the effort is the same as if no interest would have to be paid at all. The reason is that for R = C the loan repayment is a fixed cost and does not affect the expected marginal return of the project. Therefore, if C can be increased without limit then no credit rationing will ever occur in equilibrium: By raising R and C simultanously a bank can always increase its expected gross return and finance additional loanable funds. But as has been argued in earlier sections (and implicitly by Bester via his assumption W < 1) it does not seem very plausible to allow for C = R > 1.

The above result has to be slightly modified for the case of risk-aversion. Instead of (35) we get

$$(37)\quad \max \bar{u}(g(R,C,e)) = u(m-R-c(e)) - \int_{\hat{R}}^{m} u'(x-R-c(e))F(x,e)dx$$

implying the necessary condition

$$(38)\quad \frac{\partial \bar{u}}{\partial e} = -u'(m-R-c(e))c'(e) + \int_{\hat{R}}^{m} u''(x-R-c(e))c'(e)F(x,e)dx$$

$$- \int_{\hat{R}}^{m} u'(x-R-c(e))F_e(x,e)dx = 0$$

Now effort may be decreasing or increasing in R as can be seen from differentiating (29) with respect to R.

$$(39)\quad \frac{\partial^2 \overline{u}}{\partial e \partial R} = \int_0^m u''(x-R-C(e))c'(e)f(x,e) + $$

$$+ \int_0^m u''(x-R-C(e))F_e(x,e)dx$$

The sign of de/dR is generally undetermined. The reason for this difference to the case of risk-neutrality is that the marginal return of effort is now expressed through a utility index which is not independent of the fixed cost element R. It follows that the possibility of equilibrium credit rationing is unaffected by risk-aversion of borrowers. The disincentive of an increase of R, however, need not work as neatly with risk-averse borrowers as it does with risk-neutral ones. If it is possible for the bank to set C = R for arbitrary R, then, as in all other models, credit rationing disappears with the default risk.

4.6 Concluding Remarks

Bester (1984) has drawn attention to an important possibility in credit markets with asymmetric information: The use of collateral as a screening and incentive device which could remove credit rationing in equilibrium. It has turned out, however, that collateral variations cannot perform this function in general. One important reason is that in many models iso-profit curves of the bank passing through a particular credit contract are not less steep than the coresponding curves for borrowers. Together with the limited ability of loan applicants to provide collateral this limits the effectiveness of the latter as a signal of trustworthiness. It seems that asymmetric information continues to provide a fairly robust explanation for the possibility of equilibrium credit rationing.

Chapter 5:

LOAN MARKETS WITH PERFECTLY DIVISIBLE PROJECTS

5.1 Overview

A common feature of all models discussed in chapters 2-4 was the fixed size of the project to be financed. While this assumption simplifies the analysis considerably one would certainly not want the possibility of equilibrium credit rationing to depend on it. It is the purpose of this and the two following chapters to investigate the consequences of variable project and loan size for credit market equilibria. In particular, it is of interest whether an equilibrium exists and, if so, whether it may exhibit some form of rationing. The present chapter is slightly more technical in scope and discusses some of the problems which may arise if variable projects with random returns are introduced. In particular, it should become apparent how general such models can be hoped to be without becoming indeterminate. The fairly general model of *Milde* and *Riley* (1984) is presented in some detail, and it is shown that a *Nash*-equilibrium need not exist. The aim of these exercises is to indicate how the simpler models used in chapters 6 and 7 could be made more general without affecting the main conlusions.

This chapter is organized as follows: In section 2,I present a very simple model with certain returns and perfectly honest loan applicants. As is to be expected, equilibria exist and imply market clearing. In section 3 the return of the project to be financed through a loan is assumed to be a random variable. It turns out that some assumptions are required in order to ensure "well-behaved" iso-profit- and demand curves, and one set of assumptions is borrowed from a recent paper by *Milde* and *Riley* (1984; for a similar model see *Gale* and *Hellwig* (1983)). It turns out that the resulting equilibrium is Pareto-efficient, though the individual loan size is smaller than desired by borrowers at the going loan rate of interest. In section 4 a further complication is introduced as borrowers are assumed to have different, for the bank not observable abilities. In such a market a *Nash*-equilibrium does not exist in general. Equilibria do exist, however, if other definitions are used, like that of *Wilson* (1977), *Riley* (1979), *Grossman* (1979) or *Spence* (1974). The different equilibria do not coincide in general and may have quite different properties. The loan size generally differs from the desired one (given the loan rate) but it may be larger as well as smaller. It also differs in comparison to the loan in a market with symmetric information.

5.2 A Loan Market with Certain Returns

In this section a simple deterministic model of a loan market is presented which serves to highlight the peculiar features of models with various forms of uncertainty discussed in later sections. In particular, we state four simple propositions and show in sections 3 and 4 conditions, under which corresponding results hold for a stochastic model. It is assumed that borrowers have no wealth of their own. They need their loan in order to finance a one period investment project. Its return x is a strictly increasing, twice continuously differentiable concave function of the size of the loan, denoted by L, which satisfies $x'(0) = \infty$ and $x'(\infty) = 0$.

As before banks are assumed to raise loanable funds and lend them at the loan rate of interest r. The only cost they incur is the deposit rate of interest i, and the supply of loanable funds, denoted by L^s, is infinitely elastic at the going deposit rate. This simplifying assumption helps to concentrate exclusively on problems arising from imperfect information. A borrower's demand for a loan is a function of r and can be obtained as the solution of the following optimization problem:

(1) $\max_{L} g = x(L) - RL \, , \quad x' > 0 > x'', \; R := 1 + r$

which implies the necessary condition

(2) $\frac{\partial g}{\partial L} = x'(L) - R = 0$

Since

$$(3) \quad \frac{\partial^2 g}{\partial L \partial R} = -1 < 0$$

and

$$(4) \quad \frac{\partial^2 g}{\partial L^2} = x''(L) < 0$$

the following property is proved:

Proposition 1: L is a strictly decreasing function of R.

Next we derive for later reference some properties of the iso-profit-curve of a borrower. Such an iso-profit-curve for a profit level g, denoted by R(L,g), is implicitly defined by the following equation:

$$(5) \quad g = x(L) - RL$$

or

$$(5') \quad R(L,g) = (x(L) - g)/L$$

Proposition 2: The iso-profit-curve R(L,g) has the following properties:

(i) R(L,g) has at most one turning point R^* at $L^*(g)$ such that $\partial R/\partial L > 0$ for $L < L^*(g)$ and $\partial R/\partial L < 0$ for $L > L^*(g)$

(ii) $\partial L^*/\partial g > 0$

(iii) $\partial R^*(L^*(g))/\partial g < 0$

Proof: (i) Differentiating (5) twice implicitly with respect to L yields

(6) $$\frac{\partial R}{\partial L} = \frac{x'(L) - R}{L} \gtreqless 0 \text{ as } x'(L) \gtreqless R$$

(7) $$\frac{\partial^2 R}{\partial L^2} = \frac{x''(L)L - 2(x'(L) - R)}{L^2}$$

The second equation is negative for $\partial R/\partial L \geq 0$. But $\partial R/\partial L$ can change its sign only once since otherwise a pair (R,L) would exist which satisfies (2) and implies $\partial^2 R/\partial L^2 > 0$, a contradiction to (7).

(ii) Instead of (6) we may also write

(6') $$\frac{\partial R}{\partial L} = \frac{x'(L)L - (x(L) - g)}{L^2}$$

and $L^*(g)$ is obtained from (6') by setting it equal to zero and solving. Differentiating (6') partially with respect to g yields

(8) $$\frac{\partial^2 R}{\partial L \partial g} = \frac{1}{L^2} > 0$$

which implies together with (7) $\partial L^*/\partial g > 0$.

(iii) This follows immediately from (ii) since it has already been shown through (3) and (4) that $\partial R^*/\partial L^* < 0$.

Q.E.D.

Perfect competition between banks implies a zero profit per loan, hence

(9) $p(L,R) := RL = IL, \quad I := 1+i$

implying

Proposition 3: The zero profit line of a bank in (L,R) space has a slope of zero.

In later sections the role of different abilities of borrowers will be investigated. Denote the level of ability by a, which becomes an argument of the production function. The following assumption is made:

A1: (i) $\partial x(L,a)/\partial a > 0$

(ii) $\partial^2 x/\partial L \partial a > 0$

One implication of A1 is that an increase of a shifts the demand curve of an individual borrower to the right, formally we have

Proposition 4: Given A1 the optimal loan size $L^*(R)$ is increasing in a.

Proof: Differentiating $\partial g/\partial L = x_L(L,q)-R$ with respect to a yields $\partial^2 x/\partial L \partial a$ which is positive by assumption. Together with the (modified) sufficient condition (4) this implies $\partial L^*/\partial a > 0$.

Q.E.D.

Remark: $a_2 > a_1$. Dotted lines refer to a_2.

Figure 1

Propositions 1 - 4 imply that iso-profit-curves have a shape as depicted in Figure 1. Lower curves indicate a higher profit and their turning point $L^*(g)$ lies below and to the right of an iso-profit curve with a smaller profit. The demand for loans curve of a borrower connects all points $L^*(g)$ and is shifted to the right as a increases. Given our assumption of infinitely elastic supply of loanable funds there always exists an equilibrium with market clearing, i.e. each borrower gets what he wants at the going loan rate of interest. The reason is that there is no conflict between the objectives of bank and borrower: the latter will choose a loan size at a given loan rate of interest which is optimal for both parties. Thus, it does not matter whether the bank can identify a loan applicant's ability or not. In the remainder of the chapter it is shown that these nice properties are lost as soon as uncertainty is introduced into the model.

5.3 A Loan Market with Uncertain Returns

5.3.1 A General Model

In this section the simple model discussed so far is generalized by allowing the return of an investment project to be a random variable which is stochastically increasing in L. It turns out that a more specific assumption about the nature of the risk is required in order to derive results about the properties of such a market which are similar to those presented in the previous section. One possibility examined closer in section 5.3.2 is the version proposed by *Gale* and *Hellwig* (1983) and, more recently, *Milde* and *Riley* (1984).

Consider first the general case where the return of investment is a random variable X with the distribution function $F(x,L)$. The distribution of X depends on L in the sense of first degree stochastic dominance, formally

(10) $F_L(x,L) \leq 0 \leq F_{LL}(x,L)$

The two inequalities of (10) state that X is stochastically increasing in L, but at a decreasing rate. As in previous chapters it is assumed that the return of the investment project has to be used as repayment to the bank up to an amount of RL. The return can be thought of as serving as collateral. On the other hand, the borrower is not liable to pay the bank from other sources if the return is insufficient.

Consequently, instead of (1) a borrower seeks to optimize

$$(11)\quad \max_{L} \bar{g} = \int_{RL}^{m} x dF(x,L) - RL(1-F(RL,L))$$

which implies the first order condition

$$(12)\quad \frac{\partial \bar{g}}{\partial L} = 0 = -\int_{RL}^{m} F_L(x,L)dx - R(1 - F(RL,L))$$

and the second order condition

$$(13)\quad \frac{\partial^2 \bar{g}}{\partial L^2} = 2RF_L(RL,L) - \int_{RL}^{m} F_{LL}(x,L)dx + R^2 f(RL,L) < 0$$

where $\bar{g}$ denotes the expected value of g.

It is straightforward to show that without further assumptions on the distribution of X and/or on the precise nature of the stochastic increase of X as a consequence of raising L most of the properties of the deterministic model do not hold. To see this with respect to proposition 1 differentiate first (12) with respect to R:

$$(14)\quad \frac{\partial^2 \bar{g}}{\partial L \partial R} = LF_L(RL,L) - (1-F(RL,L)) + RLf(RL,L) \gtreqless 0$$

From (14) and the second order condition (13) it can be seen that a borrower's demand for L is not necessarily a decreasing function of the loan rate r. It depends on the distribution of X and in particular on the probability of non-default given by (1-F(RL,L)). If it is very small then an increase of R may conceivably lead to an increase of the desired loan size.

Similarly, no results corresponding to proposition 2 are readily available. The iso-profit curve of a borrower need not be strictly quasi-concave. From (12) and $\partial\bar{g}/\partial R = -L(1-F(RL,L))$ we get for the first derivatives of an iso-profit curve $R(L,g)$.

$$(15)\quad \frac{\partial R(L,g)}{\partial L} = -[\int_{RL}^{m} F_L(x,L)dx+R(1-F(RL,L))]/L(1-F(RL,L)) \gtreqless 0$$

and for the second derivative[1]

$$(16)\quad \frac{\partial^2 R(L,g)}{\partial L^2} = \frac{\partial^2\bar{g}/\partial L^2-(\partial R(g,L)/\partial L)[2(\partial^2\bar{g}/\partial L\partial R)-(\partial R/\partial L)(\partial^2\bar{g}/\partial R^2)]}{L(1-F(RL,L))}$$

In contrast to the properties employed for the proof of proposition 2(i) nothing can be said in general about the sign of (16). In particular, as can be seen from (13), $\partial^2\bar{g}/\partial L^2$ need not be negative, and $R(L,g)$ may change its sign more than once. Obviously, some additional assumptions about the distribution $F(x)$ and/or the precise nature of a stochastic increase of X due to an increase of L are required in order to ensure "nice" properties of the iso-profit-curves.

The same is true for the bank's zero-profit-line per borrower. It is defined by

$$(17)\quad LI = \bar{p}(L,R) := \int_0^{RL} x dF(x,L) + RL(1-F(RL,L))$$

and differentiating (17) totally yields

1) Recall that for $G(x,y) = 0$ one gets
$$\frac{d^2x}{dy^2} = -\frac{G_{yy}(G_x)^2 + G_{xx}(G_y)^2 - 2G_xG_yG_{xy}}{(G_x)^3}$$

$$(18)\quad \frac{dR}{dL} = [I-R(1-F(RL,L)) + \int_0^{RL} F_L(x,L)dx]/L(1-F(RL,L))$$

From (17) it follows that $I=R(1-F(RL,L))+\int_0^{RL} (x/L)dF(x,L)$,

and a sufficient condition for (18) to be positive would be

$$\int_0^{RL} (x/L)f(x,L) + F_L(x,L)]dx > 0 \text{ for all positive R and L.}$$

This condition, though easily derived, is rather difficult to interpret. Intuitively, it appears related to the economic notion that average product is bigger than marginal product, both taken with respect to L, but the stochastic nature of X and its relation to L does not allow such a simple interpretation.

In the light of these difficulties encountered in a very general model we turn next to a more specific model which allows for an appealing economic interpretation and requires only mild restrictions in order to yield unambigous results.

5.3.2 The Milde-Riley Model

A very simple way of introducing uncertainty into the model of section 2 is to assume that the output price of the investment project is a nonnegative random variable. Formally, the return of the project X is given by

$$(19)\quad X = q(L,a)Y$$

where q denotes the quantity produced with input L, a, as before, denotes ability and Y is a nonnegative random variable with distribution F(y). As *Milde* and *Riley* have shown recently (1984) fairly mild restrictions on q(L,a) and F(y) ensure "nice" properties of the model. In this section some of their results are summarized.

Consider first a borrower's demand for a loan as a function of R. He has to solve (a is set constant and omitted for the moment)

$$(20)\quad \max_{L} \bar{g} = q(L) \int_{\hat{y}}^{m} y dF(y) - RL(1-F(\hat{y}))$$

where $\hat{y} := RL/q(L)$.

It is convenient to express (20) in a different way. Using the fact that $\int_{\hat{y}}^{m} y dF(y) = \hat{y}(1-F(\hat{y})) + \int_{\hat{y}}^{m} (1-F(y))dy$, we can write

$$(21)\quad \max_{L} \bar{g} = q(L)[\hat{y}(1-F(\hat{y})) + \int_{\hat{y}}^{m} (1-F(y))dy] - RL(1-F(\hat{y}))$$

which implies the first order condition

$$(22)\quad \frac{\partial \bar{g}}{\partial L} = 0 = [R(e(L) - 1) + q'(L)H(\hat{y})](1-F(\hat{y}))$$

where e(L) stands for the scale elasticity of production, formally

$$e(L) := \frac{q'(L)L}{q(L)}$$

and $H(\hat{y})$ is defined as

$$H(\hat{y}) := \frac{\int_{\hat{y}}^{\infty}(1-F(y))dy}{1 - F(\hat{y})}$$

Clearly, for $F(\hat{y}) < 1$ condition (22) is only satisfied if the expression in square brackets equals zero. The second order condition equals

$$(23)\quad \frac{\partial^2 \bar{g}}{\partial L^2} = (R \frac{de}{dL} + q''H(\hat{y}) + q'H'(\hat{y})\hat{y}_L)(1-F(\hat{y})) -$$

$$- f(\hat{y})\hat{y}_L(\partial g/\partial L)/(1-F(\hat{y}))$$

Sufficient for a negative sign of (23) are together the conditions $e(L) < 1$ which implies $\hat{y}_L > 0$, and $H'(\hat{y}) < 0$. Differentiating (22) with respect to R yields

$$(24)\quad \frac{\partial^2 \bar{g}}{\partial L \partial R} = (e(L) - 1 + q'(L)H'(\hat{y})\hat{y}_R)(1-F(\hat{y}) -$$

$$- f(\hat{y})\hat{y}_R(\partial \bar{g}/\partial L)/(1-F(\hat{y}))$$

We impose the following restriction on $q(L)$:

A2: (i) $e(L) < 1$ for all $L \geq 0$,
(ii) $\partial e/\partial L \leq 0 \leq \partial e/\partial a$

The property $H'(\hat{y}) < 0$ obviously requires some restriction on $F(y)$. As *Milde* and *Riley* (1984) have shown it suffices that the so called hazard rate of F, $f/(1-F)$ is increasing in y (see appendix A1). Hence we assume

A3: The hazard rate of F, $F'(y)/(1-F(y))$ increases with y and tends to infinity as $F(y)$ approaches unity.

Since A2 and A3 together imply a negative sign of (24) the following result corresponding to Proposition 1 holds:

Proposition 5: Given A2 and A3 the demand for a loan L decreases with R.

The properties stated in Proposition 2 are also preserved under the given assumptions. In particular we have

Proposition 6: Given A2 and A3 the iso-profit-curve $R(L,g)$ has the following properties

(i) $R(L,g)$ has a unique turning point at $L^*(g)$ such that $\partial R/\partial L > 0$ for $L < L^*(g)$ and $\partial R/\partial L < 0$ for $L > L^*(g)$

(ii) $\partial L^*/\partial g > 0$

(iii) $\partial R(L^*(g))/\partial g < 0$

<u>Proof</u>: (i) Differentiating (21) with respect to R yields

$$(25)\quad \partial\bar{g}/\partial R = -L(1-F(\hat{y})) < 0$$

and consequently

$$(26)\quad \frac{\partial R}{\partial L} = \frac{-(\partial\bar{g}/\partial L)}{(\partial\bar{g}/\partial R)} \gtreqless 0 \quad \text{as} \quad \frac{\partial\bar{g}}{\partial L} \gtreqless 0$$

and

$$(27)\quad \frac{\partial^2 R}{\partial L^2} = \frac{\partial^2\bar{g}/\partial L^2-(\partial R/\partial L)[2(\partial^2\bar{g}/\partial L\partial R)-(\partial R/\partial L)(\partial^2\bar{g}/\partial R^2)]}{L(1-F(\hat{y}))}$$

Now the same argument as in the proof of Proposition 2(i) applies: Under given assumptions $\partial R/\partial L \geq 0$ implies $\partial\bar{g}/\partial L \geq 0$ which implies $\partial^2\bar{g}/\partial L^2 < 0$, as can be seen from (23). Hence $\partial R/\partial L$ can change signs at most once, since $\partial\bar{g}/\partial L = 0$ implies that (27) is negative.

The proofs of (ii) and (iii) are also analogous to those of Proposition 2(ii) and 2(iii) and therefore omitted.

Q.E.D.

In order to characterize the equilibrium in this loan market we need the shape of the zero-profit-line of the bank. It has the following important property.

<u>Proposition 7:</u> Given A2 the zero-profit-line per borrower of a bank has a strictly positive slope everywhere.

Proof: The zero-profit-line is defined as

$$(28)\quad q(L)\int_0^{\hat{y}} ydF(y) + RL(1-F(\hat{y})) - IL = 0$$

which implies

$$(29)\quad \frac{\partial R}{\partial L} = - \frac{q'(L)\int_0^{\hat{y}} ydF(y) + R(1-F(\hat{y})) - I}{L(1-F(\hat{y}))}$$

From (28) it follows that

$$(30)\quad I = (q(L)/L)\int_0^{\hat{y}} ydF(y) + R(1-F(\hat{y})), \text{ hence}$$

$$(31)\quad I > q'(L)\int_0^{\hat{y}} ydF(y) + R(1-F(\hat{y})) \qquad \text{if} \quad q(L)/L > q'(L)$$

But this last inequality is implied by A2, hence (31) holds and (29) is strictly positive.

Q.E.D.

Propositions 5 to 7 imply a situation as depicted in Figure 2. An equilibrium has to lie on the zero-profit-line p^o and it is given at that point, where p^o is tangential to the best feasible iso-profit-curve of the borrower.

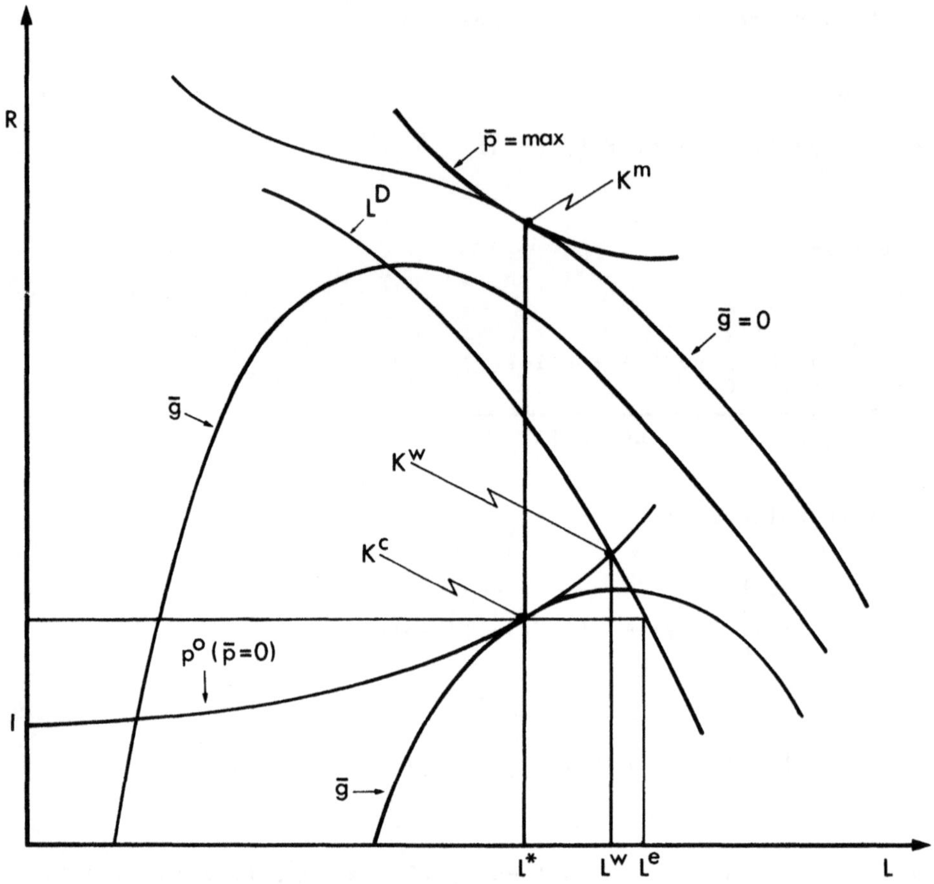

K^m: monopoly contract
K^w: market clearing
k^c: competitive contract

Figure 2

Algebraically the equilibrium is found by maximizing $\bar{g}(R,L)$ under the constraint $IL = \bar{p}(R,L) = q(L) \int_0^{\hat{y}} y dF(y) + RL(1-F(\hat{y}))$, formally

$$(32) \quad \max_{R,L} Z = \bar{g}(R,L) - \lambda(\bar{p}(R,L) - IL)$$

where λ denotes the Lagrange multiplier. The first order conditions are

$$(33)\quad q'(L)\int_{\hat{y}}^{\infty} ydF(y)-R(1-F(\hat{y})) = \lambda[q'(L)\int_{o}^{\hat{y}} ydF(y)+R(1-F(\hat{y}))-I]$$

$$(34)\quad L(1-F(\hat{y})) = -\lambda L(1-F(\hat{y}))$$

and from these conditions it follows that in equilibrium

$$(35)\quad q'(L^*)EY = I$$

must hold. But this is exactly the condition for maximizing $E(X|L) - IL$, thus the equilibrium is Pareto-efficient.

From this it also follows that the loan size offered by a monopolist would not differ from that in the competitive model. The only difference is in the loan rate of interest which a monopolist will fix at the maximum level, i.e. such that borrowers make an expected zero profit (see Figure 2).

In any case, the loan actually granted is smaller than the desired loan at the given interest rate. Hence the loan applicant is rationed in the sense that $L^e > L^*$. It has been argued, however, that it is "at best confusing" to call this "rationing", since the default risk is one characteristic of a loan, and loans of different sizes are, in that sense, different goods. Borrowers desire a larger than the Pareto-efficient loan because part of the default risk is transferred to the bank.

More interesting features of such a market appear if we allow for differences in the abilities of borrowers. We turn to this case in the next section.

5.4 The Nash-Equilibrium with Borrowers of Different Abilities

So far it has been assumed that all loan applicants are identical. In this section we investigate the consequences of differences with respect to their abilities. In particular, it is assumed that two types of borrowers exist, the high ability borrowers with ability a_2 and the low ability ones with a_1, $a_2 > a_1$.

Following once more *Milde* and *Riley* (1984) we state the following two important propositions:

Proposition 8: Given A1 and A2 an increase in a shifts
(i) the bank's zero-profit curve for any R and
(ii) the equilibrium loan size L* to the right.

Proof: (i) Keeping R fixed we differentiate (28) implicitly with respect to L and a and get

$$(36)\quad \frac{dL}{da} = \frac{q_a \int_0^{\hat{y}} y dF(y)}{q_L \int_0^{\hat{y}} y dF(y) + R(1-F(\hat{y})) - I} > 0$$

since the numerator is negative by A1 and the denominator is negative according to proposition 7 (see (31)).

(ii) Differentiating (35) with respect to a yields

$$(37)\quad EY(\partial q_L(L^*,a)/\partial a) > 0$$

because of A1, and this implies together with the second order condition corresponding to (35) $dL^*/da > 0$.

Q.E.D.

Proposition 9: The slope of the iso-profit-curve of a borrower is increasing in a at any point (R,L) if A1 - A3 hold.

Proof: Recall first (26), the slope of an iso-profit-curve:

$$(26)\quad \frac{dR}{dL} = -\frac{(\partial \bar{g}/\partial L)}{(\partial \bar{g}/\partial R)}$$

After some manipulations (see appendix A2) this can be written as

$$(26') \quad \frac{dR}{dL} = \frac{R}{L} \, [e(1 + H(\hat{y})/\hat{y}) - 1]$$

Because of A1, $\hat{y}$ is decreasing in a. Since $H(\hat{y})$ is a decreasing function, $H(\hat{y})/\hat{y}$ is increasing in a, and so is e according to A2. Therefore

$$(39) \quad \frac{\partial(dR/dL)}{\partial a} > 0$$

Q.E.D.

Economically proposition 9 states that abler loan applicants have a higher marginal willingness to pay for an increase of the loan size. Given Propositions 5 - 9 the situation of a loan market with two types of borrowers is as depicted in Figure 3.

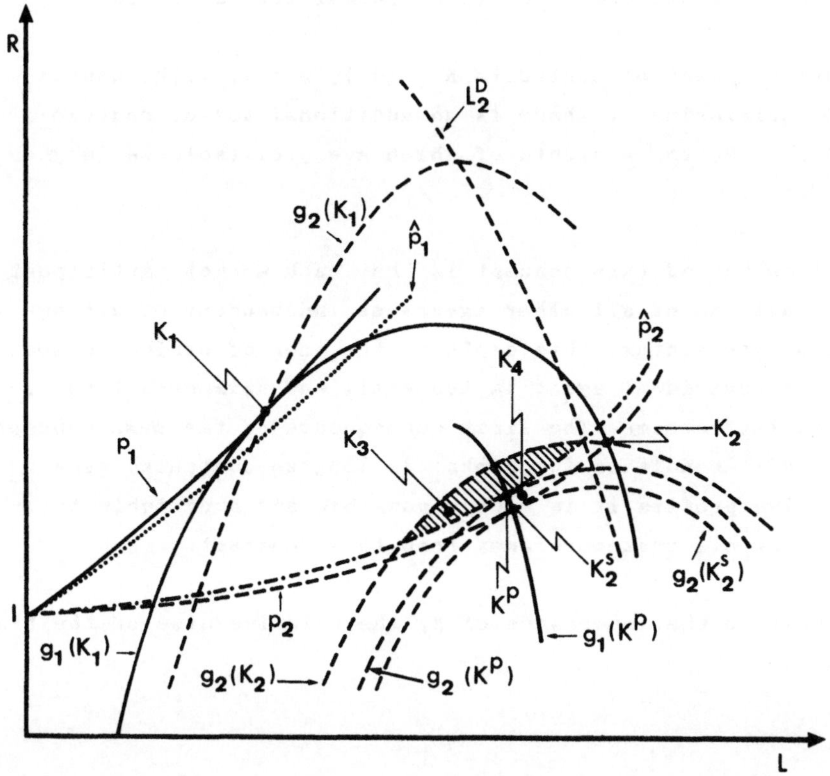

Figure 3

If banks could distinguish between the two types of borrowers the two equilibrium loan contracts would be K_1 and K_2^S. If information about borrowers' abilities is asymmetric, however, this pair of contracts could not be an equilibrium because low ability borrowers would also apply for K_2^S which is on a better iso-profit-curve than K_1. Hence, a separating equilibrium (i.e. an equilibrium with two contracts) requires that the contract for the abler borrowers does not lie below the iso-profit-curve of the less able borrowers going through the contract offered to the latter group, denoted by $g_1(K_1)$.

In Figure 3 the pair of contracts (K_1, K_2) satisfies this requirement and yields an expected profit of zero to banks. Does this mean that (K_1, K_2) constitutes an equilibrium? The answer depends on the precise definition of an equilibrium, on the relative size of both ability groups, and on the ability difference between them.

The equilibrium concept most frequently used is due to *Nash* (1951), and in the present framework it could be formulated as follows:

Nash-equilibrium: A set of contracts $K := \{K_j\}$, $j = 1,...,k$, constitutes a *Nash*-equilibrium if there is no additional set of contracts K', with $K \cap K' = \emptyset$, the elements of which are profitable as long as $K \cup K'$ are offered.

The crucial idea behind this concept is that each market participant considers the actions of all other agents as independent of his own one. In an economic context this captures the idea of perfect competition where each individual agent is too small and unimportant to influence the market outcome. The first consequence of the *Nash*-concept is the zero-profit condition for banks: As long as contracts make strictly positive profits it is always possible and profitable to undercut and draw all customers away from this contract.

Let us turn next to the importance of β, the relative size of the high ability group.

Suppose first the difference in abilites is very large and the share of the low ability group is high, then (K_1, K_2) is a *Nash*-equilibrium: The bank's zero-profit-curve for a contract demanded by both groups, denoted by $\hat{p}_1$, would be quite close to that for low-ability borrowers denoted by p_1.

Any contract to the left of K_2 and below the dotted iso-profit-curve going through K_2, denoted as $g_2(K_2)$, would attract both types of borrowers and make losses, because it is to the right of $\hat{p}_1$.

Note, that there need not be rationing in the sense that borrowers get a smaller loan than they desire at the going loan rate of interest: high ability borrowers may get a larger or a smaller loan than they would buy at an interest factor R_2 if they could determine the size. Which of the two is true depends on the location of the intersection of $g_1(K_1)$ and p_2. In fact, as *Milde* and *Riley* show, higher ability may also be signalled through a smaller loan if the stochastic framework is changed (see appendix A3). The only thing one can say safely is that in a market with asymmetric information about abilities of borrowers in a separating *Nash*-equilibrium at least some borrowers do not get the loan size they desire at the quoted loan rate, and at least some contracts offered differ from those available in a market with symmetric information.

The situation is quite different if the abilities are close to each other and the share of high quality borrowers is large. More precisely, there is no *Nash*-equilibrium if the joint-zero-profit-curve of the banks has an intersection with the high-ability iso-profit-line $g_2(K_2)$.

Inspection of Figure 3 shows that $K = (K_1, K_2)$ is no *Nash*-equilibrium if the bank's joint-zero-profit-line is $\hat{p}_2$ instead of $\hat{p}_1$. In that case any contract in the shaded region, like e.g. K_3 would make nonnegative profits, since it lies to the left and above $\hat{p}_2$. Hence there is no separating *Nash*-equilibrium. But there is also no pooling *Nash*-equilibrium. It would have to lie on $\hat{p}_2$, say at point K^P. Again any contract between p_2 and $g_2(K^P)$ and to the right of $g_1(K^P)$, like K_4, would break the equilibrium since it would attract only the high ability borrowers and make profits. K^P, on the other hand, would be demanded by low ability borrowers only and make losses. Hence, there is no *Nash*-equilibrium at all.

The possible non-existence of a *Nash*-equilibrium in the present model is not very surprising if its similarity with the insurance market model of *Rothschild* and *Stiglitz* (1976) and *Wilson* (1977) is considered. As a reaction several alternative equilibrium concepts have been proposed, and we shall investigate their implications for credit markets in due course. Before doing so, however, it is convenient to simplify the present model in the following way: Instead of assuming that the project return is a random variable satisfying restrictions that ensure "well behaved" iso-profit-curves for all parties concerned we shall concentrate on the simpler case where a project either fails and yields a return of zero or succeeds and yields a return that is determined by a neo-classical production function. It will be apparent that most conclusions that can be drawn from this simpler model carry over easily to more general models like that of *Milde* and *Riley*.

Since we also wish to analyse additional problems that arise as soon as variable loan size is admitted, like the exchange of information between banks, the analysis is continued in two subsequent chapters. The remainder of this chapter contains for the convenience of the reader a technical appendix with further details of the *Milde* and *Riley* model.

Appendix:

A1: Lemma (*Milde* and *Riley* 1984): If the hazard rate of F, F'/(1-F) is increasing, then for any y such that F(y) < 1

$$\text{(i)} \quad H(y) = \frac{\int_y^m (1-F(y))dy}{1-F(y)} \quad \text{where m is the upper limit of y.}$$

is a decreasing function of y.

Proof: By l'Hôspital's rule

$$\text{(ii)} \quad H(m) = \lim_{y \to m} \frac{-(1-F(m))}{-F'(m)} = 0$$

Differentiating (i) with respect to y yields

$$\text{(iii)} \quad H'(y) = -1 + \frac{F'(y)}{1-F(y)} H(y)$$

Differentiating again we get

$$\text{(iv)} \quad H''(y) = \frac{d[(F'(y)/(1-F(y))]}{dy} H(y) + \frac{F'(y) \cdot H'(y)}{1-F(y)}$$

By hypothesis, F'/(1-F) is increasing. Therefore, whenever H(y) is positive the first term on the right hand side of (iv) is positive. Then $H'(y) = 0 \Rightarrow H''(y) > 0$, i.e. any turning point of H(y) is a minimum. But $H(y) \geq 0$ and $H(m) = 0$. Thus there can be no turning points and H(y) is decreasing everywhere.

Q.E.D.

$$\text{A2: (i)} \quad \left.\frac{dR}{dL}\right|_{\bar{g}} = - \frac{(\partial \bar{g}/\partial L)}{(\partial \bar{g}/\partial R)} = \frac{R}{L} [e(1+H(\hat{y})/\hat{y})) - 1]$$

<u>**Proof**</u>:

$$\text{(ii)} \quad \bar{g}(R,L) = q(L)\int_{\hat{y}}^{\infty} y dF - (1-F(\hat{y}))RL$$

$$\text{(iii)} \quad \frac{\partial \bar{g}}{\partial L} = q'(L)\int_{\hat{y}}^{\infty} y dF - (1-F(\hat{y}))R$$

$$\text{(iv)} \quad \frac{\partial \bar{g}}{\partial R} = -(1-F(\hat{y}))L$$

Integrating by parts yields

$$\text{(v)} \quad \int_{\hat{y}}^{\infty} y dF = \hat{y}(1-F(\hat{y})) + \int_{\hat{y}}^{\infty}(1-F(y))dy$$

Substituting first (iii) and (iv) we get

$$\text{(vi)} \quad \frac{dR}{dL}\Big|_{\bar{g}} = \frac{q'(L)\int_{\hat{y}}^{\infty} y dF - (1-F(\hat{y}))R}{(1-F(\hat{y}))L} =$$

$$= \frac{R}{L}\left[\frac{Lq'(L)}{q} \cdot \frac{\int_{\hat{y}}^{\infty} y dF}{\hat{y}(1-F(\hat{y}))} - 1\right]$$

Substituting (v) into the last term we get

$$\text{(vii)} \quad \frac{dR}{dL}\Big|_{\bar{g}} = \frac{R}{L}\left[\frac{Lq'((L)}{q}\left[1 + \frac{H(\hat{y})}{\hat{y}}\right] - 1\right]$$

Q.E.D.

A3: Replace (19) by the stochastic production function

(i) $X = q(L) + YL + a$

For a given deposit rate of interest the optimal loan size L* is obtained from the condition

$$\text{(ii)} \quad \frac{\partial(x-IL)}{\partial L} = 0 = \frac{\partial}{\partial L}\{q(L)L - \bar{y}L - IL + a\} =$$

$$= \{1 + e(q,L^*)\}q(L^*) + \bar{y} - I$$

The optimal loan size is independent of ability a. The qualitative properties of the bank's zero profit curve are the same as for (19), i.e. proposition 7 and 8 still hold. Instead of proposition 9, however, we now get

Proposition (9'): If (19) is replaced by (i), other assumptions as before, then the slope of the iso-profit curve of a borrower is decreasing in a at any point (R,L)

Proof: $$\text{(iii)} \quad \left.\frac{dR}{dL}\right|_{\bar{g}} = \frac{\int_{\hat{y}}^{m}[q + Lq' + y - R]dF}{(1-F(\hat{y}))L}$$

where $y = \dfrac{RL - q(L)\cdot L - a}{L}$, consequently $\dfrac{\partial\hat{y}}{\partial a} < 0$

Reformulating (ii) we get

$$\text{(iii)} \quad \left.\frac{dR}{dL}\right|_{\bar{g}} = [q + Lq' - R + \frac{\int_{\hat{y}}^{m} ydF}{(1-F(\hat{y}))}]/L$$

$$= [q + Lq' - R + \hat{y} + H(\hat{y})]/L$$

Differentiating (iii) with respect to a yields

$$\frac{\partial [dR/dL]}{\partial a}\Big|_{\bar{g}} = \frac{\partial \hat{y}}{\partial a}[1 + H'(\hat{y})]/L < 0$$

since $1+H'(\hat{y}) > 0$ (see A1, (iii)).

Q.E.D.

Economically, proposition 9' states that abler loan applicants have a smaller marginal willingness to pay for an increase of the loan size. Consequently, in a separating equilibrium they get a smaller loan than the less able one.

Chapter 6:

VARIABLE LOAN SIZE, SIGNALLING AND ENDOGENOUS INFORMATION

6.1 Overview

In chapter 5 the assumption of an exogenously given project and loan size for each borrower was replaced by the more appealing assumption that the return of the project is a positive, concave function of the loan size according to a conventional neoclassical production function. It turned out that changing from a deterministic to a stochastic world where the project return is a random variable leads to complications which require some restrictions on the random distributions concerned in order to keep the model 'well behaved'. Then it was shown that even if appropriate assumptions are made no Nash-equilibrium may exist if there is asymmetric information about the abilities of borrowers.

The present chapter continues this analysis by introducing in the next section a very simple stochastic framework which facilitates especially the diagrammatic presentation considerably: Following an approach also used by *Bester* (1984b) it is assumed that projects either succeed with probability q and yield a return which is determined by the above mentioned production function, or they fail with probability 1-q and yield a return of zero.

In this version again no *Nash*-equilibrium may exist and alternative equilibrium concepts which ensure existence are introduced. As it happens, the resulting equilibria do not coincide in general, and one wonders which of these, if any, is the appropriate one. Section 3 presents an attempt to answer this question by modelling the credit market as a signalling game and applying the type of refinements of the *Nash*-equilibrium as proposed recently e.g. by *Kreps* and *Wilson* (1982), *Kohlberg* and *Mertens* (1982), *Kreps* (1985), *Milgrom* and *Roberts* (1984) and others. It turns out that the *Wilson*-equilibrium emerges as the most plausible solution.

In sections 4 and 5 we look at equilibria in variable loan size variants of model R and model H respectively. In section 6 we investigate a problem peculiar to variable loan size models: the endogenously determined exchange of information about borrowers between banks.

6.2 Success-Failure Projects and Different Abilities

6.2.1 The Nash-Equilibrium

The model we use in the remainder of this chapter and in chapter 7 bears close resemblance to that of chapter 5.2. In particular, recall that borrowers' iso-profit curves are concave, that the size of a loan demanded by individuals is a decreasing function of the loan rate r, and that this function and the iso-profit curves are shifted to the right as the ability a is increased. The only difference to the model of chapter 5.2 is that the investment project may fail completely with probability 1-q and yield a return of zero. If it is successful, which happens with probability q, its return x is determined by the positive, concave function x(L).

Now assume there are two types of loan applicants with abilities $a_2 > a_1$ and probabilities of success $q_2 > q_1$.

A graphical presentation of this model is given in Figure 1. The borrowers' iso-profit curves are the same as in Figure 5.1, dotted lines correspond again to high ability borrowers. What is different now are the bank's zero-profit curves: They are different for different abilities and satisfy $R_i = I/q_i$, i=1,2, hence $R_2 < R_1$.

If the banks knew the ability of a loan applicant the equilibrium would be the pair of contracts $(K_1, K_2^{\S})$, both maximizing the borrowers' profits given $R_i = I/q_i$. With asymmetric information, however, this could not be an equilibrium since low ability borrowers prefer $K_2^{\S}$ to K_1 and banks would make losses. An additional requirement for an equilibrium is therefore incentive compatibility, formally $g_1(K_1) \geq g_1(K_2)$. Given K_1, the best incentive compatible contract able borrowers can get without inflicting losses on the banks is K_2, the intersection of $g_1(K_1)$ and $R_2 = I/q_2$.

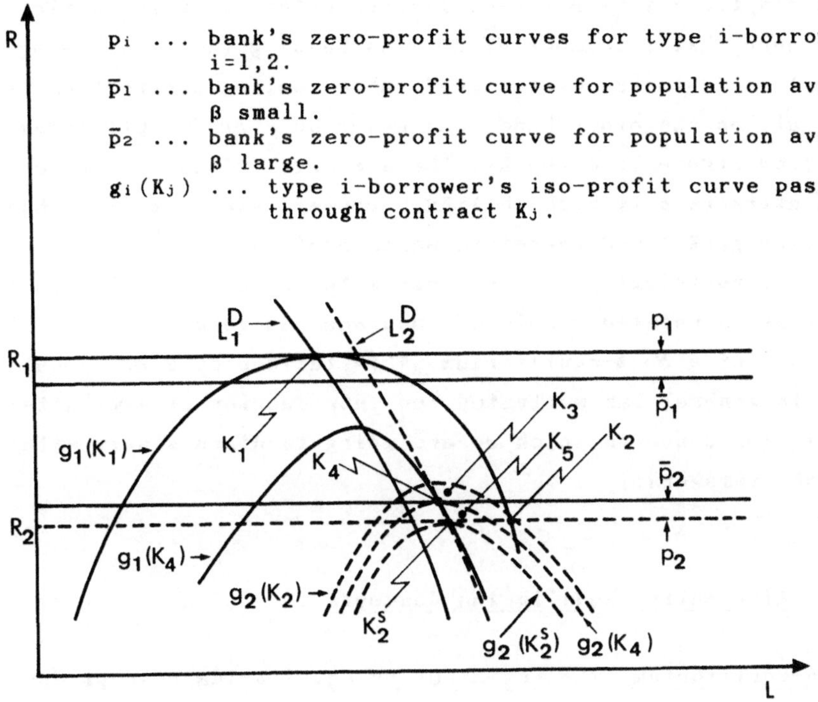

Figure 1

Whether (K_1,K_2), in fact, constitutes an equilibrium depends on β, the share of able borrowers, and/or on the equilibrium concept employed. Define $R^*: = I/(\beta q_2 + (1-\beta)q_1)$ as the average zero-profit line which is relevant if all borrowers get the same contract. If β is sufficiently small then R^* lies above $g_2(K_2)$, the able borrowers' iso-profit curve passing through K_2, and (K_1,K_2) is a *Nash*-equilibrium. One remarkable property of (K_1,K_2) pointed out by *Bester* (1984b) is that high ability borrowers get a larger rather than a smaller loan than they desire at R_2.

As in chapter 5.4 no *Nash*-equilibrium exists if β is sufficiently large such that a segment of R^* lies below $g_2(K_2)$: The separating pair (K_1, K_2) is dominated by the profitable pooling contract K_3. A pooling contract, on the other hand, can never be a *Nash*-equilibrium as can be seen from Figure 1: Given K_4, there always exists a contract like K_5 which attracts only high ability borrowers since it lies above $g_1(K_4)$ and below $g_2(K_4)$ and therefore makes profits.
So, not surprisingly, we are faced with the same problem as in chapter 5.4 or as in related models of insurance markets: The possible non-existence of a *Nash*-equilibrium. This failure of a *Nash*-equilibrium to exist in general has motivated the introduction of some alternative equilibrium concepts which we are going to discuss next within the present framework.

6.2.2 Alternative Equilibrium Concepts

Wilson-equilibrium: The anticipatory equilibrium concept due to *Wilson* (1977) states that a set of contracts $\{K_j\}$, $j=1,..,k$ constitutes an equilibrium if there exists no contract K_{k+1} that is profitable after all contracts of $\{K_j\}$ which make losses because of the introduction of K_{k+1} have been withdrawn.

If a *Nash*-equilibrium exists, i.e. if β is sufficiently small, it coincides with the *Wilson*-equilibrium. The more interesting case arises for large β and non-existence of a *Nash*-equilibrium.

The separating pair of contracts (K_1, K_2) is no *Wilson*-equilibrium for an analogous reason for which it is no *Nash*-equilibrium: A contract like K_3 would not be turned into a lossmaker by withdrawal of K_1 and/ or K_2. The unique *Wilson* equilibrium is, in fact, the pooling contract K_4. If, in addition to it, K_5 were offered only high ability borrowers would buy it and K_4 would make losses and disappear from the market. But then all borrowers would have to buy K_5 which would make losses because it is below the bank's zero profit line of the population average. Now according to the *Wilson* concept banks would anticipate this and renounce from offering K_5 in addition to K_4.

The *Wilson*-equilibrium has been criticized at least on two grounds: *Milde* and *Riley* (1984) complain that it requires an immediate reaction of all banks if one of them deviates from the equilibrium and suggest that this is not very plausible. ***Rothschild*** and ***Stiglitz*** (1976) noted earlier that the ***Wilson***-equilibrium is a 'curious half-way house' since it only considers passive reactions of banks, i.e. the withdrawal of existing contracts and not the introduction of new ones.

The first criticism seems somewhat besides the point because it only makes sense if there is less than perfect information about the contracts actually offered in the market. Now while this may be a reasonable assumption it would lead to an altogether different model where, as related work on insurance markets seems to suggest, existence problems of the kind described above may not occur at all (***Zink*** 1985).

The second criticism, however, seems more serious, and is taken care of to some extent in the next equilibrium concept defined below: Riley-equilibrium: The reactive equilibrium concept due to ***Riley*** (1979) states that a set of contracts $\{K_j\}$, j=1,...k, constitutes an equilibrium if for each additional contract K_{k+1} which is profitable if $\{K_j\}$ continues to be offered there is another profitable contract K_{k+2} which induces a loss on K_{k+1} and cannot be turned into a loss-maker itself as long as $\{K_j\}$ and K_{k+1} are in the market.

Again the interesting case is the one where no ***Nash***-equilibrium exists since otherwise it coincides with the ***Riley***-equilibrium. The pooling contract K_4 cannot be a ***Riley***-equilibrium: A contract like K_5 can never make losses as long as K_4 continues to be offered, hence nothing prevents banks from offering K_5 in addition to K_4.

The pair (K_1,K_2), however, is a ***Riley***-equilibrium: Any contract like K_3 could be turned into a loss maker by offering some additional contract above $g_1(K_3)$ and below $g_2(K_3)$, hence no bank has an incentive to offer K_3 in addition to (K_1,K_2).

It is noteworthy that the pooling contract K_4 is Pareto-better than the separating contracts (K_1,K_2) in the case where β is too large for a ***Nash***-equilibrium to exist. Both types of borrowers are on a better iso-profit-curve with K_4 than they would be at (K_1,K_2), and the bank's expected profit is the same in both cases.

The *Riley*-equilibrium can be criticized for exactly the opposite reason as the *Wilson* concept: It implies that banks continue to offer unprofitable contracts even though they very cleverly foresee the reactions of competitors to their own actions. Both, the *Wilson*- and the *Riley*-concept, are of course difficult to reconcile with the assumption of perfect competition: Either individual firms are so small that the market does not react to their actions (or so they believe), or they are big enough to have an effect on other banks, but then we have an oligopolistic market. This, on the other hand, would be hard to analyze, and one cannot help feeling that both, the *Wilson*- and the *Riley*-concept are something of a compromise between models of perfect and of oligopolistic competition.

What all concepts discussed so far neglect is the behaviour of loan applicants. In particular, upsetting a pooling-contract as described in the *Nash*- and *Riley*-concept implies that low ability borrowers do not mind being identified even though this will mean that they will be made worse off. In many instances they will have a strong incentive to disguise their true ability, and this motivates the next equilibrium concept.

Grossman-equilibrium: The dissembling equilibrium concept due to *H.I.Grossman* (1979) states that a set of contracts $\{K_j\}$, $j=1,...k$, constitutes an equilibrium if there is no contract K_{k+1} which is profitable after less able borrowers have decided whether to disguise their true status by buying a contract intended for able ones or not. The crucial point is that identified less able borrowers will not get a better contract than K_1, hence they will often have an incentive to act as if they belonged to the other group.

In the present model this implies that, given non-existence of a *Nash*-equilibrium, K_4 is a *Grossman*-equilibrium: K_3 could never be profitable since it would be purchased by all borrowers, for those sticking to K_4 would be deemed less able.

All the above equilibrium concepts imply a high degree of rationality particularly on behalf of the banks who never miss a profitable opportunity. A somewhat weaker and less demanding equilibrium concept is the following:

Spence-equilibrium: The concept of an informationally consistent equilibrium due to *Spence* (1973, 1974) states that a set of contracts constitutes an equilibrium if no bank makes (expected) losses, i.e. if the behaviour of borrowers generated by the supply of contracts satisfies the expectations of the lenders. Hence, any pooling contract or pair of separating contracts with non-negative expected profits for borrowers on the bank's zero-profit lines is a *Spence*-equilibrium. Obviously, there is a continuum of equilibria, and many are not Pareto-efficient. The underlying behavioural assumptions, however, seem particularly hard to swallow in this model. It is difficult to see why banks and customers should stop experimenting with new contracts as soon as the bank-profit is zero.

Another potential equilibrium appears if we relax the assumption that each type of contract has to break even in equilibrium. In principal it is conceivable that a bank offers a pair of contracts which together satisfy the zero-profit constraint, and one makes a loss which is exactly offset by the gains of the other. Such a pair of contracts (K_1^*, K_2^*) is shown in Figure 2. Clearly, (K_1^*, K_2^*) is Pareto-better than (K_1, K_2), and it is incentive compatible. The question arises whether such a pair of "subsidizing contracts" could ever constitute an equilibrium.

The answer depends on the equilibrium concept and is "yes" only for the *Wilson*-approach or, more precisely, for a version of the *Wilson* concept that has been proposed by *Miyazaki* (1977): A bank acting according to the *Nash*- or the *Riley*-concept has no reason to offer loss-making K_1^* since it assumes all (or at least some) other banks do. With dissembling behaviour, on the other hand, low ability borrowers would buy K_2^* rather than K_1^* because they are afraid to be rejected or get K_1 once they are identified. Anticipation of withdrawals of K_1^* by all banks once one bank starts withdrawing it motivates banks to stick to (K_1^*, K_2^*) once it is in the market. In fact, if banks behave according to the *Wilson*-approach, their optimal strategy is to attract high ability borrowers with a contract K_2^* and prevent low ability borrowers from purchasing the same contract by offering an alternative contract which results in a tolerably small loss. Taking into account incentive compatibility and the zero-profit condition, in equilibrium the following optimization problem will be solved:

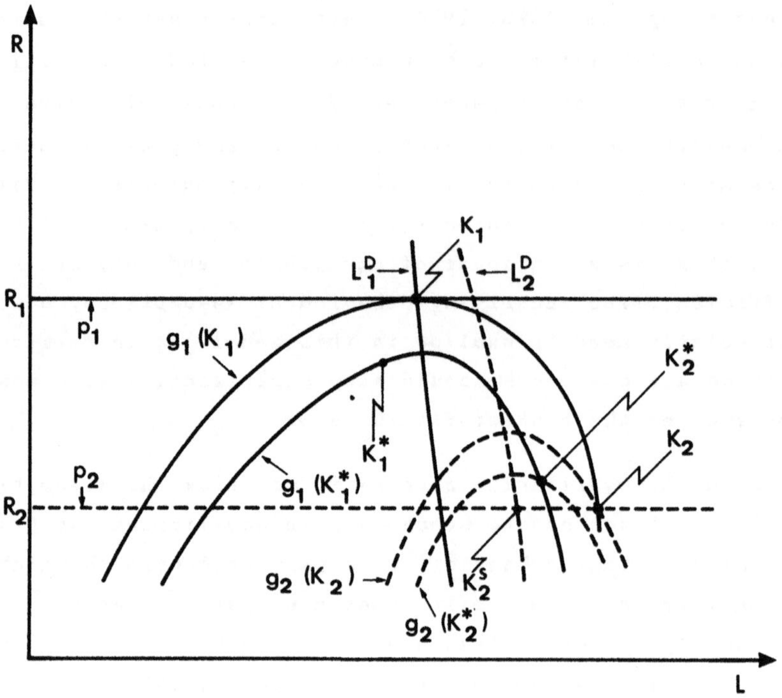

Figure 2

$$\max_{K_1, K_2} \bar{g}_2(K_2) = q_2(x_2(L_2) - R_2 L_2) \tag{10}$$

s.t.

$$\bar{g}_1(K_2) - \bar{g}_1(K_1) \le 0 \tag{11}$$

$$\beta(q_2 R_2 L_2 - I L_2) + (1-\beta)(q_1 R_1 L_1 - I L_1) = 0 \tag{12}$$

$$L_1, L_2, R_1, R_2 \ge 0 \tag{13}$$

where $K_j = (R_j, L_j)$, $j = 1,2,$. (11) is the condition of incentive compatibility and (12) is the zero-profit condition. It is straightforward to show that at an interior solution one has (see Appendix).

$$(14)\quad \beta > \frac{x_2'(L_2^*) - x_1'(L_2^*)}{(q_2/q_1)(R_2^* - x_2'(L_2^*)) + x_2'(L_2^*) - x_1'(L_2^*)} =: Z(L_2^*)$$

where $(R_2^*, L_2^*) = K_2^*$, the optimal subsidizing contract for high ability borrowers. Now it is easy to check that $x_2''(L) - x_1''(L) \leq 0$ implies $dZ(L)/dL < 0$. Suppose this assumption is satisfied, then (14) provides a simple criterion for determining whether a *Nash*-equilibrium solves the above optimization problem: Let (R_2^{**}, L_2^{**}) denote the high ability contract of a *Nash*-equilibrium. If we have $\beta < Z(L_2^{**})$ then the *Nash*-solution is optimal also with respect to all subsidizing pairs of contracts, since for L_2 smaller than L_2^{**} (14) cannot be satisfied either. In particular, suppose the differences of abilities are so large that K_2^S is to the right of K_2. In that case $R_2 = x_2'(L)$ and obviously (14) can never hold since $\beta < 1$. On the other hand, if K_2^S is to the left of K_2 one can always make β sufficiently small such that the *Nash*-equilibrium is optimal. Inspection of (14) shows that the optimality of a truly subsidizing pair of contracts is more likely the larger the difference between probabilities of success and the smaller the differences of abilities.

Now even the sympathetic reader may feel, as with other signalling models, that the above analysis is rather unsatisfactory: Conclusions appear very sensitive with respect to the equilibrium concept chosen (and this will be even more so in chapter 7), and it seems unclear which concept is to be preferred for economic reasons. The next section attempts to offer some guidance as to which is the appropriate equilibrium by modelling the credit market as an extensive signalling game.

6.3 Strategic Stability of Credit Market Equilibria

This section is something of a digression from the main theme of the book since it contains an explicit application of game theoretic concepts which are not used elsewhere in this investigation. There are two reasons for its inclusion in the present chapter: Firstly, as just remarked, recent developments in the theory of (extensive) signalling games carry the promise to shed some light on the problem of the choice of an appropriate equilibrium concept. Secondly, these very same developments seem to suggest that in the near future much of the analysis of markets with imperfect information will profitably be recast in a game theoretic framework. This section indicates how this can be done as far as credit markets are concerned.

It must also be stated, however, that at its present stage the work on signalling games has not yet come up with a unified terminology or analytical framework, hence the task of reformulating the entire analysis of this book in game theoretic terms should better be performed after the appropriate concepts have taken a clearer shape than is the case presently.

So let us turn next to a game theoretic formulation of the credit market model of the previous section. Suppose there are two Banks, B_1 and B_2, who compete for a continuum of loan applicants who have a share β of high ability types with (a_2,q_2) and a share $(1-\beta)$ of low ability types with (a_1,q_1), $a_2 > a_1$, $q_2 > q_1$. The game has three stages:

Stage 1: Each bank announces a set of credit contracts of the form (R,L).

Stage 2: Each borrower applies for one contract at one bank. If both banks offer the same contracts each applicant tosses a fair coin to determine the bank at which he applies (if he applies at all)

Stage 3: The bank decides whether to accept or to reject applications.

An extensive game like this has a large number of *Nash*-equilibria, because the definition of a *Nash*-equilibrium does not restrict the 'beliefs' of the players which, of course, govern their behaviour if they are faced with actions of other players which would not occur in equilibrium. The response of game theorists has been to develop criteria which rule out certain beliefs or behaviour as "implausible" or "irrational" and therefore eliminate many *Nash*-equilibria. Ideally, one hopes to find refinements of the *Nash*-concept which lead to a unique equilibrium, and as will be shown below this is indeed possible for the credit market game under consideration. But let us first have a look at some of the *Nash*-equilibria of the present game. To that purpose, consider Figure 3.

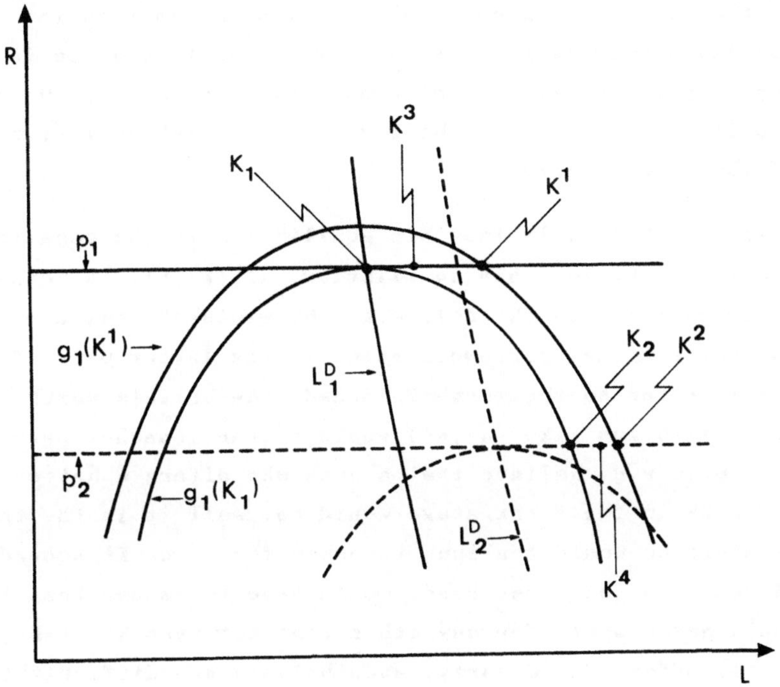

Figure 3

Considering only equilibria in pure strategies of the banks there are two types of *Nash*-equilibria

(i) Separating equilibria, where each bank offers two contracts K^1, K^2, which satisfy the following conditions:

Incentive compatibility: $\bar{g}_1(K^1) \geq \bar{g}_1(K^2)$ and
$\bar{g}_2(K^2) \geq \bar{g}_2(K^1)$

Acceptability: $\bar{g}_1(K^1), \quad \bar{g}_2(K^2) \geq 0$

Zero-profit for banks: $\bar{p}_1(K^1) = \bar{p}_2(K^2) = I$

Consulting Figure 3 it is obvious that there is a continuum of pairs like (K^1, K^2) on R_1 and R_2 which satisfy the above requirements. A Nash equilibrium would be, e.g. the following combination of strategies: B_1 and B_2 offer both (K^1, K^2), low ability borrowers demand K^1, high ability borrowers apply for K^2, and both banks accept all applicants. Clearly, each player's strategy is a best response to the strategies of all other players. In particular, given the application for K^2 of high ability borrowers it does not pay a bank to deviate from K^2 by offering a (profitable) pair of contracts like (K^3, K^4). On the other hand, applying for K^2 is the best choice for high ability borrowers if only (K^1, K^2) are offered.

What makes (K^1, K^2) an implausible equilibrium is the behaviour implied for situations outside this equilibrium. If (K^3, K^4) is actually offered in addition to (K^1, K^2), e.g. "by mistake", how can it be explained that rational borrowers stick to the latter pair of contracts, which is inferior to the former? Indeed, the beliefs which could support an equilibrium like (K^1, K^2) would appear somewhat peculiar: A borrower could e.g. believe that a bank who offers a better contract than K^1 or K^2 in the first stage would not sell it in the third stage and therefore he would continue to apply for K^1 or K^2 according to his type. A bank, on the other hand, would have to assume that the applicant would never apply for any other contract than K^1 or K^2, hence she would never offer one. Clearly, such beliefs are difficult to reconcile with intuitive notions of rational behaviour.

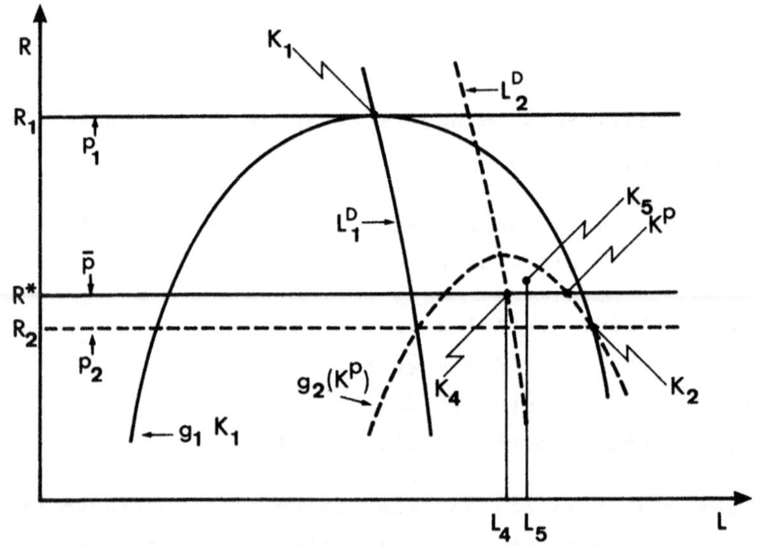

Figure 4

(ii) Pooling equilibria like K^P, which have to satisfy the acceptability and the zero-profit condition as depicted in Figure 4. Again, there is a continuum of pooling equilibria, which result from the following combination of strategies: Both banks offer K^P, all borrowers apply for it and are accepted by both banks. However, such an equilibrium carries little conviction as far as the behaviour of market participants outside the equilibrium is concerned. Beliefs of the following type have to be invoked: Suppose K^P is the equilibrium contract and a bank offers a contract like K_5 between R^* and $g_2(K^P)$. If this bank believes that the share of low ability applicants for the additional contract is larger than for the set of all applicants it would reject all applications in the third stage. If borrowers anticipate this they would not apply for a contract other than K^P which therefore is a *Nash*-equilibrium of this game. As with (K^1, K^2) the beliefs required to support such an equilibrium do not look very plausible.

As hinted above several authors have proposed refinements of the *Nash*-equilibrium which in one way or other restrict 'admissible' beliefs and reduce the number of equilibria. Examples are perfectness (*Selten* 1975), sequentiallity (*Kreps* and *Wilson* 1982), iterated elimination of weakly dominated (*Milgrom* and *Roberts* 1985) or of useless strategies (*McLennan* 1983), and structural or strategic stability (*Kohlberg* and *Mertens* 1982). In some cases the different criteria lead to the same outcomes, but as yet there is neither full agreement on the terminology nor is the relationship between the various concepts entirely clear (a lucid discussion of these issues is contained in *Kreps* (1985)). The stability criterion of *Kohlberg* and *Mertens* is the strongest in the sense that each equilibrium that is strategically stable is also perfect, sequential etc., but not vice versa. The original presentation of *Kohlberg* and *Mertens* is rather abstract and not easily accessable, and its application to specific games leads to a rather involved analysis except for very simple examples. In addition, applicability is so far only possible for finite games. Fortunately *Kreps* (1985) and *Hellwig* (1985b) have shown that for games like the one above quite often there exist intuitive criteria which can be used to single out an equilibrium as particularly convincing, and which yield the same result as the formal concept of *Kohlberg* and *Mertens*.

In the present model it is fairly easy to get rid of all separating equilibria except for (K_1, K_2) and of all pooling equilibria except for K_4: One could invoke, e.g. iterated elimination of weakly dominated strategies: Clearly, all pooling contracts on R are dominated for high ability borrowers by K_4 and can be eliminated. Similarly, all separating contracts like (K^1, K^2) on R_1 and R_2 respectively are dominated by (K_1, K_2) for all borrowers and therefore are implausible equilibria. Provided the game is reformulated in a discrete version the concepts of perfectness or sequentiality would achieve the same.

Now the really interesting question is whether for some β sufficiently large to rule out a separating *Nash*-equilibrium in the model of section 2 it is possible to decide whether in the corresponding game the separating (= *Riley*)-equilibrium or the pooling (= *Wilson*)-equilibrium emerges as the most plausible.

Consider first the separating equilibrium (K_1, K_2). Is this equilibrium stable with respect to all possible perturbations? Suppose a contract like K_5 is offered by one of the banks. How can borrowers be expected to react? Since the contract, if applications are accepted, is better for both types of borrowers, they can be expected to apply for it with the same mix as their total, and the bank should accept all applications. Given this, all borrowers will apply for it, hence the separating (*Riley*) equilibrium is not stable.

The pooling equilibrium K_4, in contrast, is stable: Suppose a bank offers K_5 in addition to K_4. This bank, however, would not accept applicants for the following reason: High ability applicants prefer K_4 to K_5. Hence, a bank offering K_4 expects a deterioration of the mix of its applicants and refuses to sell K_4. This induces also low ability borrowers to apply for K_5, which therefore would make losses if actually sold, hence the bank offering K_5 would reject applicants. Consequently, no bank has an incentive to deviate from K_4. The reader may check that for small β a pooling contract cannot be a stable equilibrium since it can be removed through the offer of an appropriate pair of separating contracts. In that situation (K_1, K_2) is stable.

Finally, it is worth mentioning that a pair of subsidizing contracts which could be a *Miyazaki-Wilson* equilibrium could not be a strategically stable equilibrium: Low ability borrowers would not expect to get a contract that inflicts a loss on the bank, and banks actually have no reason to accept one in the present framework.

Thus we may conclude that the Wilson-equilibrium corresponds to the unique strategically stable equilibrium in the game corresponding to our credit market model. This result has been established also for an insurance market by *Hellwig* (1985a).

Does this settle the quarrel between advocates of the *Riley*- and the *Wilson*-concept? Some caution seems in order.

First of all, the credit market just discussed is essentially static. It is a somewhat arbitrary specification that the game has exactly three stages. In particular, the justification of the separating *Riley*-equilibrium implicitly assumes a fourth stage which allows a bank to react to an offer of K_5 by offering another contract that turns K_5 into a loss maker. However, the dissembling behaviour of low ability borrowers presumably destroys separating equilibria with large β even in more complicated versions of the game.

Second, and somewhat more seriously, there are results obtained by *Kreps* (1985) which state exactly the opposite from our conclusions above: He shows that in three-stage signalling games the *Riley*-equilibrium is the only stable equilibrium if the informed players, in our case the loan applicants, have to move first. Such a game would have the following structure.

Stage 1: Loan applicants announce the loan size they desire
Stage 2: Banks offer a loan rate for each loan size
Stage 3: Applicants buy the most preferred contract.

Now let us consider only the case with large β and ask why borrowers would prefer to announce L_1 and L_2 rather than L_4, even though the latter is preferred by all types. The reason is that given L_4 it always pays the high ability applicant to demand a larger loan, say L_5: banks would interpret this (correctly) as showing high ability, since low ability borrowers are worse off with L_5 than with L_4 (and K_4) even if they make the bank believe with certainty they have high ability. Now a combination of signals L_4 and L_5 could not be an equilibrium either: Banks would raise R for L_4 applicants thus creating an incentive for all borrowers to announce L_5. The resulting pooling contract would be no strategically stable equilibrium for the same reason as K_4. Consider, in contrast, the signals L_1 and L_2: Banks would offer R_1 and R_2 for the following reason: They would not believe that a low ability borrower would demand L_2 because even if he is then classified as a high ability type with probability one he would not be better off than with K_1. This is exactly the restriction on beliefs which is implied by the stability concept of *Kohlberg* and *Mertens* (1982) and leads to the above stated conclusion of *Kreps* (1985).

So it seems all we have gained is a switch from the choice between *Wilson* and *Riley* to a choice between *Hellwig* and *Kreps*, i.e. to a determination of which player moves first, the uninformed or the informed.

Now in many cases the latter choice is quite easy and arises naturally from the economic context under consideration. But even if we are more cautious and decide that nature makes the first move and determines which of the players has to take the opening action it seems likely that the *Wilson* equilibrium emerges if the strategy spaces are sufficiently rich. Suppose nature has decided that loan applicants have to start the credit market game. Since they are extremely rational and smart players they should realize that signalling their type before receiving offers from banks works in their disfavour regardless of their type. Why don't we allow them to solicit offers from banks without announcement of a particular loan size? Banks, in contrast, gain nothing by withholding offers and passing the ball back to borrowers. Hence, the *Kreps* result does not look very convincing in cases where the informed party is worse off by immediate, fully revealing signalling - if we enlarge the strategy space in a reasonable way we are most likely to switch into a *Hellwig* regime.

But even if for some reason the borrowers have to announce their desired loan size and end up in a separating equilibrium it is difficult to see why the process should stop after stage 3. What should stop a bank, possibly a market entrant, to offer a Pareto-better pooling contract? Usually loans are allowed to be repaid before they are due, and in the present context (with large β) this would be profitable for borrowers even if they had to incur (small) additional costs.

To conclude this lengthy section, it seems that there are two lessons to be learned: A game theoretical version of our credit market model seems to suggest strongly that the *Wilson*-equilibrium is the most convincing one of all proposed so far. The second lesson, however, is even more obvious. There is still a long way to go until we can expect game theory to provide really clear-cut and satisfactory solutions to problems encountered in markets with imperfect information.

6.4 Projects of Different Riskiness

We now return to our basic model and analyze how variable loan size affects equilibria in variant R and H (see section 6.5. Moral hazard model E is taken up in chapter 7.6).

In contrast to the two preceding sections we assume now that ability a and probability of success q are negatively correlated, i.e. there are two types of applicants with $a_2 > a_1$ and $q_1 > q_2$. The *Rothschild* and *Stiglitz* concept of increasing riskiness suggests the following formulation of the project returns: $y_i = a_i x(L)$, $q_i = 1/a_i$, $i = 1,2$ where $x(L)$ is the production function introduced in chapter 5.1. Potential equilibria in that market are shown in Figure 5.

The main difference between Figure 1 and Figure 5 is the location of the zero profit lines of banks: In Figure 5 type 2 borrowers have a lower probability of success and consequently the corresponding bank-zero-profit line is higher than that referring to low ability, high-success probability borrowers. The iso-profit curves of the able borrowers are, as before, to the right of those of the low ability borrowers. In a separating equilibrium incentive compatibility requires $g_2(K_2) \geq g_2(K_1)$ and this may imply, as is shown in Figure 5, that loan applicants with the safer project get a loan which is smaller than they desire. This result has been established first by *Bester* (1984b).
As in model A discussed in section 2 the pair (K_1, K_2) is only a *Nash*-equilibrium if the share of type 2 borrowers is sufficiently large, otherwise we encounter the by now familiar problem of the choice of an appropriate equilibrium concept which is not repeated at this point. We only note in passing that in a pooling equilibrium type 2 borrowers get a smaller loan than they desire at the ruling interest factor.

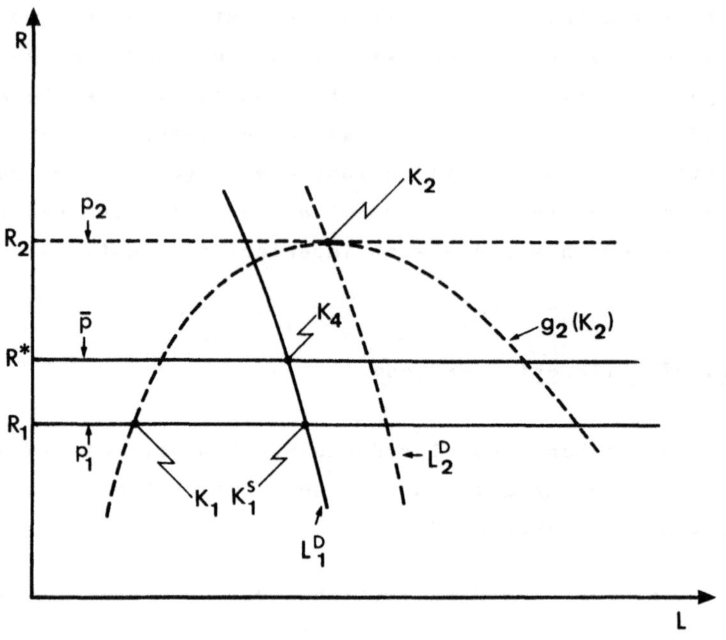

Figure 5

6.5 Borrowers With Different Default Costs

Next we turn to approach H and present it with the assumption of variable loan size. It is assumed that all projects are identical and as described in chapter 5.2. The only uncertainty stems from the borrowers' unknown costs of default which determine whether a particular contract will be honoured or not.

Suppose there are two types of loan applicants, the "honest" ones with extremely high default costs, who always fulfill their contract, and the "dishonest" ones who only repay their debt (including interest) if it is not larger than their costs of default. Denote the share of the former by β.
A graphical representation of such a loan market is given in Figure 6.

As has been shown in section 2 the supply of loans is infinitely elastic at R = I as long as full repayment of debts is granted. In

Figure 6 this is the case up to L_1, where total repayment RL equals the default cost of the "dishonest" group, denoted by D_1. Through the contract K_1 passes the line $R(D_1) := D_1/L$, and the dishonest borrowers will default at any contract to the north-east of it.

At K_1 the supply of loans curve jumps and continues as a parallel of the ordinate at a level of R satisfying
$R_2 := I/\beta$, i.e. at the level at which the honest borrowers exactly compensate the banks for their losses incurred with loans to dishonest borrowers. The maximum possible loan size is given by L* which satisfies $I/\beta = R_2 = D_2/L^*$, i.e. if L is increased further all borrowers would default. Given R_2 the desired contract of honest borrowers is given at K_2.

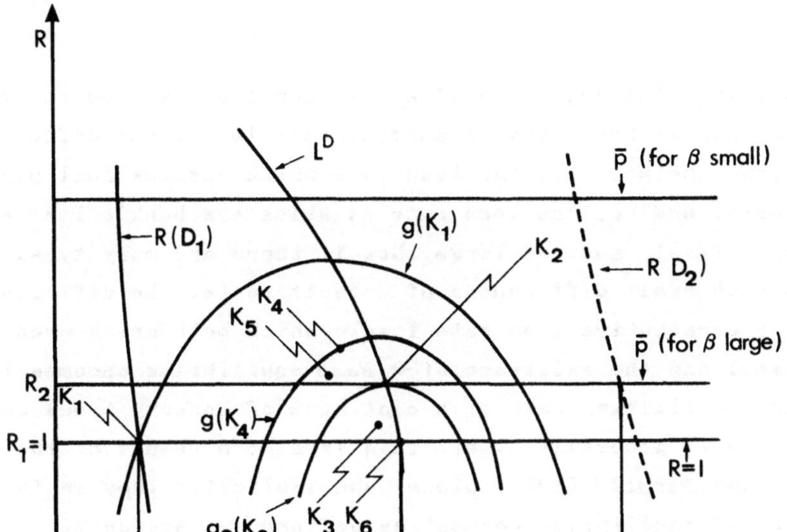

Figure 6

Next we turn to the question of the existence of an equilibrium. Assume first D_2 is sufficiently large such that L* is to the right of K_2.

Whether a *Nash*-equilibrium exists in the present model or not, depends once more on the size of β, the share of honest borrowers. If it is small then the difference between I and R_2 is large and the indifference curve of honest borrowers passing through K_1 lies entirely below the upper branch of the bank's zero-profit line. In this case K_1 is a *Nash*-equilibrium since there is no other contract which attracts borrowers and is profitable at the same time.

Suppose next that β is very large. In that case the iso-profit-curve $g(K_1)$ contains points greater than or equal to R_2 and no Nash-equilibrium exists. K_1 is not an equilibrium since any contract above R_2 and below $g(K_1)$ such as K_4 would yield a positive profit. K_4 is not an equilibrium precisely because it yields a positive profit. K_2 satisfies the zero-profit condition for banks, but it is no *Nash*-equilibrium either: Any contract below $g(K_2)$, between R_1 and R_2 and to the left of L_2 will make a profit because it will attract only honest borrowers.

As a consequence the existence of a *Nash*-equilibrium requires that the share of dishonest borrowers be sufficiently large. Put differently, the difference between r_1, the loan rate which ensures full payment by all borrowers, and r_2, the loan rate at which the bank's losses due to default are offset, must be large. Now if there are many types of borrowers with small differences of default costs, the difference between two consecutive loan rate levels which both break even also becomes small and the existence of a *Nash*-equilibrium becomes less likely. In the limiting case of a continuum of honesty-types no *Nash*-equilibrium will generally exist. This is also a result of the original *Jaffee* and *Russell* (1976) piece, and implicitly they in fact use a *Wilson*-type of equilibrium concept as defined in section 2.
Suppose β is large and no *Nash*-equilibrium exists. K_1 is no *Wilson*-equilibrium because K_4 would make profits with or without K_1. The unique *Wilson*-equilibrium is K_2: Any contract like K_3, which would be purchased by honest borrowers only, would make losses as soon as K_2 is withdrawn. Since the latter would make losses, because it would be stuck with dishonest borrowers only, any bank who considers offering K_3 in addition to K_2 would anticipate the withdrawal of K_2 and renounce from offering K_3.

Consider next the *Riley* concept for large β: The *Wilson*-equilibrium K_2 cannot be a *Riley*-equilibrium: A contract like K_3 can never be turned into a loss-maker as long as K_2 remains in the market. The unique *Riley*-equilibrium is K_1: Any additional profitable contract like K_4 would make losses as soon as a third profit-making contract like K_5 is introduced. In addition, K_5 can never make losses as long as K_4 is in the market.

One problem common to all equilibrium concepts discussed so far is the rather silly behaviour of dishonest borrowers who reveal themselves if they demand, say K_2 even if K_3 is offered and preferred by all honest borrowers.

Hence, there is particular good reason for introducing *Grossman*'s dissembling equilibrium. Clearly, K_2 is a *Grossman* equilibrium: all dishonest borrowers would immediately purchase a contract like K_3 in order to disguise their plan to default and it would be bound to make losses.

Finally, any point on the bank's zero profit line is a *Spencian* informationally consistent equilibrium.

The reader will easily realize that the *Wilson*-equilibrium is (at least weakly) Pareto better than the *Riley*-equilibrium and almost all *Spence* equilibria. Possible policy implications are left for future research.

6.6 Exchange of Information Between Banks

The analysis of this section is again somehow a digression from the main thread of the book since it touches upon a problem not further considered in other chapters (or in the relevant literature, for that matter): The exchange of information about borrowers between banks.

This issue has been raised first in the context of insurance markets by *Jaynes* (1978) whose argument would run as follows in the present framework: All equilibria discussed in the preceding 4 sections require that each borrower can get loans only from one bank which in turn presupposes that banks inform each other about the loans they have granted and the clients who got them. But this is a rather strong assumption and it would be desirable to show that such a complete exchange of information is indeed in the mutual interest of all banks. Now it is easy to find examples where this is not the case: Suppose there is a separating equilibrium where the loan size corresponding to the low interest rate is smaller than that granted at the high interest rate, as it may be the case in model R of section 4. Clearly, borrowers who purchase the latter contract (K_2 in Figure 5) could improve their expected profit if they could purchase K_1, pay R_1, and supplement it with a loan of the size they desire at an interest factor R_2. While banks offering loans for R_1 clearly have an incentive to share information about borrowers, exactly in order to prevent high risk borrowers from financing large projects through several loans from different banks, some other bank would not risk anything by offering loans for R_2 and keeping quiet. Consequently, situations are conceivable in which some banks have an incentive to withhold information about their clients. Thus, it seems worthwhile to explore the implications of an endogenous exchange of information.

The first point to note is that a situation like the one just described could not persist in equilibrium since banks who sell at the lower R make losses as soon as high risk borrowers get the same contract as those with the smaller one. Hence, if high risk borrowers can finance their project through a combination of loans then the contract sold to both types must be on the bank-zero-profit line for the population average.

The second point to note is that in some variants of the adverse selection model of credit markets there is no incentive for high risk borrowers to purchase a loan contract in addition to an equilibrium pooling contract. This is true for the version of model A analyzed in section 2: The loan size of the pooling contract is already to the right of the individual demand curve of low ability borrowers.

The third point to note is that in model H banks have a very strong incentive to exchange all their information. If they do not then all applicants (except for those with infinite default costs) would collect a total loan size that makes it worthwhile to take the money and run.

Consequently, endogenization of information exchange is only a problem for models where the loan size offered at a pooling equilibrium is smaller than desired by borrowers with the riskier project. This is true for model R presented in section 4, and we shall focus attention on this one.

We shall demonstrate now, using Figure 7 below, that the unique *Nash*-equilibrium with endogenous exchange of information has the following form: One set of banks offers contracts on R*, the break even interest factor for the population average, up to a loan size L, which corresponds to the pooling equilibrium contract of section 4 and maximizes the expected profit of the safe project given R*.

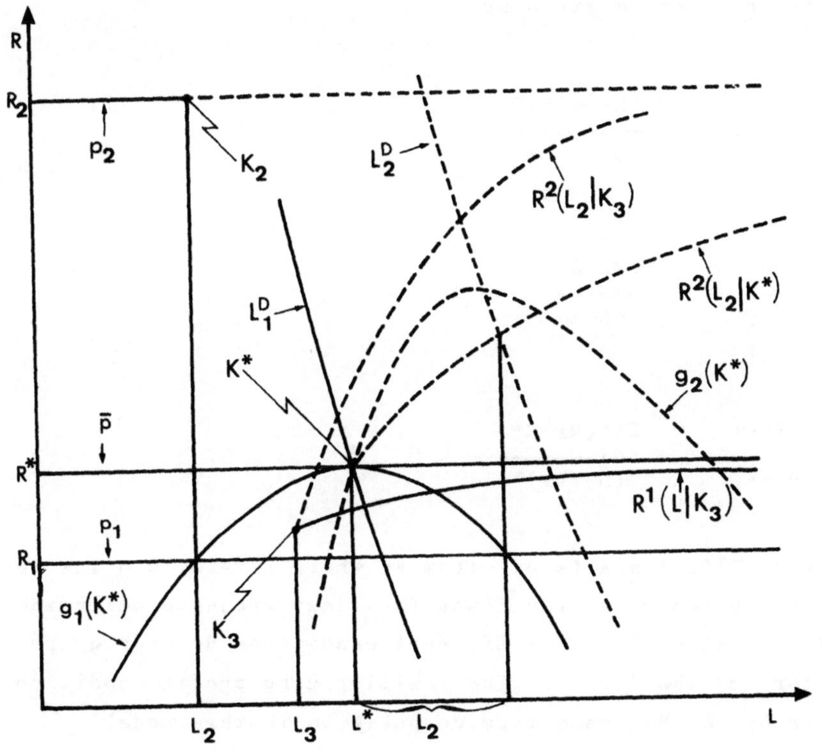

$R^i(L|K)$ ... contract K plus further contract on p_2 for i=2 and on $\bar{p}$ for i=1.

Figure 7

In fact, only $K^* = (R^*, L^*)$ will be purchased, but the other contracts are required in order to support the equilibrium. All banks offering K^* and contracts on R^* to the left of it exchange all their information about clients in order to prevent borrowers with the risky project from purchasing more than one contract and inflicting losses on these banks.

A second set of banks offers contracts on R_2 up to an amount of L_2. The customers of these banks are borrowers with the risky project who only purchase K_2 if they are promised that the information about this deal is not passed on to the banks where they already got K^*. The amount L_2 is determined as follows: The average interest factor they have to consider is given by

$$(15) \qquad R^2(L_2) = \frac{L^*R^* + L_2R_2}{L^* + L_2}$$

with

$$(16) \qquad \frac{dR^2}{dL_2} = \frac{L^*(R_2 - R)}{(L^* + L_2)^2} > 0$$

and

$$(17) \qquad \frac{d^2R^2}{dL_2{}^2} = -\frac{2L^*(R_2 - R^*)}{(L^* + L_2)^3} < 0$$

The curve $R^2(L_2)$ starts off from K^* where $L_2 = 0$, and its intersection with the demand curve for loans for risky projects determines the total loan size $L^2 = L^* + L_2$. What conditions do we require to hold in equilibrium? The first is the familiar zero-profit condition for banks implied by the Bertrand type competition in this model.

The second requires that banks and borrowers pass on information if and only if it is profitable for them.

The third is the *Nash*-condition that it does not pay any agent to deviate from his strategy, given the strategies of all other market participants.

Now as has been mentioned above banks offering contracts on R^* have an incentive to share their information with all other banks except for one case that will not occur in equilibrium (see below). Clearly, a bank that does not publicize the identity of its clients will attract all high risk applicants and make losses. Banks offering contracts on R_2, on the other hand, can only attract borrowers if they do not disclose any information about their clients. One can imagine, e.g. that contracts on R^* include a clause that involves a heavy penalty on borrowers who purchase additional loans from other banks. This motivates the discretion of banks about their clients on R_2.

It remains to be shown that it does not pay a bank to offer a contract to the left and below of K^*, more precisely in the "triangle" between R_1 and the dotted (high risk) and the solid (low risk) iso-profit curves passing through K^*. Clearly, if such a contract attracts only borrowers with the safe projects such a contract would be profitable and destroy the supposed equilibrium. The crucial point is whether a bank offering K_3 can prevent applicants from getting an additional loan on R^*. If it can, then high risk borrowers may not apply for K_3: It is easy to see that for some $L^{**} := L^* + L_2 = L_3 + L_2^*$ it is possible that $(R_3 L_3 + R_2 L_2^*)/L^{**} > (R^* L^* + R_2 L_2)/L^{**}$. If this inequality is reversed for $L^{**} = L^*$ then there is no problem since high risk borrowers would also apply for K_3 and make it unprofitable. Otherwise, K_3 would be profitable, because only low risk borrowers demand it, and (K^*, K_2) could not be an equilibrium.

But clearly it pays borrowers with the safe project to supplement K_3 with some contract on R^*. Can they really be prevented from doing so? As has been noted by *Hellwig* (1985a) for the insurance market model this may indeed be possible: Since banks publicize all clients who purchase a contract on R^* the bank who has sold K_3 would learn any additional purchase and could invoke the clause mentioned above. Hence K_3 would destroy an equilibrium like the one described, because only borrowers with the safe project would buy it. However, this line of reasoning is not entirely convincing. If a low risk borrower can improve his expected profit by purchasing a contract on R^* in addition to K_3 he could ask a bank not to tell the bank from which he got K_3, and clearly it would pay the supplier of the additional contract to keep the information secret from the seller of K_3. But then buyers of K_3 cannot effectively be prevented from purchasing an additional contract on R*, and K_3 becomes also profitable for high risk borrowers - inducing losses on the bank who supplies it. Hence the combination of contracts on R* and R_2 described above is indeed a *Nash*-equilibrium for sufficiently rich strategy spaces.

The analysis becomes more complicated if we leave the convenient world of success-failure projects and return to more general models like that of *Milde* and *Riley* (1984, see chapter 5). If a pooling contract is supplemented by a contract for risky projects this involves certain externalities: It is reasonable to assume that the order in which banks get project proceeds if these are insufficient to cover the entire debt, is fixed in advance, presumably according to a rule that gives priority to the older contract. This means that the first bank benefits from the larger project size since the likelihood increases that the actual project return covers her claim. The opposite is obviously true for the second bank. It is a priori unclear whether a combination of two contracts is actually beneficial for a borrower. The reason for this complication is, of course, that in contrast to the simpler model the probability of default depends now on the total debt and, from an individual bank's point of view, on the order in which loans have been granted.

Instead of going into the (tedious) details of an analysis of these issues we conclude this section with a couple of remarks on the importance of this problem.

First of all, as has been argued above, the issue of information exchange between banks arises only in some variants of our basic credit market model and is not of general interest. Second, as far as business loans are concerned, it is presumably not too difficult for a bank to figure out whether the project its loan is supposed to finance looks like the one that has been proposed or whether it looks as if it requires additional means the borrower is asked to account for.

Hence we consider it justifiable to continue our analysis under the assumption of perfect information about the total amount of loans each applicant gets.

6.7 Concluding Remarks

The purpose of this chapter was to show some of the problems and peculiarities that arise in credit market models with asymmetric information and variable endogenous loan size per borrower. Probably the most striking insight concerns the sensitivity of the equilibrium with respect to apparently innocent variations of assumptions, even in the rather simple stochastic framework employed. A rather general result of potentially great importance is certainly the possible Pareto-inefficiency at least of some equilibria.

What has been left out of the analysis is an investigation of type II Rationing, which clearly is incompatible with the assumption of an infinitely elastic supply of loanable funds. This theme will be taken up in the next chapter.

Appendix: Proof of condition (14)

$$\text{(i)}\quad \max_{K_1, K_2} \bar{g}_2(K_2) = q_2(x_2(L_2) - R_2 L_2) \qquad K_i = (R_i, L_i),\ i=1,2$$

s.t.

$$\bar{g}_1(K_2) - \bar{g}_1(K_1) \leq 0$$

$$\beta(q_2 R_2 L_2 - I L_2) + (1-\beta)(q_1 R_1 L_1 - I L_1) = 0$$

$$L_1,\ L_2,\ R_1,\ R_2 \geq 0$$

Reformulating (i) using the Lagrange function V yields

$$\text{(ii)}\quad \max_{K_1, K_2} V = q_2(x_2(L_2) - R_2 L_2) - \lambda_1 [x_1(L_2) - R_2 L_2 - x_1(L_1) + R_1 L_1] - \lambda_2 [\beta(q_2 R_2 L_2 - I L_2) + (1-\beta)(q_1 R_1 L_1 - I L_1)]$$

which implies the Kuhn-Tucker-conditions

$$\text{(iii)}\quad \frac{\partial V}{\partial R_1} R_1 = (-\lambda_1 L_1 - \lambda_2 (1-\beta) q_1 L_1) R_1 = 0$$

$$\text{(iv)}\quad \frac{\partial V}{\partial R_2} R_2 = (-q_2 L_2 + \lambda_1 L_2 - \lambda_2 \beta q_2 L_2) R_2 = 0$$

$$\text{(v)}\quad \frac{\partial V}{\partial L_1} L_1 = (\lambda_1 (x_1'(L_1) - R_1) - \lambda_2 (1-\beta)(q_1 R_1 - I)) L_1 = 0$$

$$\text{(vi)}\quad \frac{\partial V}{\partial L_2} L_2 = (q_2 (x_2'(L_2) - R_2) - \lambda_1 (x_1'(L_2) - R_2) - \lambda_2 (\beta q_2 R_2 - I))) L_2 = 0$$

Now consider a solution with L_1, L_2, R_1, $R_2 > 0$. From (iii) and (iv) one gets

$$\text{(vii)}\quad \lambda_1 = -\lambda_2 (1-\beta) q_1$$

$$\text{(viii)}\quad \lambda_1 = \lambda_2 \beta q_2 + q_2$$

which implies

(ix) $\lambda_2 = -q_2/((1-\beta)q_1 + \beta q_2)$

Substituting for λ_1 and λ_2 in (vi) yields

$$\text{(x)}\quad q_2(x'_2(L_2)-R_2)-[(1-\beta)q_1q_2/((1-\beta)q_1+\beta q_2)](x'_1(L_2)-R_2) + $$
$$+ [q_2\beta/((1-\beta)q_1+\beta q_2)](q_2R_2-I) = 0$$

Multiplying (x) by $[(1-\beta)q_1 + \beta q_2]/q_2$ yields

$$\text{(xi)}\quad (1-\beta)q_1x'_2(L_2)-(1-\beta)q_1R_2+\beta q_2x'_2(L_2)-\beta q_2R_2-(1-\beta)q_1x'_1(L_2) +$$
$$+ (1-\beta)q_1R_2 + \beta(q_2R_2-I) = 0$$

or

$$\text{(xii)}\quad \beta[q_1x'_2(L_2)-q_2x'_2(L_2)-q_1x'_1(L_2)+I] = q_1[x'_2(L_2)-x'_1(L_2)]$$

or

$$\text{(xiii)}\quad \beta = \frac{q_1(x'_2(L_2) - x'_1(L_2))}{I - q_2x'_2(L_2) + q_1(x'_2(L_2) - x'_1(L_2))}$$

But if in the optimum $p_2(K_2) > 0$ we have $q_2R_2 > I$, and replacing I by q_2R_2 leads to inequality (14), i.e.

$$\text{(xiv)}\quad \beta > \frac{q_1(x'_2(L_2) - x'_1(L_2))}{q_2(R_2-x'_2(L_2)) + q_1(x'_2(L_2)-x'_1(L_2))}$$

Q.E.D.

Chapter 7:

VARIABLE LOAN SIZE AND TYPE II RATIONING

7.1 Overview

In the preceding two chapters it has been analyzed at some length what problems may arise with respect to the equilibria of credit markets with asymmetric information and variable, endogenously determined loan size. In particular, it has become apparent that allocative efficiency will not be achieved in general, which leaves room for potentially beneficial policy measures, an issue not pursued further in this study. It has also turned out that some variant of Type I Rationing may occur (see 6.4, 6.5), though in some situations borrowers will feel induced to demand a larger loan size than they actually want at the quoted loan rate in order to signal their credit worthiness (see 6.2). What has not occurred, however, is Type II Rationing which has been the main theme of chapters 2-4. This is hardly surprising since it has been assumed that the supply of loanable funds is infinitely elastic, but apparently some authors attach even more weight to the endogenization of the individual loan size. So we read in *Milde* and *Riley* (1984) "...once we drop this assumption [of a fixed loan size] the stickiness result no longer arises".

It is analyzed below whether this claim is still valid if the supply of loanable funds is limited, i.e. if it is an increasing function of the deposit rate of interest i. To this purpose the models discussed in chapter 6 are slightly modified.

In particular, the supply of loanable funds is introduced on a per capita basis. For easy reference this is done in a perfect information framework in the next section.

In the subsequent four sections each variant of the basic asymmetric information model is analysed in turn. Model H, where borrowers have different default costs, does not allow for Type II Rationing once the loan size is endogenous. The possibility of Type II Rationing in moral hazard model E, on the other hand, looks fairly robust with respect to the introduction of variable loan size. As far as the adverse selction models R and A are concerned, however, this possibility depends on the equilibrium concept employed. Only if there is a pooling contract in equilibrium then it may happen that some applicants are rejected randomly. This requires that a *Wilson* - or a *Grossman*-type of equilibrium is deemed plausible. Considering the discussion of chapter 6 this is a fairly convincing possibility.

The above mentioned results are derived from the simplest possible model, but they look fairly general: Certainly they are true also for the variants discussed in chapter 5, though a graphical presentation would be still messier than the present one already is.

7.2 The Basic Model

The starting point for the following analysis is the simple credit model of chapter 5.2. The only modification introduced in this section concerns the supply of loanable funds: Instead of being infinitely elastic it is now assumed to be an increasing function of the deposit interest factor I. Furthermore, it is assumed that the total number of potential loan applicants is exogenously given. Hence the per capita supply of loanable funds is given by

(1) $L^s = L^s(I), \quad dL^s/dI > 0$

As has been shown in chapter 5.2, the loan size demanded by an applicant with ability a is determined by the loan interest factor R and his production function $x = x(L,a)$ with $x_L, x_a, x_{La} > 0 > x_{LL}$, and the Inada-conditions $x_L(0,a) = \infty$, $x_L(\infty) = 0$, unless stated otherwise. The following equations hold:

(2) $L^D = L^D(R,a), \quad \partial L^D/\partial R < 0, \quad \partial L^D/\partial a > 0$

i.e. the size of a loan demanded is increasing in ability and decreasing in the loan rate.

Define $R(L,g^*,a)$ implicitly by the equation $g(R(L,g^*,a),L) = g^*$, i.e. $R(L,g^*,a)$ is an iso-profit-curve of a borrower with ability a in R-L-space.

Then we have for two abilities $a_2 > a_1$

(3) $R(L,g^*,a_2) > R(L,g^*,a_1) \quad \forall \quad L,g^* > 0,$

i.e. an increase of a shifts the iso-profit curve of a borrower, in the figure below denoted by g, upwards.

Finally, there is a given number of banks. They are assumed to be risk neutral maximizers of their expected profit, which equals the expected gross return p(R,L) minus their costs which are assumed to consist only of interest payments to depositors. Perfect competition between banks implies a zero profit in equilibrium. It is assumed that all banks are identical in all respects, hence we may concentrate on the analysis of a representative bank and its customers. Each bank has an equal share of the total number of customers, and the term $L^s(R)$ denotes the loan size per loan applicant.

Now in the absence of default risk, the zero profit constraint can be written as

(4) $p(L,R) = RL = IL, \quad I: = 1 + i$

If all loan applicants are identical then the equilibrium in such a market is as depicted in Figure 1.

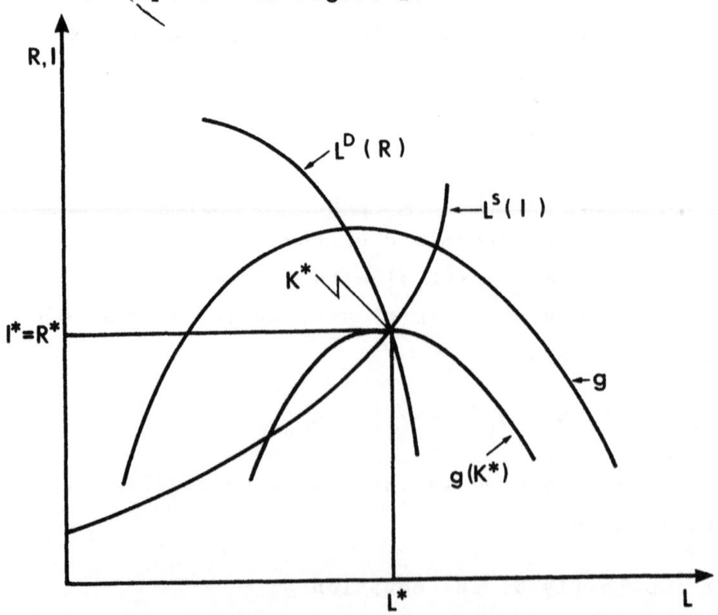

Figure 1: Identical, honest borrowers, certain returns

The per capita demand for a loan function $L^D(R)$ can be found graphically by connecting the maximum points of the borrowers' iso-profit-curves.

There is a unique, market clearing equilibrium with R = I and $L^S(I) = L^D(R)$

Suppose next that there are two groups of borrowers, group 1 with ability a_1 and group 2 with ability a_2, such that $a_2 > a_1$. Let the share of group 2 be denoted by β. A market clearing equilibrium has to satisfy two conditions

(E1) $R = I$

(E2) $L^s(I) = \beta L_2(R) + (1-\beta)L_1(R)$

where $L_i(R)$ denotes the per capita demand of group i-borrowers, i = 1,2.

The population per capita loan demand $L^D(R)$ is now a weighted average of the per capita demand of the two groups.

Equilibria of this market are depicted in Figures 2 and 3 below.

It is obvious that in such a market there is never an equilibrium with credit rationing as defined earlier. In the upper right panel of Figure 2 below the iso-profit and loan demand curves of the two types of borrowers are depicted, where dotted curves refer to the able borrowers. To each level of I(=R) belongs an average loan size demanded, which is projected into the upper left panel via the two lower panels. It is useful at this stage to distinguish between two cases, which carry quite different implications for the possibility of credit rationing in a stochastic model:

C1: The production function is concave and satisfies the Inada-conditions, and there are no fixed costs of setting up a project. In that case we have $L^D(R) > 0$ for all R, and, more important, the borrower's zero profit line has a non-positive slope for all positive L. To see the latter point recall that a zero profit implies

$$RL = x(L) = \int_0^L x'(h)dh > \int_0^L x'(L)dh = Lx'(L) \qquad R > x'(L) \Rightarrow \partial R/\partial L < 0$$

The first inequality follows from the concavity of x(L). Consequently we get a conventional aggregate demand function as depicted in Figure 2. Clearly, there is no room for equilibrium credit rationing.

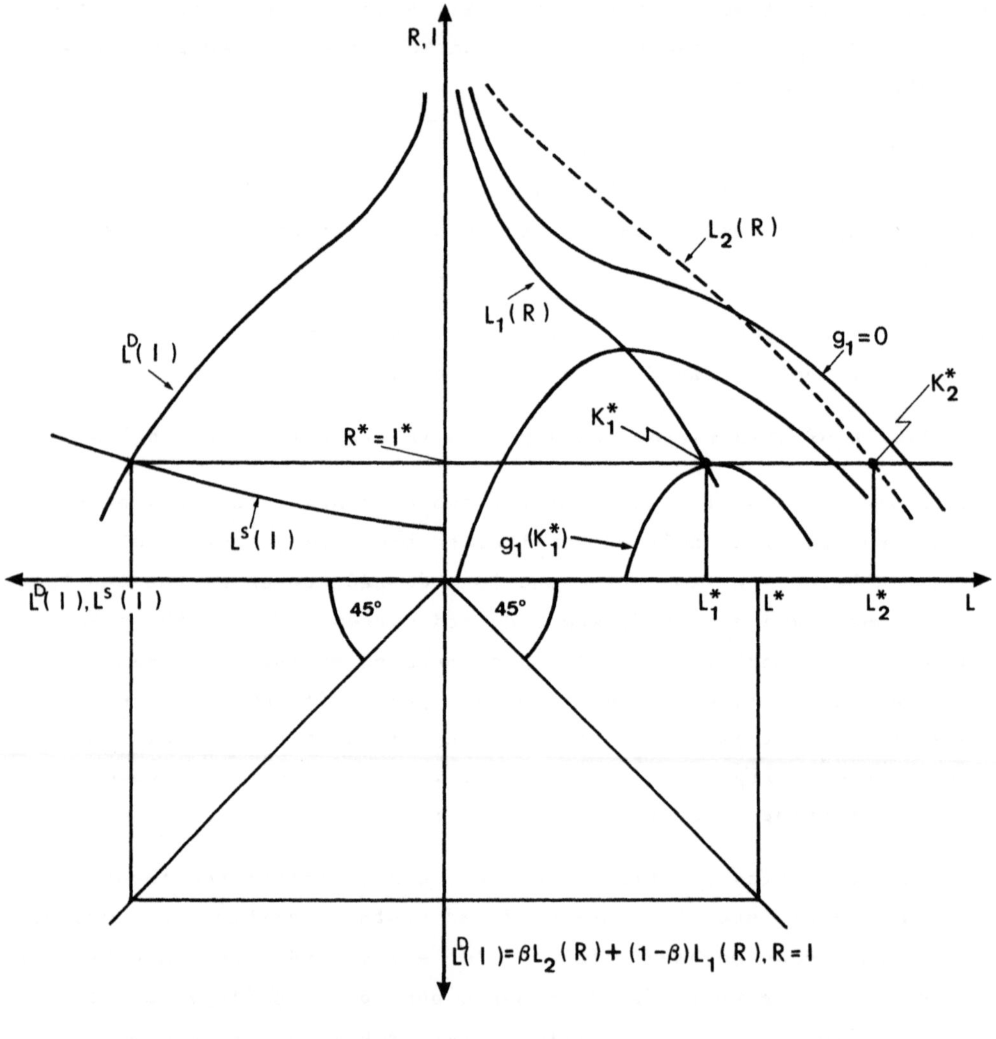

Certain returns, different abilities, β = 1/3, case C1

<u>**Figure 2**</u>

C2: We either have (a) a production function as in C1, but fixed costs of $k > 0$, or (b) an S-shaped production function with the properties $x'(0) < \infty$ and L^{***} such that $x''(L^{***}) = 0$, $x''(L) > 0$ for $L < L^{***}$ and $x''(L) < 0$ for $L > L^{***}$ instead of the Inada-conditions. As a consequence, in case (a), a loan will only be demanded if $x(L)-RL \geq k$, i.e. there exists a critical iso-profit curve for borrowers starting with a positive slope and a unique turning point such that no contract $K = (R,L)$ above it will be purchased. In case (b) the zero-profit-curve of a borrower starts with a positive slope. To see this recall again

$$RL = x(L) = \int_0^L x'(h)dh < \int_0^L x'(L)dh \text{ for } L \leq L^{***} \text{ which implies}$$

$R < x'(L)$ and $\partial R/\partial L > 0$. In both cases the per-capita demand curves obtained in such a situation are as depicted in Figure 3. The crucial difference to Figure 2 lies in the discontinuity of the per capita demand curve. However, if an equilibrium exists it implies market clearing: If there is no equilibrium at or below I_1, the highest value of R at which the unable borrowers still make a nonnegative profit, then this group drops out and only the able borrowers continue to demand a loan. At $R = I_2$ this group is indifferent between getting a loan or being rejected. Hence, even though some applicants may be denied a loan, there is no Type II Credit Rationing as defined above.

Note, that in the absence of any default risk, the bank need not be informed about the ability of its clients. At any given loan rate of interest each borrower chooses an optimal loan size (provided he himself knows his ability) and there is no reason for the bank to ration credits in any way.

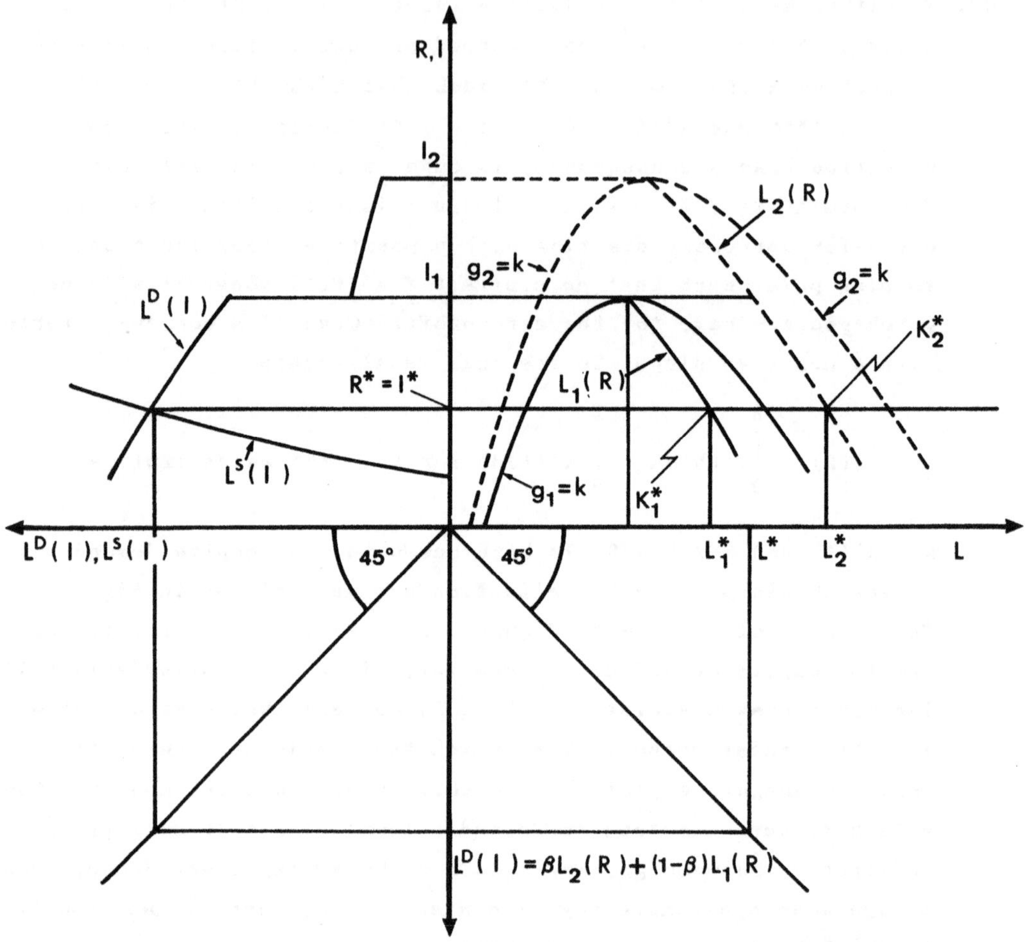

Certain returns, different abilities, $\beta = 1/3$, case C2(a)

Figure 3

In the following sections it is shown how these conclusions have to be changed if different types of uncertainty are taken into account.

7.3 Loan Applicants With Different Default Costs

The first form of uncertainty we want to deal with concerns the "honesty" of borrowers. Following *Jaffee* and *Russell* (1976) it is assumed that borrowers have identical abilities, but differ with respect to their costs of default, denoted by D (which are exogenous and constant). A borrower will honour his commitments to the bank only if $D > RL$. The following analysis applies to both cases, C1 and C2.

Suppose there are two groups of borrowers with default costs D_1 and D_2, where $D_2 > D_1$. Denote the share of 'honest' borrowers by β. All 'dishonest' borrowers default if the loan contract (R,L) is to the north-east of the curve $R(D_1)=D_1/L$. In that case the interest payments of the honest borrowers have to compensate banks for the losses incurred because of the defaults, i.e. $\beta R=I$ or $R=I/\beta$.

The determination of an equilibrium is depicted in Figure 4.

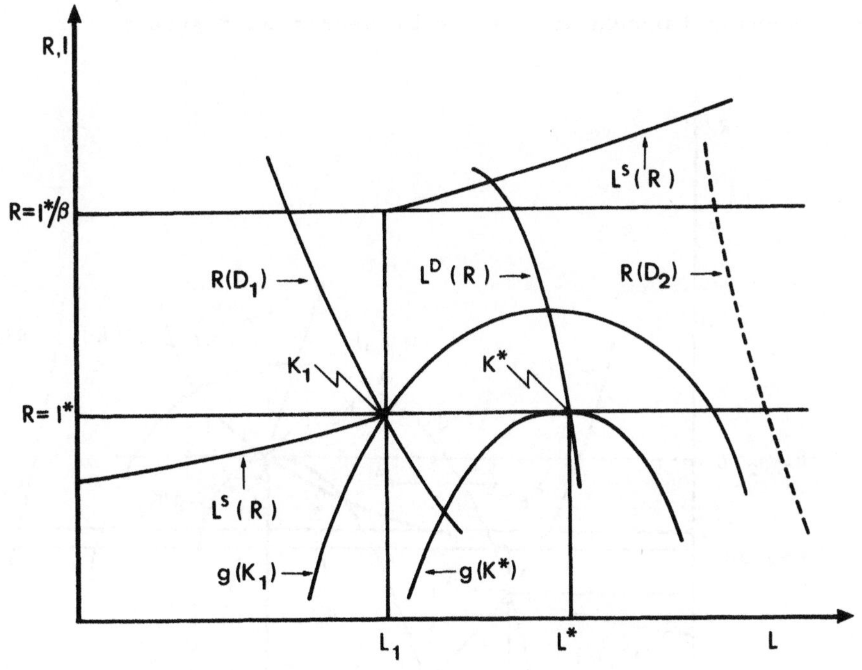

Figure 4: Different default costs, β small

Figure 4 has essentially the same interpretation as Figure 1 except for the "demarcation line" $R(D_1) = D_1/L$. In particular, to the south-west of this curve I=R, and the supply of loanable funds curve $L^s(I)$ coincides with the bank's loan supply curve $L^s(R)$. At the intersection of $L^s(I)$ and $R(D_1)$, denoted as K_1, $L^s(R)$ jumps to a level such that $R=I/\beta$ is satisfied. Of course, the size of this jump depends on the share of honest borrowers, β. In Figure 4, β is sufficiently small to make K_1 the unique (*Nash-*) equilibrium: Banks compete for clients by offering contracts (R,L). At R_1, honest (and, of course, even more so, dishonest) borrowers would prefer a larger loan size, but any loan contract with non-negative expected profits and a larger volume than L_1 would be on $L^s(R)$ and hence above the borrowers' iso-profit curve going through K_1. So there is Type I Rationing since at R_1 honest borrowers would prefer $L^* > L_1$, but there is no Type II Rationing: each applicant gets a loan.

A mild complication arises if β is sufficiently large as to make the jump of $L^s(R)$ so small that $L^s(R)$ lies partly below the iso-profit curve passing through K_1, as can be seen from Figure 5.

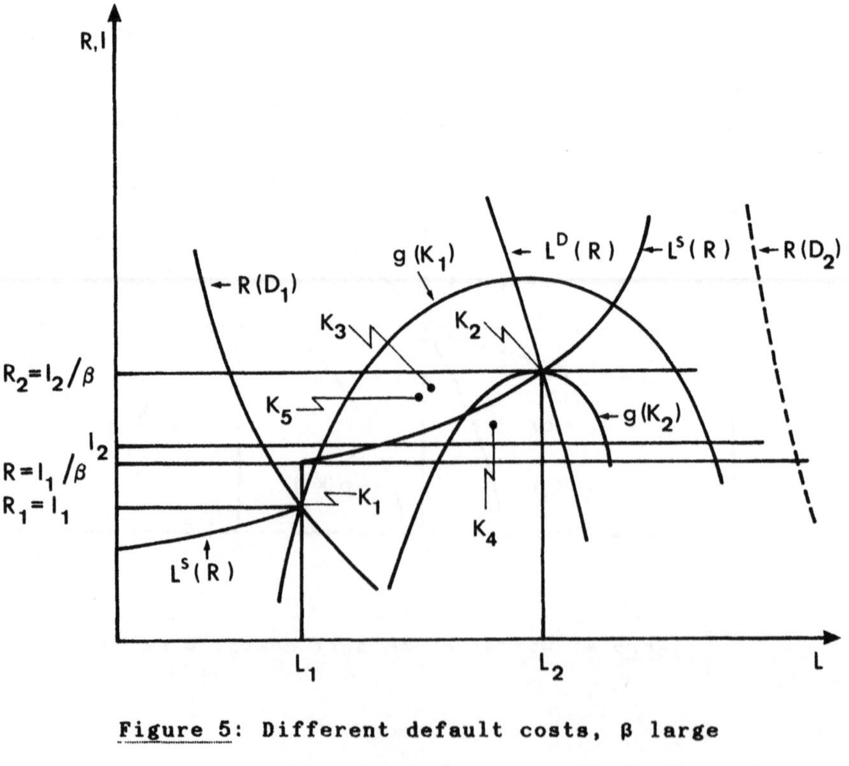

Figure 5: Different default costs, β large

Whether an equilibrium exists and, if so, how it is characterized, depends on the equilibrium concept employed (see chapter 6). Recall the three most commonly used concepts for this type of market with asymmetric information:

(i) A ***Nash***-equilibrium is a set of contracts $\{K_i\}$, $i=1,\ldots,k$, such that there does not exist an additional profitable contract K_{k+1}. It is straightforward to see that in Figure 4 no ***Nash***-equilibrium exists (K_3 is profitable if K_1 rules, K_4 is profitable if K_2 rules).

(ii) A ***Wilson***-equilibrium (***Wilson*** 1977) is a set of contracts $\{K_i\}$, $i=1,\ldots,k$, such that any additional profitable contract K_{k+1} incurs losses as soon as those contracts of $\{K_i\}$ which make losses because of the introduction of K_{k+1} are withdrawn from the market. In Figure 5, K_2 is a ***Wilson***-equilibrium (K_4 would induce withdrawal of K_2 and make losses afterwards, K_3 would be unaffected by a withdrawal of K_1).

(iii) A ***Riley***-equilibrium (***Riley*** 1975, 1979) is a set of contracts $\{K_i\}$, $i=1,\ldots,k$, such that any additional profitable contract K_{k+1} can be turned into a loss maker through the introduction of a further profitable contract. In Figure 5, K_1 is a ***Riley***-equilibrium (K_3 would make losses if in addition K_5 is offered, K_4 can never make losses as long as K_2 is in the market).

The choice of a particular equilibrium concept is of great importance for the existence and the properties of an equilibrium (see chapter 6), but, at least in the model of this section, it does not affect our conclusion about the non-existence of Type II Rationing. This can be seen from Figure 5.

If the ***Riley***-equilibrium K_1 rules, then we have the same situation as in Figure 4. At the ***Wilson***-equilibrium K_2 there is neither Type I nor Type II rationing (if we ignore the potentially infinite demand of the dishonest borrowers). If D_2 is sufficiently small then the equilibrium would be given (for large β) at the intersection of $L^s(R)$ and $R(D_2)$. Again no rationing would occur (neglecting again the unsatiable demand of dishonest borrowers).

Hence we may conclude that models of type H do not offer an explanation of Type II Credit Rationing once the assumption of a fixed loan size is relaxed. This conclusion remains valid even if we allow for a continuum of honesty types: The main difference to Figures 4 and 5 would be that $L^s(R(I))$ does not display discrete jumps but is, for each $L > L_1$, steeper than and above $L^s(I)$. Since any equilibrium contract will still be on $L^s(R(I))$ there is no Type II Rationing.

7.4 Loan Applicants With Different Abilities

In chapter 2.4 it has been shown that equilibrium credit rationing may occur because borrowers have different abilities, which are assumed to be positively correlated with the size of some alternative income. In that case an increase of R may induce able borrowers to withdraw their demand from the credit market and the resulting adverse selection prevents the banks from reacting to an excess demand by raising the loan rate of interest. It is now investigated whether this possibility continues to hold once the assumption of a fixed size of the loan is dropped.

As in chapter 6, consider a market with two types of loan applicants, the able ones with ability a_2 and probability of success q_2, and the unable ones, where $a_2 > a_1$ and $q_2 > q_1$. The zero bank-profit condition requires $I = q_1 R_1 = q_2 R_2$ if $R_1 \neq R_2$ or $I=(\beta q_2+(1-\beta)q_1)R$ if $(R_1,L_1)=(R_2,L_2)=(R,L)$, where β denotes the share of able borrowers. Whether the latter situation can persist in equilibrium depends, once more, on the equilibrium concept chosen. The following analysis is basically the same for both cases mentioned above, C1 and C2, if it is assumed as in chapter 2.4 that borrowers have opportunity costs $w(a_i)$, with $w(a_2) > w(a_1)$. Consider case C1: For $w(a_i) > 0$ the borrower's critical iso-profit curve has a branch with positive slope, as depicted in Figure 3: $w(a_i)$ simply takes the place of k in case C2. Since $w(a_2) > w(a_1)$ a situation may arise as presented in Figure 6.

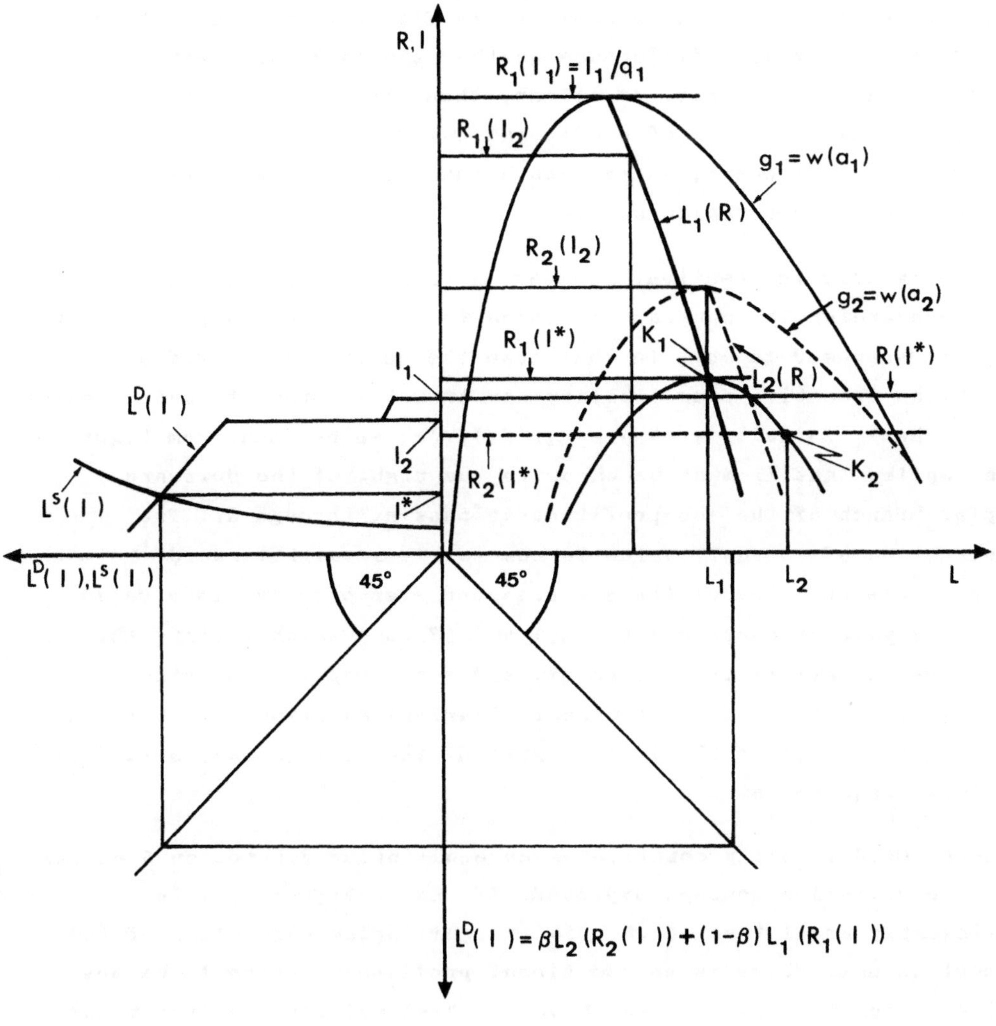

__Figure 6__: Uncertain returns, different abilities, $q_2=1/2$, $q_1=1/3$, $\beta=1/3$.

7.4.1 __The Case with Small β__

Figure 6 bears close resemblance to Figure 3 and is constructed in a very similar fashion. The main difference is that because of the possibility of default we no longer have I=R, instead there are two zero-profit lines of the bank, each belonging to one ability group, which are denoted by $R_1(I)=I/q_1$ and $R_2(I)=I/q_2$. In contrast to the case with certain returns as depicted in Figure 3, with uncertain returns it does make a difference whether the bank can identify a borrower's ability or not. If it can, then there is a separating equilibrium with no form of credit rationing, i.e. one contract for each group of borrowers, where each breaks even, and with per capita demand equal to per capita supply.

With asymmetric information, however, a problem arises if low ability borrowers prefer the contract intended for the other group to the one they are supposed to buy. In that case the contracts offered have to satisfy an incentive compatibility constraint in order to avoid losses for the bank, formally $g_1(K_1) \geq g_1(K_2)$. As can be seen from Figure 6 this implies that K_2 must be on or to the right of the downward sloping branch of the iso-profit-curve passing through K_1. The construction of an equilibrium is now fairly straightforward. To each deposit rate of interest there correspond even breaking loan rates R_1 and R_2, a pair of contracts (R_1, L_1) and (R_2, L_2) which satisfy the incentive compatibility constraint, and a per capita loan size $L^D(I) = \beta L_2 + (1-\beta)L_1$. In (a market clearing) equilibrium, it is also required that $L^s(I) = L^D(I)$. In Figure 6, the pair (K_1, K_2) satisfies all three requirements.

Whether (K_1, K_2) really constitutes an equilibrium depends on β and/or on the equilibrium concept employed. If, as in Figure 6, β is sufficiently small then (K_1, K_2) is an equilibrium regardless of the concept in use: There is no additional profitable contract, because $R(I) = I/(\beta q_2 + (1-\beta)q_1)$ lies above the high-ability iso-profit-curve passing through K_2. Let us concentrate first on this case and postpone the dicussion of consequences of a large β to the next subsection.

The first thing to note is that (K_1, K_2) does not entail any form of credit rationing but, on the contrary, overinvestment of high ability borrowers. Hence, we reach the same conclusion as in the case of infinitely elastic supply of loanable funds analysed in chapter 6.1.

Secondly, it is obvious that there is no room for Type II Rationing in equilibrium. As long as there is an excess demand for loans (i.e. $L^D(I) > L^s(I)$), the deposit rate will be increased with a consequent reduction of $L^D(I)$ and an increase of $L^s(I)$. At the deposit rate I_2 the loan rate $R_1(I_2)$ is such that high ability applicants are indifferent between getting a loan or not and drop out at the slightest further increase of I (and R_1), but there is no rationing (at I_1 also low ability borrowers become indifferent, hence $L^D(I)$ has three kinks).

7.4.2 The Case with Large β

Suppose next that β is sufficiently large such that no *Nash*-equilibrium exists. It will be recalled from chapter 6.1 that a *Riley*-equilibrium is a separating equilibrium, hence for that concept the same argument applies as in the preceding subsection and no Type II Rationing will occur.

A *Wilson*-equilibrium, however, will be a pooling equilibrium for sufficiently large β (i.e. all borrowers are offered the same contract), and this implies the possibility of Type II Rationing, as is shown in Figure 7.

Figure 7 should be interpreted as follows: At deposit rate I^* the corresponding pooling loan rate equals $R(I^*)$, the highest loan rate acceptable for able applicants since $g_2 := g(R,L) = w(a_2)$. Now suppose we have $L^D(R(I^*)) > L^s(I^*)$, as depicted in the left upper panel. Banks are left with the choice between offering K and rejecting some applicants at random or trying to raise additional funds by offering a higher deposit rate and charging a higher loan rate. But if they do the latter they lose immediately all able clients. Hence they would have to raise R substantially in order to finance a higher deposit rate. This jump of R may be so large that the low ability borrowers would also drop out. Hence there is no alternative profitable contract and K is indeed a *Wilson*-equilibrium with Type II Rationing (and overinvestment of low ability borrowers). Hence we may conclude that credit market models of type A may display Type II Rationing despite a variable loan size if we employ an equilibrium concept that allows for the possibility of a pooling equilibrium. In the light of the discussion in section 6.2 the plausibility of such a pooling equilibrium appears convincing. Note, that it is indeed true that in a multi-stage game all applicants prefer the pooling contract to the

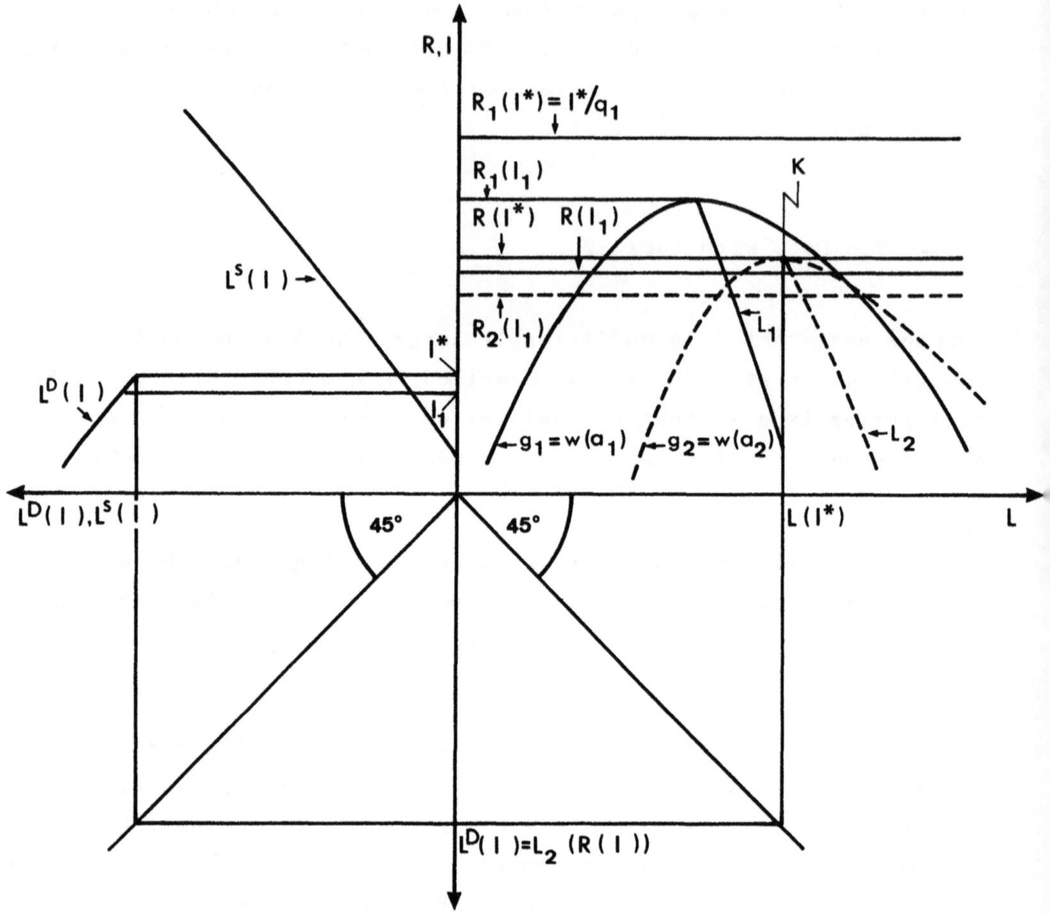

Figure 7: Uncertain returns, different abilities, $\beta=3/4$.

separating ones, even if this implies the possibility of being rationed: The expected return of a separating contract for high ability borrowers is at the mininum level, hence they prefer the pooling contract. This may, but need not be true for low ability borrowers. But even if they were better off with a separating contract, they would not demand it, because at the third stage they would be rejected.

The above conclusions continue to hold if the return of a project is a more general random variable as long as it satisfies certain conditions like those discussed in chapter 5.

7.5 Projects of Different Riskiness

Stiglitz and ***Weiss*** (1981) have shown that projects of fixed size are, at any loan rate of interest, more profitable for the borrower the riskier they are in the sense of ***Rothschild*** and ***Stiglitz*** (1970). As a consequence, less risky projects are withdrawn first as the loan rate of interest is increased and Type II Rationing may occur.

As in section 6.3 it is assumed that there are two groups of loan applicants characterized through the parameters a_1 and a_2, with $a_2 > a_1 > 1$ and β as the relative size of group 2. Dotted lines in Figure 8 belong to group 2 which has the "riskier" project. Since $q_2 < q_1$ it follows that $R_2(I) > R_1(I)$. By similar reasoning as in the preceding section it can be shown that for large β (i.e. a large share of risky projects) the equilibrium is a separating equilibrium like (K_1, K_2) in Figure 8 which satisfies an incentive compatibility constraint. Note that now applicants with the "safer" project are subjected to Type I Rationing.

If β is small then no ***Nash***-equilibrium will exist, but there still is a separating ***Riley***-equilibrium and a pooling ***Wilson***-equilibrium. As has been argued in the preceding section, in a separating equilibrium Type II Rationing is ruled out.

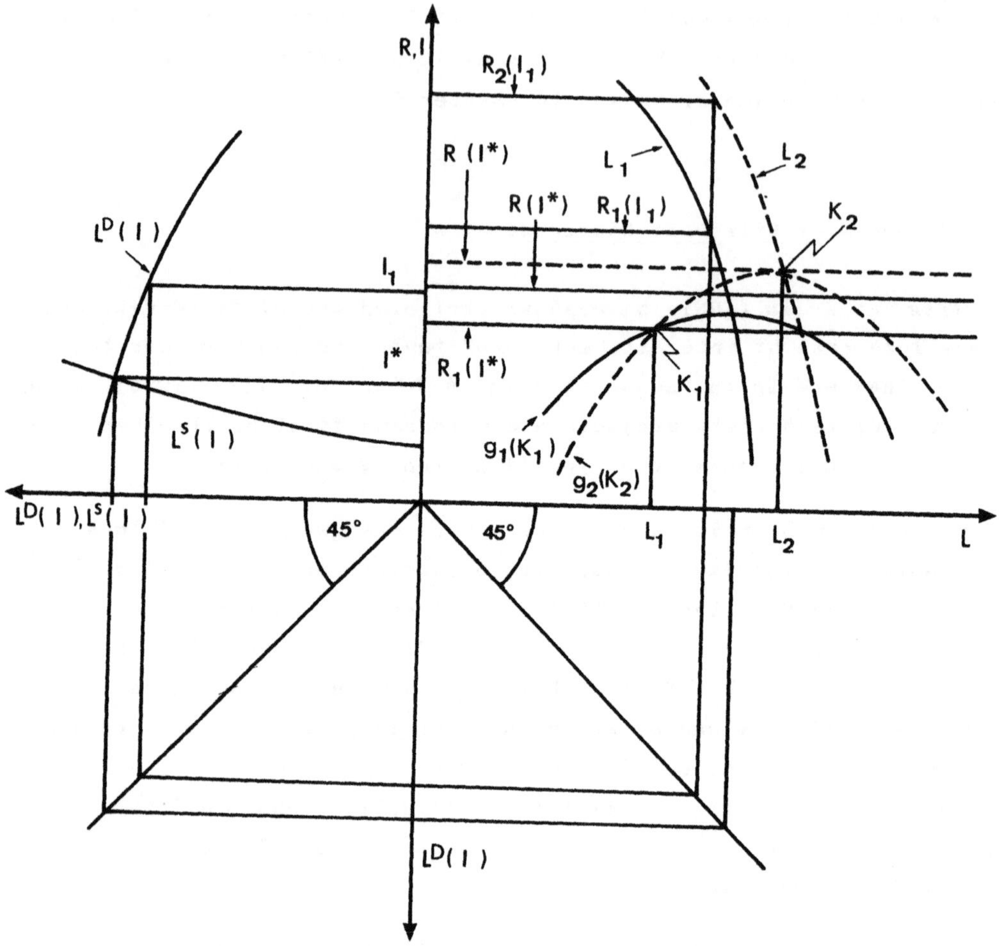

<u>Remark</u>: The demand curves $L_i(R)$ correspond to case C1; in case C2 the per capita demand curve $L^D(I)$ would have a kink at that level of I at which low risk borrowers would drop out (compare Figures 3,6,7 and 9)

<u>Figure 8</u>: Projects with different riskiness
$q_1=3/4$, $q_2=1/2$, $\beta=2/3$

Consider next a pooling equilibrium: It must be at that point of $R(I) = I/(\beta q_2 + (1-\beta)q_1)$ which is tangential to a (solid) iso-profit curve of the safe project. Now at this stage it is crucial whether we consider case C1 or case C2. Suppose first we have case C1. In that case the pooling contract is on the loan demand curve of borrowers with the safe project which is to the left of the demand curve induced by the risky project. Consequently, borrowers with the risky project get a smaller loan than they desire at the ruling loan rate, but there is no Type II Rationing: An excess demand for loans induces an increase of R and a reduction of L along L_1 until the market is cleared.

The situation is quite different for case C2. Suppose the fixed costs k are the same for all borrowers. The zero-profit curve for the safe project, implicitly defined by $q_1(a_1x(L)-RL)-k = 0 = x(L)-q_1RL-k$ lies inside the corresponding zero-profit curve of the risky project, obtained from $x(L)-q_2RL-k = 0$, since $q_1 > q_2$. Consequently, a situation as depicted in Figure 9 emerges: As I is increased it will be the safe project that is withdrawn first as R(I) reaches first the highest point of the zero-profit-line of group 1 borrowers. A further marginal increase of I would require a big jump of R to $R_2(I^*)$ which may not be feasible if it takes R above the zero-profit curve of the risky project, hence Type II Rationing can be generated. Such a situation is depicted in Figure 9.

The similarity between this model and the one of section 4 is obvious: In both models we need a pooling equilibrium and a mechanism which leads to the withdrawal of projects with high probabilities of success first as the deposit rate and consequently the loan rate are increased. It is noteworthy, however, that model R requires special assumptions about the production function in order to generate the possibility of Type II Rationing despite a variable loan size. Model A, on the other hand, works without such an assumption but requires some exogenously given opportunity costs. It is left to the reader to judge how plausible either requirement is.

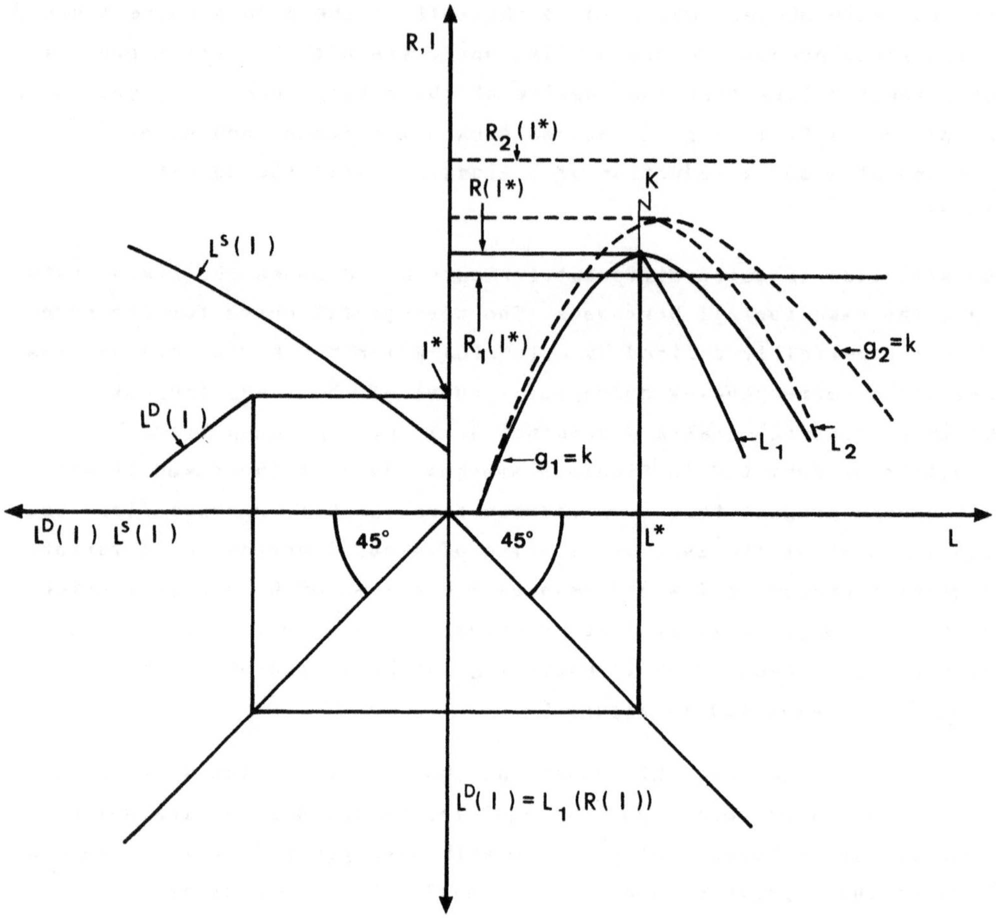

<u>Remark</u>: $L_1(R)$ correspond to case C2; in case C1 there may be a pooling equilibrium, but no type II rationing is possible, because L can always be made sufficiently small to yield a nonnegative profit for any R.

<u>Figure 9</u>: $q_1 = 1/2$, $q_2 = 1/3$, $\beta = 1/5$

7.6 <u>The Role of Effort</u>

Finally, we turn to the last factor which is likely to influence the outcome of a project: the effort of the applicant. If one assumes that this effort is costly and cannot be observed directly by the bank one gets a principal-agent problem with the possibility of Type II Rationing if the loan size is fixed. Now, in contrast, it is assumed that the return of the project is determined by the production function of case C1, whereas the probability of success is determined by the effort e. For the sake of simplicity assume that $0 \leq e \leq 1$ equals this success probability, and that the costs depend on e and on the project size L in the following way:

(5) $c = c(e,L), \quad \infty > c_e, c_L, c_{ee}, c_{LL}, c_{eL} > 0$

The level of effort chosen by a borrower for a contract (R,L) is the solution to

(6) $\max \bar{g} = e(x(L) - RL) - c(e,L)$

which implies the necessary condition

(7) $\partial\bar{g}/\partial e = x(L) - RL - c_e(e,L) = 0$

and the second order condition

(8) $\partial^2\bar{g}/\partial e^2 = -c_{ee} < 0$

Differentiating (7) with respect to L and R yields

(9) $\partial^2\bar{g}/\partial e\partial L = x'(L) - R - c_{eL}(e,L) \gtrless 0$

and

(10) $\partial^2\bar{g}/\partial e\partial R = -L < 0$

From (10) it follows immediately that for any level of L an increase of R reduces the level of effort, formally

(11) $\partial e/\partial R =: e_R = -L/c_{ee} < 0$

The effect of a marginal change of the loan size, given a particular loan rate of interest R, is slightly more complicated. From (6) and (7) we get

(12) $\partial e/\partial L =: e_L = (x'(L)-R-c_{eL}(e,L))/c_{ee}(e,L) \gtrless 0$

Since by assumption $x'(0) = \infty$ and because of continuity we have a positive sign of (12) for sufficiently small L and finite c_{eL}. Differentiating (7) twice implicitly with respect to L and e yields

$$(13)\ \partial^2 e/\partial L^2 = ((x''(L)-c_{eLL}(e,L))+(\partial e/\partial L)(c_{eee}(\partial e/\partial L)-2c_{eeL}))/c_{ee}$$

It is easy to see that $c_{eLL} \geq 0$ is sufficient for $\partial e/\partial L$ to change its sign at most once: For any L with $\partial e/\partial L = 0$ (13) is negative. Thus under suitable conditions there exists $L^*(R)$ for each R such that $e(R,L)$ reaches a maximum with respect to L.

Now in equilibrium either there is market clearing or the contract offered yields a maximum gross return for the bank per Dollar lent. In the latter case the bank would not change the contract even in the face of an excess demand for loans. Hence, in a credit rationing equilibrium the following maximization problem would be solved.

$$(14)\quad \max \bar{p} = e(R,L).R$$

with the first order conditions

$$(15)\quad \partial\bar{p}/\partial R = e_R(R,L)R + e(R,L) = 0$$

$$(16)\quad \partial\bar{p}/\partial L = e_L(R,L).R = 0$$

Suppose there is a unique solution (L^*,R^*). The zero-profit-constraint implies

$$(17)\ e(R^*,L^*)R^* = I^*$$

Clearly, it is possible to construct examples such that there exists an optimal contract that will not be changed even if there is an excess demand for loans. A bank, who has to pay a deposit rate I, would inevitably make losses by offering a contract other than (R^*,L^*). Therefore, if in per capita terms $L^s(I) < L^*$, there will be Type II Rationing. Note, that this possibility does not depend on the equilibrium concept in use.

It is also easy to see that unobservable effort may lead to Type I Rationing: Given R^* a borrower would choose e and L in order to satisfy

$$(7)\quad x(L) - RL - c_e(e,L) = 0$$

(18) $e(R^*,L)(x'(L) - R^*) - c_L = 0$

But for the optimal contract (R^*,L^*) we have from (12)

(19) $x'(L^*) - R^* - c_{eL} = 0$

which implies, in general (i.e. for $[1-e(R^*,L)][x'(L)-R^*] \neq c_{eL}-c_L$), $L^* \neq L$. Whether there is over- or underinvestment cannot be determined a priori, but even in the absence of Type II Rationing an equilibrium does not imply market clearing.

It appears to this author that the criticisms raised against models which explain credit rationing by referring to asymmetric information are quite unconvincing if unobservable effort is the key variable. It remains to be seen whether appropriate incentive mechanisms can be devised in order to mitigate the consequences of this principal agent problem.

7.7 Concluding Remarks

It has been shown that credit rationing by random rejection of applicants may occur even if the individual loan size is variable. However, this possibility depends on the factor about which there is asymmetric information. If it is the willingness to pay of borrowers, then there is no Type II Rationing, and if it is ability of borrowers or riskiness of projects, its existence is sensitive with respect to the underlying equilibrium concept, and, at least for model R, also with respect to the production function of the project. The most robust explanation of rationing appears to be model E, and on the whole there are convincing theoretical arguments in favour of the possibility of Type II Rationing.

This concludes our theoretical analysis of equilibrium credit rationing. It has been shown that it is a convincing possibility under a variety of circumstances. In contrast to what many authors suggested it does not hinge on irrational behaviour of economic agents, on restrictions imposed from outside or on certain simplifying assumptions like fixed loan size, fixed collateral or confinement to one period. The picture that emerges from the above analysis appears quite clear: If one is ready to accept that there is imperfect information in credit markets, one should also be willing to accept that equilibrium credit rationing is a plausible possibility.

This does not mean that all theoretical problems concerning credit markets are solved. Far from it. But at least in the opinion of this author the theoretical grounds on which credit rationing rests seem already safe enough to take first steps in a potentially very important direction: What are the policy implications of equilibrium credit rationing? The concluding remarks of the following epilogue sketch the lines of future research.

Chapter 8:

Epilogue: Whither Now

It would certainly be an exaggeration to claim that the preceding analysis has exhausted its subject. However, it has been shown that equilibrium credit rationing is possible under a variety of circumstances, and it is time to take stock of what has been achieved, and to identify areas of future research. The second aspect is discussed in the next two sections, where at first the potential of regulatory measures is considered, and afterwards macro-economic consequences of imperfect information in credit markets are treated. Let me turn first to an assessment of the analysis contained in the preceding six chapters.

The analysis is in the spirit of the "New Information Economics" (henceforth NIE), a term coined by one of its leading proponents, (*Stiglitz* 1985a). It refers to the attempts, intensified in the last two decades, to incorporate informational problems into economic theory in a rigorous way. The foregoing analysis of credit markets is - in my view - a good example of achievements and shortcomings of the NIE, so let me add a few words on this.

The main deficiency of the NIE is that it has not yet come up with a general theory comparable to the *Arrow-Debreu* model and its numerous variants. Instead, "there seems to be a myriad of special cases and few general principles" (*Stiglitz* 1985a, p.21). The problem is, of course, that there is only one way of being perfectly informed, but a myriad of possibilities for information to be incomplete. It must be emphasized that the informational assumptions of traditional general equilibrium theory are, in fact, very special and not at all "general". Consequently, the NIE has been quite successful in questioning certain theorems derived from *Arrow-Debreu* type models by devising counterexamples, e.g. models where no equilibria exist, where equilibria do neither display market clearing nor Pareto-efficiency organization or not. So the best one can usually hope for is to show that certain phenomena may occur under some plausible conditions, but not that they must occur under all plausible (let alone imaginable) circumstances.

The present analysis of credit markets is a good illustration of these points. Only one market is considered, the loan market, and a second market where the allocation of saving deposits takes place is modelled, if at all, only in a rudimentary fashion. Linkages with other markets are completely ignored. It is shown that equilibrium rationing is compatible with a variety of model specifications, but it is not possible to reach the conclusion that rationing may occur under all plausible circumstances. How reliable then is the above credit rationing theory as a basis for further research?

Clearly, it is little consolation that these problems reflect the state of the art within the NIE. However, my claim is that the two basic shortcomings just mentioned do not weigh as heavily as it may look at first sight. Consider first the potential effect of markets neglected in this analysis. As far as the market for saving deposits is concerned, I have argued earlier (cf. ch.1) that it also has its information problems. In particular, there is the trust of depositors in banks which induces the latter to be particularly careful in the loan market. A bank's costs in case of a lender's default can be partially explained by a loss of reputation with depositors. In short, I do not see how a fuller treatment of the market for saving deposits should adversely affect the possibility of credit rationing.

A more serious problems seems to be the neglect of alternative means for financing investment projects, in particular, the neglect of equity markets. Again, this is an apparent rather than a real shortcoming of the analysis: As *Gale* and *Hellwig* (1983) have shown, in many situations with asymmetric information a debt contract as used in our credit market models is an efficient arrangement. *Stiglitz* and *Weiss* (1985) have shown that from the point of view of the bank it is immaterial whether a borrower invests his own wealth directly into the project or whether he provides it as collateral for a loan. Finally, and most importantly, the equity market faces very similar informational problems as the credit market. *Ross* (1977) has developed a theory of the financial structure of a firm which is based on incentive signalling. It states that debt financing signals a project with a higher probability of success than does financing through raising equity because in the former case the penalty for managers is higher if the firm defaults. *Greenwald*, *Stiglitz* and *Weiss* (1984) use this approach as a building stone of a theory of macro-economic fluctuations and argue that because of its adverse signalling effects equity financing may not be feasible when it is needed most, i.e. when credits are rationed. In view of these results it is quite safe to say that a neglect of equity markets does not affect seriously the validity and relevance of credit rationing examples.

Finally there remains the objection that credit rationing theory is not embedded in a general equilibrium model. An attempt to do this is not only beyond the scope of this analysis but also, as I have argued above, beyond the present limits of the NIE. A definitive assessment of conclusions derived from partial models is therefore not possible, but I find it difficult to imagine that credit rationing caused by information imperfections should disappear through the influence of other markets which, in general, can safely be assumed to struggle with informational problems of their own. I conclude that the partial nature of credit rationing models is not a decisive deficiency as regards the result that equilibrium rationing is a plausible possibility.

The second objection against the NIE in general and against credit rationing theory in particular is the arbitrariness of its (informational) assumptions. But while it has turned out that certain rationing examples can be refuted if all possible actions of market participants are taken into account, no general results have been obtained proving the impossibility of equilibrium rationing. Moral hazard explanations have appeared particularly robust (this has been shown for the model of this book as well as for that developed by *Stiglitz* and *Weiss* 1985). The preceding analysis has shown that variable loan size, collateral-loan rate variations, or the extension of the model to several periods are all compatible with rationing. Models, where moral hazard and adverse selection are combined, though only at a very early stage, suggest that informational problems cannot be overcome in general and strengthen the plausibility of rationing results. It is unsatisfactory that we have to make do with numerous examples and counterexamples, but as long as only the possibility of equilibrium rationing is at stake and not its precise manifestations and causes we seem to be on fairly safe grounds: "Unemployment and credit rationing are not phantasms" (*Stiglitz* and *Weiss* 1981, p.409).

The second question I want to discuss briefly concerns the directions in which research on credit rationing should be continued or intensified. Again I think the answer I offer below is applicable to many branches of the NIE.

Firstly, the kind of analysis performed in the preceding six chapters needs to be continued. Though a point may be reached where the setting up of more and more examples and counterexamples becomes a bit tedious it is indispensable as long as no truly general results are obtainable. There is hope for the latter, however, if more complex models with imperfect information about several aspects can be developed: The still scarce literature on multidimensional signalling suggests that it is possible only under very special circumstances to overcome informational constraints by devices as analyzed in ch.4 (see *Kohlleppel* 1983a,b, *Engers* and *Fernandez* 1984).

Secondly, and this point is closely related to the first, it seems worthwhile to intensify the research on new methodological approaches. In particular, I have in mind new developments of game theory like those quoted in ch.6. Possibly, these developments will also improve the modelling of dynamic processes. In any case, certain refinements of the *Nash*-equilibrium have already helped to single out certain market outcomes and make some of our results more definitive.

Thirdly, I think the time has come to put theoretical results of the NIE to empirical tests. Given the scarcity of data no spectacular results are to be expected, but a beginning has been made (e.g. *Kugler* 1985, *Sealy* 1979), and there seems hope for fruitful empirical research.

Fourthly, and this may seem even more daring than point three to many theorists, the NIE and in particular credit rationing theory seem sufficiently advanced by now to enter the admittedly dangerous area of policy advice. Theorists like *Hahn* are certainly right when they point out that economics has not reached and possibly never will reach a state that allows to make clear, unambiguous policy recommendations which are well grounded in a firm, widely accepted body of theory. However, given the realities of present day economic policy making such purism, while respectable, simply leaves the fore to economists who cannot offer better theories, but less scruples when they spread their gospel. Since economic policy virtually all over the (capitalist) world is presently dominated by "laissez faire" ideas, the least advocates of a NIE can be expected to do is to publicize their many, many examples of market failures. To be sure, should there be a turn in economic policy towards more regulation, more government influence etc., the NIE would have no difficulties to offer examples of failures of policy making institutions. But my claim is that the latter task is, at the moment, far less urgent than the former. Showing that there is a potential for Pareto-improving policy making is, of course, only a first step. It is still very difficult to decide which policy measures are appropriate in a particular situation, and even less so is there much reason to believe that policy authorities will automatically choose the best available actions. In any case, there is plenty of room for interesting future reseach.

It is my hope that I have succeeded in a) providing an overview of the current state of credit rationing theory, b) giving an impression of the potential of the NIE, and c) convincing the reader that equilibrium credit rationing is a highly plausible and important possibility. I certainly have succeeded in convincing myself that I have not reached the end, but at best the end of the beginning of an interesting line of research.

Bibliography

Aigner, D., and C. Sprenkle, '68: A Simple Model of Information and Lending Behaviour, Journal of Finance 23: 151-66.

Akerlof,G. '70: The Market for Lemons: Quality Uncertainty and the Market Mechanism. Quarterly Journal of Economics 84: 488-500.

Allen, F. '83: Credit Rationing and Payment Incentives, Review of Economic Studies 50: 639-46.

Arrow, K.J. '63: Uncertainty and the Welfare Economics of Medical Care, American Economic Review 53: 941-73.

Arzac, E.R., R.A. Schwartz and D.K. Whitcomb, '81: A Theory and Test of Credit Rationing: Some Further Results, American Economic Review 71: 735-37.

Azariades, C. '75: Implicit Contracts and Underemployment Equilibria, Journal of Political Economy 83: 1183-1202.

Azzi, C.F. and J.C. Cox, '76: A Theory and Test of Credit Rationing: Comment, American Economic Review 66: 911-17.

Baily, M. '74: Wages and Employment Under Uncertain Demand. Review of Economic Studies 41: 37-50.

Baltensperger, E. '76: The Borrower-Lender Relationship, Competitive Equilibrium, and the Theory of Hedonic Prices, American Economic Review 66: 401-405.

________________ '78: Credit Rationing. Issues and Questions, Journal of Money, Credit and Banking 10: 170-83.

________________ '80: Alternative Approaches to the Theory of the Banking Firm, Journal of Monetary Economics 6: 1-37.

________________ and T.M. Devinney '85: Credit Rationing Theory: A Survey and Synthesis, Zeitschrift für die gesamte Staatswissenschaft 141: 475-502.

Baron, D.P. '79: The Incentive Problem and the Design of Investment Banking Contracts, Journal of Banking and Finance 3: 157-75.

Barro, R.J. '74: Are Government Bonds Net Wealth? Journal of Political Economy 82: 1095-117.

____________ '76: The Loan Market, Collateral, and the Rate of Interest. Journal of Money, Credit and Banking 8: 439-56.

Bernanke, B.S. '81: Bankruptcy, Liquidity and Recession, American Economic Review, Papers and Proceedings 71: 155-59.

Bester, H. '84a: Screening Versus Rationing in Credit Markets with Imperfect Information, University of Bonn, Discussion Paper No.136.

________ '84b: The Level of Investment in Credit Markets with Imperfect Information, University of Bonn, Discussion Paper No.150.

Blackwell, N.R. and A.M. Santomero, '82: Bank Credit Rationing and the Customer Relation, Journal of Monetary Economics 9: 121-29.

Blinder, A.S. '84: Credit Rationing and Effective Supply Failure, Princeton University, mimeo.

Blinder, A.S. and J. Stiglitz, '83: Money, Credit Constraints, and Economic Activity, American Economic Review, Papers and Proceedings, 73: 297-302.

Bull, C. '83: Implicit Contracts in the Absence of Enforcement and Risk Aversion, American Economic Review 73: 655-71.

Bulow, J.I. and J.B. Shoven, '78: The Bankruptcy Decision, Bell Journal of Economics 9: 437-56.

Cable, I. and P. Turner '84: Asymmetric Information and Credit Rationing: Another View of Industrial Bank Lending and Britain's Economic Problem, University of Warwick, mimeo.

Campbell, T. and W. Kracaw, '80: Information Production, Market Signalling and the Theory of Financial Intermediation, Journal of Finance 35: 863-81.

Chaing, R. and J. Finkelstein, '82: An Incentive Framework for Evaluating the Impact of Loan Provisions on Default Risk, Southern Economic Journal 48: 962-69.

Chan, Y.-S. and G. Kanatas '85: Asymmetric Valuation and the Role of Collateral in Loan Agreements, Journal of Money, Credit and Banking, 17: 84-95.

Chateau, J.P. '83: Credit Rationing as a (Temporary) Suboptimal Equilibrium With Imperfect Information, European Economic Review 23: 195-201.

Clemenz, G. '83: Märkte mit asymmetrischer Qualitätsinformation, Universität Wien, mimeo.

________ '84a: Theorien der Kreditrationierung, University of Vienna, Department of Economics, Working Paper No.8402.

________ '84b: Credit Rationing in the Absence of Direct Observability of Efforts and Abilities of Borrowers, University of Vienna, Department of Economics, Working Paper No.8405.

________ '85: Existence and Efficiency of Equilibria in Credit Markets with Asymmetric Information, in: H.Göppl und R.Henn (Hrsg.): Geld, Banken und Versicherungen, VVW Karlsruhe.

Cukierman, A. '78: The Horizontal Integration of the Banking Firm, Credit Rationing and Monetary Policy, Review of Economic Studies 45: 165-78.

Davidson, P. '72: Money and the Real World, New York: Wiley, Halistad Press.

Devinney, T.M. '85a: Incentives and Multi-Period Rationing in Loan Contracts, in: H. Göppl and R. Henn (eds.), Geld, Banken und Versicherungen, VVW Karlsruhe.

——— '85 b: Rationing in a Theory of the Banking Firm, Vanderbilt University, Working Paper 84-121.

Diamond, P. and J. Stiglitz, '74: Increases in Risk and Risk Aversion. Journal of Economic Theory, 8: 337-60.

Eaton, J. and M. Gersowitz '80: Debt with Potential Repudiation: Theoretical and Empirical Analysis, Review of Economic Studies, 47: 389-409.

Engers, M. and L. Fernandez '84: On the Existence and Uniqueness of Signalling Equilibria, UCLA mimeo.

Freimer, M. and M. Gordon '62: Why Bankers Ration Credit, Quarterly Journal of Economics 79: 397-410.

Fried, J. and P. Howitt '80: Credit Rationing and Implicit Contract Theory, Journal of Money, Credit and Banking, 12: 471-87.

Gale, D. and M. Hellwig '83: Incentive Compatible Debt Contracts I: The One Period Problem, University of Bonn, Discussion Paper No.124.

Garella, P. and J.J. Gabszewicz '84: Informational Asymmetries in a Duopolistic Credit Market. Core Discussion Paper No. 8431.

Gordon, D.F. '74: A Neoclassical Theory of Keynesian Unemployment, Economic Inquiry 12: 431-59.

Greenwald, B. '79: Adverse Selection in the Labour Market, New York: Garland Publishing Co.

Greenwald, B. and J.E. Stiglitz '84: Pecuniary and Markets Mediated Externalities: Towards a General Theory of the Welfare Economics with Imperfect Information and Incomplete Markets, NBER Working Paper 1304.

——— '85: Money, Imperfect Information, and Economic Fluctuations, Lecture presented by J.E. Stiglitz at the Second International Meeting on Monetary Economics and Banking, June 6/7, 1985, Nice-Sophia Antipolis.

Greenwald, B., J.E. Stiglitz and A. Weiss '84: Informational Imperfections in the Capital Market and Macro-economic Fluctuations, American Economic Review, Papers and Proceedings 74: 194-9.

Grossman, H.I. '79: Adverse Selection, Dissembling, and Competitive Equilibrium, Bell Journal of Economics 10: 336-43.

Guttentag, B. and R. Herring '84: Credit Rationing and Financial Disorder, Journal of Finance, 39: 1359-82.

Hahn, F. '84: Uses and Misuses of Equilibrium in Economics, Schumpeter Lectures 1984, Wirtschaftsuniversität Wien, Ordinariat VW5, Discussion Paper No. 1.

Harris, D '74: Credit Rationing at Commercial Banks: Some Empirical Evidence, Journal of Money, Credit and Banking 6: 227-40.

Hayek, F.A. '69: Three Elucidations of the Ricardo Effect, Journal of Political Economy 77.

Hellwig, M. '77: A Model of Borrowing and Lending With Bankruptcy, Econometrica, 45: 1879-1906.

Hellwig, M. '85a: A Note on the Specification of Inter-Firm Communication in Insurance Markets with Adverse Selection, Journal of Economic Theory, forthcoming.

Hellwig, M. '85b: Modelling Competition in Markets with Adverse Selection, paper presented at the Workshop on Information, Incentives, and Strategic Behaviour. June 14/15, 1985, Bonn.

Hess, J.D. '84: Imperfect Information, Uncertainty, and Credit Rationing: Comment, Quarterly Journal of Economics, 99: 865-68.

Ho, T. and A. Saunders '80: A Catastrophe Model of Bank Failure, Journal of Finance, 35: 1189-1207.

Ho, T. and Kazu Voda '81: Tests of the Equilibrium Hypothesis in Disequilibrium Econometrics: An International Comparison of Credit Rationing: International Economic Review 22: 691-708.

Hodgman, D. '60: Credit Risk and Credit Rationing, Quarterly Journal of Economics, 74: 258-78.

Jackman, R. and J. Sutton '82: Imperfect Capital Markets and the Monetarist Black-Box: Liquidity Constraints, Inflation, and the Asymmetric Effects of Interest Rate Policy, Economic Journal, 92: 108-28.

Jaffee, D. '72: Credit Rationing and the Commercial Loan Market, New York: John Wiley.

Jaffee, D. and F. Modigliani '69: A Theory and Test of Credit Rationing, American Economic Review 59: 850-72.

Jaffee, D. and F. Modigliani '76: A Theory and Test of Credit Rationing: Reply, American Economic Review 66: 918-20.

Jaffee, D.. and T. Russell '76: Imperfect Information, Uncertainty, and Credit Rationing, Quarterly Journal of Economics 90: 651-66.

Jaffee, D. and T. Russell '84: Reply to Hess and Vandell, Quarterly Journal of Economics, 99: 869-72.

Jaynes, G.G. '78: Equilibrium in Monopolistically Competitive Insurance Markets, Journal of Economic Theory, 19: 394-422.

Johansen, L. '61: The Role of the Banking System in a Macroeconomic Model, International Economic Papers, 8: 91-110.

Kalay,A. and R. Rabinovitch '78: On Individual Loans' Pricing, Credit Rationing and Interest Rate Regulation, Journal of Finance, 33: 1071-85.

Kane, E. and B.G. Malkiel '65: Bank Portfolio Allocation, Deposit Variability and the Availability Doctrine, Quarterly Journal of Economics, 79: 113-34.

Keeton, W.R. '79: Equilibrium Credit Rationing, New York & London, Garland Publishing Inc.

Kletzer, K.M. '84: Asymmetries of Information and LDC Borrowing with Souvereign Risk, Economic Journal, 94: 287-307.

Keynes, J.M. '30: A Treatise on Money, London: Macmillan

________ '36: The General Theory of Employment, Interest and Money, London: Macmillan.

King, M. '84: Tax Policy and the Business Cycle, London School of Economics, mimeo.

Kohlberg, E. and J.F. Mertens, '82: On the Strategic Stability of Equilibria, Core Discussion Paper.

Kohlleppel, L. '83a: Multidimensional Market Signalling, Universität Bonn, Institut für Gesellschafts- und Wirtschaftswissenschaften, Discussion Paper No. 125.

________ '83b: Properties of Sorting Equilibria, Universität Bonn, Institut für Gesellschafts- und Wirtschaftswissenschaften, Discussion Paper No. 133.

Koskela, F. '76: A Study of Bank Behaviour and Credit Rationing, Helsinki: Annales Academiae Scientiarum Fennicae.

________ '79: On the Theory of Rationing Equilibrium With Special Reference to Credit Markets: A Survey, Zeitschrift für Nationalökonomie 39: 63-82.

________ '83: Credit Rationing and Non-Price Loan Terms: A Re-Examination, Journal of Banking and Finance 7: 405-16.

Krahnen, J.P. '84: Intermediation and the Structure of Credit Contracts: Towards a Microeconomic Understanding of the Banking Firm, Freie Universität Berlin, F.B. Wirtschaftswissenschaft, Diskussionsbeiträge Nr. 15.

Kreps, D.M. '85: Signalling Games and Stable Equilibria, Stanford Graduate School of Business, mimeo.

Kreps, D. and R. Wilson '82: Sequential Equilibria, Econometrica 50: 863-94.

Kugler, P. '85: Credit Rationing: Evidence from Disequilibrium Interest Rate Equations, Universität Basel, Working Paper No. 32.

Laffont, J.J. and R. Garcia '77: Disequilibrium Econometrics for Business Loans, Econometrica 45: 1187-1204.

Leland,H. and D. Pyle '77: Informational Asymmetries, Financial Structure and Financial Intermediation, Journal of Finance, 32: 371-87.

Lindbeck, A. '62: The New Theory of Credit Control in the United States, Stockholm Economic Studies.

Melitz, J. and M. Dardue '73: The Demand and Supply of Commercial Bank Loans, Journal of Money, Credit and Banking 5: 669-92.

Milde, H. '80: Kreditrationierung, Zinsdispersion und Sequentialsuche, Zeitschrift für die gesamte Staatswissenschaft 136: 266-85.

Milde, H., J.H. Shim and S.H. Yoon '85: Credit Markets with Private Information, in: H.Göppl and R.Henn (Hrsg.): Geld, Banken und Versicherungen, VVW Karlsruhe.

Milde, H. and J.G. Riley '84: Signalling in Credit Markets, University of Konstanz, Diskussionsbeiträge Serie A-No.185.

Milgrom, P. and J. Roberts '84: Price and Advertising Signals of Product Quality, mimeo, Stanford University.

Miller, M. '62: Credit Risk and Credit Rationing: Further Comment, Quarterly Journal of Economics, 76: 480-88.

Minsky, H.P. '75: John Meynard Keynes, New York: Macmillan.

Miyazaki, H. '77: The Rat Race and Internal Markets, Bell Journal of Economics 8: 394-418.

Myerson, R. '78: Refinements of the Nash Equilibrium Concept, International Journal of Game Theory, 7: 73-80.

Nash, J. '51: Noncooperative Games, Annals of Mathematics, 54: 286-95.

Nelson, P. '70: Information and Consumer Behaviour, Journal of Political Economy, 78.

Riley, J.G. '75: Competitive Signalling, Journal of Economic Theory 10: 174-86.

________ '79: Informational Equilibrium, Econometrica 47: 331-60.

________ '84: Competitive Signalling Reconsidered, UCLA, Department of Economics, Working Paper 294.

Roosa, R. '51: Interest Rates and the Central Bank, in Money, Trade and Economic Growth: Essays in Honour of John H. Williams, New York: Macmillan.

Rosen, S. '74: Hedonic Prices and Implicit Markets Product Differentiation in Pure Competition, Journal of Political Economy 82: 34-55.

Ross, S. '77: The Determination of Financial Structure: The Incentive Signalling Approach, Bell Journal of Economics, 8: 23-40.

Rothschild, M. and J.E. Stiglitz '70: Increasing Risk I: A Definition, Journal of Economic Theory, 2: 225-43.

________________ '76: Equilibrium in Competitive Insurance Markets: An Essay on the Economics of Imperfect Information, Quarterly Journal of Economics 80: 628-49.

Russell, T. '74: The Effects of Improvements in the Consumer Loan Markets, Journal of Economic Theory 9: 327-39.

Ryder, H. '62: Credit Risk and Credit Rationing: Comment, Quarterly Journal of Economics, 76: 471-79.

Saunders, A. '83: The Determinants of Country Risk: A Selection Survey of the Literature, International Monetary Fund, DM/83/64.

Schultze, C.L. '85: Microeconomic Efficiency and Nominal Wage Stickiness, American Economic Review 75: 1-15.

Scott, I. Jr. '57: The Availability Doctrine: Theoretical Underpinnings, Review of Economic Studies, 25: 41-48.

________ '57: The Availability Doctrine: Development and Implications, Canadian Journal of Economics and Political Science, 23: 532-39.

Sealy, G.W. Jr. '79: Credit Rationing in the Commercial Loan Market: Estimates of a Structural Model under Conditions of Disequilibrium, Journal of Finance, 34: 689-702.

Selten, R. '75: A Re-examination of the Perfectness Concept for Equilibrium Points in Extensive Games, International Journal of Game Theory, 4: 25-55.

Smith, B. '83: Limited Information, Credit Rationing, and Optimal Government Lending Policy, American Economic Review, 73: 305-18.

Smith, C. '80: On the Theory of Financial Contracting: The Personal Loan Market, Journal of Monetary Economics, 6: 337-57.

Smith, V. '72: A Theory and Test of Credit Rationing: Some Generalizations, American Economic Review, 62: 477-83.

Spence, A.M. '73: Job Market Signalling, Quarterly Journal of Economics 80: 628-49.

________ '74: Market Signalling, Harvard University Press, Cambridge, MA.

Stiglitz, J.E. '79: Equilibrium in Product Markets with Imperfect Information, American Economic Review, Papers and Proceedings, 69: 339-45.

________ '83: On the Relevance or Irrelevance of Public Financial Policy: Indexation, Price Rigidities and Optimal Monetary Policy, NBER Working Paper No. 1106.

________ '84: Price Rigidities and Market Structure, American Economic Review, Papers and Proceedings, 74: 350-56.

________ '85a: Information and Economic Analysis: A Perspective, Economic Journal Supplement, 95: 21-42.

________ '85b: Credit Markets and the Control of Capital, Journal of Money, Credit and Banking, 17: 133-152.

Stiglitz, J.E. and A. Weiss '81: Credit Rationing in Markets with Imperfect Information, American Economic Review 71, 393-410.

________ '83: Incentive Effects of Termination: Applications to the Credit and Labour Markets, American Economic Review, 73: 912-27.

________ '85: Credit Rationing, mimeo, Bell Communications Research.

Streißler, E. and G. Tichy '78: Die Transmission monetärer Impulse über den Kreditmarkt, in Ehrlicher, W. and A. Oberhauser (Hrsg.): Probleme der Geldmengensteuerung, Schriften des Vereins für Socialpolitik, Berlin.

Vandell, K.D. '84: Imperfect Information, Uncertainty and Credit Rationing: Comment and Extension, Quarterly Journal of Economics, 99: 841-64.

Watson, H. '84: Credit Markets and Borrower Effort, Southern Economic Journal 50, 802-13.

Webb, D.C. '81: The Net Wealth Effect of Government Bonds When Credit Markets are Imperfect, Economic Journal, 91: 405-14.

Wette, H. '83: Collateral in Credit Rationing in Markets With Imperfect Information: Note, American Economic Review, 73: 442-45.

Williamson, S.D. '84: Costly Monitoring, Financial Intermediation and Equilibrium Credit Rationing, Queen's University, Discussion Paper 583.

Wilson, C.A. '77: A Model of Insurance Markets with Incomplete Information, Journal of Economic Theory 16: 167-207.

Wilson, R. '83: Multidimensional Siganlling, mimeo: Stanford University.

Yanelle, M.-O. '85: Bertrand Competition Among Intermediaries, Paper presented at the Workshop on Information, Incentives, and Strategic Behaviour, June 14/15, 1985, Bonn.

Yellen, J.L. '84: Efficiency Wage Models of Unemployment, American Economic Review, Papers and Proceeding, 74: 200-205.

Zink, H. '84: The Role of the Market Intransparency in Insurance Market Models, mimeo, Berne University.

Vol. 184: R. E. Burkard and U. Derigs, Assignment and Matching Problems: Solution Methods with FORTRAN-Programs. VIII, 148 pages. 1980.

Vol. 185: C. C. von Weizsäcker, Barriers to Entry. VI, 220 pages. 1980.

Vol. 186: Ch.-L. Hwang and K. Yoon, Multiple Attribute Decision Making – Methods and Applications. A State-of-the-Art-Survey. XI, 259 pages. 1981.

Vol. 187: W. Hock, K. Schittkowski, Test Examples for Nonlinear Programming Codes. V. 178 pages. 1981.

Vol. 188: D. Bös, Economic Theory of Public Enterprise. VII, 142 pages. 1981.

Vol. 189: A. P. Lüthi, Messung wirtschaftlicher Ungleichheit. IX, 287 pages. 1981.

Vol. 190: J. N. Morse, Organizations: Multiple Agents with Multiple Criteria. Proceedings, 1980. VI, 509 pages. 1981.

Vol. 191: H. R. Sneessens, Theory and Estimation of Macroeconomic Rationing Models. VII, 138 pages. 1981.

Vol. 192: H. J. Bierens: Robust Methods and Asymptotic Theory in Nonlinear Econometrics. IX, 198 pages. 1981.

Vol. 193: J.K. Sengupta, Optimal Decisions under Uncertainty. VII, 156 pages. 1981.

Vol. 194: R. W. Shephard, Cost and Production Functions. XI, 104 pages. 1981.

Vol. 195: H. W. Ursprung, Die elementare Katastrophentheorie. Eine Darstellung aus der Sicht der Ökonomie. VII, 332 pages. 1982.

Vol. 196: M. Nermuth, Information Structures in Economics. VIII, 236 pages. 1982.

Vol. 197: Integer Programming and Related Areas. A Classified Bibliography. 1978 – 1981. Edited by R. von Randow. XIV, 338 pages. 1982.

Vol. 198: P. Zweifel, Ein ökonomisches Modell des Arztverhaltens. XIX, 392 Seiten. 1982.

Vol. 199: Evaluating Mathematical Programming Techniques. Proceedings, 1981. Edited by J.M. Mulvey. XI, 379 pages. 1982.

Vol. 200: The Resource Sector in an Open Economy. Edited by H. Siebert. IX, 161 pages. 1984.

Vol. 201: P. M. C. de Boer, Price Effects in Input-Output-Relations: A Theoretical and Empirical Study for the Netherlands 1949–1967. X, 140 pages. 1982.

Vol. 202: U. Witt, J. Perske, SMS – A Program Package for Simulation and Gaming of Stochastic Market Processes and Learning Behavior. VII, 266 pages. 1982.

Vol. 203: Compilation of Input-Output Tables. Proceedings, 1981. Edited by J. V. Skolka. VII, 307 pages. 1982.

Vol. 204: K.C. Mosler, Entscheidungsregeln bei Risiko: Multivariate stochastische Dominanz. VII, 172 Seiten. 1982.

Vol. 205: R. Ramanathan, Introduction to the Theory of Economic Growth. IX, 347 pages. 1982.

Vol. 206: M.H. Karwan, V. Lotfi, J. Telgen, and S. Zionts, Redundancy in Mathematical Programming. VII, 286 pages. 1983.

Vol. 207: Y. Fujimori, Modern Analysis of Value Theory. X, 165 pages. 1982.

Vol. 208: Econometric Decision Models. Proceedings, 1981. Edited by J. Gruber. VI, 364 pages. 1983.

Vol. 209: Essays and Surveys on Multiple Criteria Decision Making. Proceedings, 1982. Edited by P. Hansen. VII, 441 pages. 1983.

Vol. 210: Technology, Organization and Economic Structure. Edited by R. Sato and M.J. Beckmann. VIII, 195 pages. 1983.

Vol. 211: P. van den Heuvel, The Stability of a Macroeconomic System with Quantity Constraints. VII, 169 pages. 1983.

Vol. 212: R. Sato and T. Nôno, Invariance Principles and the Structure of Technology. V, 94 pages. 1983.

Vol. 213: Aspiration Levels in Bargaining and Economic Decision Making. Proceedings, 1982. Edited by R. Tietz. VIII, 406 pages. 1983.

Vol. 214: M. Faber, H. Niemes und G. Stephan, Entropie, Umweltschutz und Rohstoffverbrauch. IX, 181 Seiten. 1983.

Vol. 215: Semi-Infinite Programming and Applications. Proceedings, 1981. Edited by A.V. Fiacco and K.O. Kortanek. XI, 322 pages. 1983.

Vol. 216: H.H. Müller, Fiscal Policies in a General Equilibrium Model with Persistent Unemployment. VI, 92 pages. 1983.

Vol. 217: Ch. Grootaert, The Relation Between Final Demand and Income Distribution. XIV, 105 pages. 1983.

Vol. 218: P. van Loon, A Dynamic Theory of the Firm: Production, Finance and Investment. VII, 191 pages. 1983.

Vol. 219: E. van Damme, Refinements of the Nash Equilibrium Concept. VI, 151 pages. 1983.

Vol. 220: M. Aoki, Notes on Economic Time Series Analysis: System Theoretic Perspectives. IX, 249 pages. 1983.

Vol. 221: S. Nakamura, An Inter-Industry Translog Model of Prices and Technical Change for the West German Economy. XIV, 290 pages. 1984.

Vol. 222: P. Meier, Energy Systems Analysis for Developing Countries. VI, 344 pages. 1984.

Vol. 223: W. Trockel, Market Demand. VIII, 205 pages. 1984.

Vol. 224: M. Kiy, Ein disaggregiertes Prognosesystem für die Bundesrepublik Deutschland. XVIII, 276 Seiten. 1984.

Vol. 225: T.R. von Ungern-Sternberg, Zur Analyse von Märkten mit unvollständiger Nachfragerinformation. IX, 125 Seiten. 1984

Vol. 226: Selected Topics in Operations Research and Mathematical Economics. Proceedings, 1983. Edited by G. Hammer and D. Pallaschke. IX, 478 pages. 1984.

Vol. 227: Risk and Capital. Proceedings, 1983. Edited by G. Bamberg and K. Spremann. VII, 306 pages. 1984.

Vol. 228: Nonlinear Models of Fluctuating Growth. Proceedings, 1983. Edited by R.M. Goodwin, M. Krüger and A. Vercelli. XVII, 277 pages. 1984.

Vol. 229: Interactive Decision Analysis. Proceedings, 1983. Edited by M. Grauer and A.P. Wierzbicki. VIII, 269 pages. 1984.

Vol. 230: Macro-Economic Planning with Conflicting Goals. Proceedings, 1982. Edited by M. Despontin, P. Nijkamp and J. Spronk. VI, 297 pages. 1984.

Vol. 231: G.F. Newell, The M/M/∞ Service System with Ranked Servers in Heavy Traffic. XI, 126 pages. 1984.

Vol. 232: L. Bauwens, Bayesian Full Information Analysis of Simultaneous Equation Models Using Integration by Monte Carlo. VI, 114 pages. 1984.

Vol. 233: G. Wagenhals, The World Copper Market. XI, 190 pages. 1984.

Vol. 234: B.C. Eaves, A Course in Triangulations for Solving Equations with Deformations. III, 302 pages. 1984.

Vol. 235: Stochastic Models in Reliability Theory. Proceedings, 1984. Edited by S. Osaki and Y. Hatoyama. VII, 212 pages. 1984.

Vol. 236: G. Gandolfo, P.C. Padoan, A Disequilibrium Model of Real and Financial Accumulation in an Open Economy. VI, 172 pages. 1984.

Vol. 237: Misspecification Analysis. Proceedings, 1983. Edited by T.K. Dijkstra. V, 129 pages. 1984.

Vol. 238: W. Domschke, A. Drexl, Location and Layout Planning. IV, 134 pages. 1985.

Vol. 239: Microeconomic Models of Housing Markets. Edited by K. Stahl. VII, 197 pages. 1985.

Vol. 240: Contributions to Operations Research. Proceedings, 1984. Edited by K. Neumann and D. Pallaschke. V, 190 pages. 1985.

Vol. 241: U. Wittmann, Das Konzept rationaler Preiserwartungen. XI, 310 Seiten. 1985.

Vol. 242: Decision Making with Multiple Objectives. Proceedings, 1984. Edited by Y. Y. Haimes and V. Chankong. XI, 571 pages. 1985.

Vol. 243: Integer Programming and Related Areas. A Classified Bibliography 1981–1984. Edited by R. von Randow. XX, 386 pages. 1985.

Vol. 244: Advances in Equilibrium Theory. Proceedings, 1984. Edited by C. D. Aliprantis, O. Burkinshaw and N. J. Rothman. II, 235 pages. 1985.

Vol. 245: J. E. M. Wilhelm, Arbitrage Theory. VII, 114 pages. 1985.

Vol. 246: P. W. Otter, Dynamic Feature Space Modelling, Filtering and Self-Tuning Control of Stochastic Systems. XIV, 177 pages. 1985.

Vol. 247: Optimization and Discrete Choice in Urban Systems. Proceedings, 1983. Edited by B. G. Hutchinson, P. Nijkamp and M. Batty. VI, 371 pages. 1985.

Vol. 248: Plural Rationality and Interactive Decision Processes. Proceedings, 1984. Edited by M. Grauer, M. Thompson and A. P. Wierzbicki. VI, 354 pages. 1985.

Vol. 249: Spatial Price Equilibrium: Advances in Theory, Computation and Application. Proceedings, 1984. Edited by P. T. Harker. VII, 277 pages. 1985.

Vol. 250: M. Roubens, Ph. Vincke, Preference Modelling. VIII, 94 pages. 1985.

Vol. 251: Input-Output Modeling. Proceedings, 1984. Edited by A. Smyshlyaev. VI, 261 pages. 1985.

Vol. 252: A. Birolini, On the Use of Stochastic Processes in Modeling Reliability Problems. VI, 105 pages. 1985.

Vol. 253: C. Withagen, Economic Theory and International Trade in Natural Exhaustible Resources. VI, 172 pages. 1985.

Vol. 254: S. Müller, Arbitrage Pricing of Contingent Claims. VIII, 151 pages. 1985.

Vol. 255: Nondifferentiable Optimization: Motivations and Applications. Proceedings, 1984. Edited by V. F. Demyanov and D. Pallaschke. VI, 350 pages. 1985.

Vol. 256: Convexity and Duality in Optimization. Proceedings, 1984. Edited by J. Ponstein. V, 142 pages. 1985.

Vol. 257: Dynamics of Macrosystems. Proceedings, 1984. Edited by J.-P. Aubin, D. Saari and K. Sigmund. VI, 280 pages. 1985.

Vol. 258: H. Funke, Eine allgemeine Theorie der Polypol- und Oligopolpreisbildung. III, 237 pages. 1985.

Vol. 259: Infinite Programming. Proceedings, 1984. Edited by E. J. Anderson and A. B. Philpott. XIV, 244 pages. 1985.

Vol. 260: H.-J. Kruse, Degeneracy Graphs and the Neighbourhood Problem. VIII, 128 pages. 1986.

Vol. 261: Th. R. Gulledge, Jr., N. K. Womer, The Economics of Made-to-Order Production. VI, 134 pages. 1986.

Vol. 262: H. U. Buhl, A Neo-Classical Theory of Distribution and Wealth. V, 146 pages. 1986.

Vol. 263: M. Schäfer, Resource Extraction and Market Structure. XI, 154 pages. 1986.

Vol. 264: Models of Economic Dynamics. Proceedings, 1983. Edited by H. F. Sonnenschein. VII, 212 pages. 1986.

Vol. 265: Dynamic Games and Applications in Economics. Edited by T. Başar. IX, 288 pages. 1986.

Vol. 266: Multi-Stage Production Planning and Inventory Control. Edited by S. Axsäter, Ch. Schneeweiss and E. Silver. V, 264 pages. 1986.

Vol. 267: R. Bemelmans, The Capacity Aspect of Inventories. IX, 165 pages. 1986.

Vol. 268: V. Firchau, Information Evaluation in Capital Markets. VII, 103 pages. 1986.

Vol. 269: A. Borglin, H. Keiding, Optimality in Infinite Horizon Economies. VI, 180 pages. 1986.

Vol. 270: Technological Change, Employment and Spatial Dynamics. Proceedings 1985. Edited by P. Nijkamp. VII, 466 pages. 1986.

Vol. 271: C. Hildreth, The Cowles Commission in Chicago, 1939–1955. V, 176 pages. 1986.

Vol. 272: G. Clemenz, Credit Markets with Asymmetric Information. VIII, 212 pages. 1986.

GPSR Compliance

The European Union's (EU) General Product Safety Regulation (GPSR) is a set of rules that requires consumer products to be safe and our obligations to ensure this.

If you have any concerns about our products, you can contact us on ProductSafety@springernature.com

In case Publisher is established outside the EU, the EU authorized representative is:

Springer Nature Customer Service Center GmbH
Europaplatz 3
69115 Heidelberg, Germany

Batch number: 10844827

Printed by Printforce, the Netherlands